# Lecture Notes in Computer Science 7755

*Commenced Publication in 1973*
Founding and Former Series Editors:
Gerhard Goos, Juris Hartmanis, and Jan van Leeuwen

T0218385

Raghunath Nambiar   Meikel Poess (Eds.)

# Selected Topics in Performance Evaluation and Benchmarking

4th TPC Technology Conference, TPCTC 2012
Istanbul, Turkey, August 27, 2012
Revised Selected Papers

 Springer

Volume Editors

Raghunath Nambiar
Cisco Systems Inc.
Data Center Group
3800 Zanker Road, San Jose, CA 95134, USA
E-mail: rnambiar@cisco.com

Meikel Poess
Oracle Corporation
Server Technologies
500 Oracle Parkway, Redwood Shores, CA 94065, USA
E-mail: meikel.poess@oracle.com

ISSN 0302-9743                          e-ISSN 1611-3349
ISBN 978-3-642-36726-7                  e-ISBN 978-3-642-36727-4
DOI 10.1007/978-3-642-36727-4
Springer Heidelberg Dordrecht London New York

Library of Congress Control Number: 2013931551

CR Subject Classification (1998): C.4, H.2.7-8, H.2.4, D.2.8, J.1, K.6.2, C.2.4

LNCS Sublibrary: SL 2 – Programming and Software Engineering

*Typesetting:* Camera-ready by author, data conversion by Scientific Publishing Services, Chennai, India

Printed on acid-free paper

Springer is part of Springer Science+Business Media (www.springer.com)

# Preface

The Transaction Processing Performance Council (TPC) is a non-profit organization established in August 1988. Over the years, the TPC has had a significant impact on the computing industry's use of industry-standard benchmarks. Vendors use TPC benchmarks to illustrate performance competitiveness for their existing products and to improve and monitor the performance of their products under development. Many buyers use TPC benchmark results as points of comparison when purchasing new computing systems.

The information technology landscape is evolving at a rapid pace, challenging industry experts and researchers to develop innovative techniques for the evaluation, measurement, and characterization of complex systems. The TPC remains committed to developing new benchmark standards to keep pace with these rapid changes in technology. One vehicle for achieving this objective is the TPC's sponsorship of the Technology Conference Series on Performance Evaluation and Benchmarking (TPCTC) established in 2009. With this conference series, the TPC encourages researchers and industry experts to present and debate novel ideas and methodologies in performance evaluation, measurement, and characterization.

The First TPC Technology Conference on Performance Evaluation and Benchmarking (TPCTC 2009) was held in conjunction with the 35th International Conference on Very Large Data Bases (VLDB 2009) in Lyon, France, during August 24–28, 2009.

The Second TPC Technology Conference on Performance Evaluation and Benchmarking (TPCTC 2010) was held in conjunction with the 36th International Conference on Very Large Data Bases (VLDB 2010) in Singapore during September 13–17, 2010.

The Third TPC Technology Conference on Performance Evaluation and Benchmarking (TPCTC 2011) was held in conjunction with the 37th International Conference on Very Large Data Bases (VLDB 2011) in Seattle, Washington, from August 29 to September 3, 2012.

This book contains the proceedings of the 4th TPC Technology Conference on Performance Evaluation and Benchmarking (TPCTC 2012), held in conjunction with the 38th International Conference on Very Large Data Bases (VLDB 2012) in Istanbul, Turkey, during August 27–31, 2012, including ten selected peer-reviewed papers, a report from the TPC Public Relations Committee (PR), two invited papers from industry and academic leaders in the field of performance engineering, and a report from the Workshop on Big Data Benchmarking (WBDB 2012).

The hard work and close cooperation of a number of people have contributed to the success of this conference. We would like to thank the members of TPC and the organizers of VLDB 2012 for their sponsorship; the members of the Program Committee and Publicity Committee for their support; and the authors and the participants who are the primary reason for the success of this conference.

January 2013

Raghunath Nambiar
Meikel Poess

# TPCTC 2012 Organization

## General Chairs

Raghunath Nambiar (Cisco)
Meikel Poess (Oracle)

## Program Committee

Chaitanya Baru (San Diego Supercomputer Center)
Daniel Bowers (Ideas International)
Michael Brey (Oracle)
Alain Crolotte (Teradata)
Masaru Kitsuregawa (University of Tokyo)
Harumi Kuno (HP Labs)
Michael Molloy (Dell)
Coskun Nurcan (Intel)
Tilmann Rabl (University of Toronto)
Marco Vieira (University of Coimbra)

## Publicity Committee

Forrest Carman (Owen Media)
Matt Emmerton (IBM)
Michael Majdalany (L&M Management Group)
Andrew Masland (NEC)
Reza Taheri (VMware)

## Keynote

Michael Carey (University of California, Irvine)

## Invited Talk

Karl Huppler (IBM)

# About the TPC

## Introduction to the TPC

The Transaction Processing Performance Council (TPC) is a non-profit organization that defines transaction processing and database benchmarks and distributes vendor-neutral performance data to the industry. Additional information is available at http://www.tpc.org/.

## TPC Memberships

### Full Members

Full Members of the TPC participate in all aspects of the TPC's work, including development of benchmark standards and setting strategic direction. The Full Member application can be found at
http://www.tpc.org/information/about/app-member.asp.

### Associate Members

Certain organizations may join the TPC as Associate Members. Associate Members may attend TPC meetings, but are not eligible to vote or hold office. Associate membership is available to non-profit organizations, educational institutions, market researchers, publishers, consultants, governments, and businesses that do not create, market, or sell computer products or services. The Associate Member application can be found at http://www.tpc.org/information/about/app-assoc.asp.

### Academic and Government Institutions

Academic and government institutions are invited join the TPC and a special invitation can be found at http://www.tpc.org/information/specialinvitation.asp.

# Contact the TPC

TPC
Presidio of San Francisco
Building 572B (surface)
P.O. Box 29920 (mail)
San Francisco, CA 94129-0920
Voice: 415-561-6272
Fax: 415-561-6120
E-mail: info@tpc.org

## How to Order TPC Materials

All of our materials are now posted free of charge on our website. If you have any questions, please feel free to contact our office directly or by e-mail at info@tpc.org.

## Benchmark Status Report

The TPC Benchmark Status Report is a digest of the activities of the TPC and its technical subcommittees. Sign-up information can be found at the following URL: http://www.tpc.org/information/about/email.asp.

# TPC 2012 Organization

## Full Members

AMD
Bull
Cisco
Dell
Fujitsu
HP
Hitachi
Huawei
IBM
Intel
Microsoft
NEC
Oracle
Redhat
Sybase (An SAP Company)
Teradata
Unisys
VMware

## Associate Members

Ideas International
ITOM International Co
San Diego Super Computing Center
Telecommunications Technology Association
University of Coimbra, Portugal

# TPC 2012 Organization

## Steering Committee

Karl Huppler (IBM), Chair
Mike Brey (Oracle)
Charles Levine (Microsoft)
Raghunath Nambiar (Cisco)
Wayne Smith (Intel)

## Public Relations Committee

Raghunath Nambiar (Cisco), Chair
Andrew Masland (NEC)
Matt Emmerton (IBM)
Meikel Poess (Oracle)
Reza Taheri (VMware)

## Technical Advisory Board

Jamie Reding (Microsoft), Chair
Andrew Bond (Red Hat)
Matthew Emmerton (IBM)
John Fowler (Oracle)
Bryon Georgson (HP)
Andrew Masland (NEC)
Wayne Smith (Intel)

# Table of Contents

# TPC Benchmark Roadmap 2012

Raghunath Nambiar[1], Meikel Poess[2], Andrew Masland[3], H. Reza Taheri[4],
Matthew Emmerton[5], Forrest Carman[6], and Michael Majdalany[7]

[1] Cisco Systems, Inc., 3800 Zanker Road, San Jose, CA 95134, USA
rnambiar@cisco.com
[2] Oracle Corporation, 500 Oracle Pkwy, Redwood Shores, CA 94065, USA
meikel.poess@oracle.com
[3] NEC Corporation of America, 14335 NE 24th Street, Bellevue, WA 98007, USA
andy.masland@necam.com
[4] VMware, Inc., 4301 Hillview Ave, Palo Alto CA 94304, USA
rtaheri@vmware.com
[5] IBM Canada, 8200 Warden Ave, Markham, ON L6G 1C7, Canada
memmerto@ca.ibm.com
[6] Owen Media, 3130 E. Madison St., Suite 206, Seattle, WA 98112, USA
forrestc@owenmedia.com
[7] LoBue & Majdalany Mgmt Group, 572B Ruger St. San Francisco, CA 94129, USA
majdalany@lm-mgmt.com

**Abstract.** The TPC has played, and continues to play, a crucial role in providing the computer industry with relevant standards for total system performance, price-performance and energy efficiency comparisons. Historically known for database-centric standards, the TPC is now developing standards for consolidation using virtualization technologies and multi-source data integration, and exploring new ideas such as Big Data and Big Data Analytics to keep pace with rapidly changing industry demands. This paper gives a high level overview of the current state of the TPC in terms of existing standards, standards under development and future outlook.

**Keywords:** Industry Standard Benchmarks, Transaction Processing Performance Council.

## 1  Introduction

In the 1980s, many companies practiced something known as "benchmarketing" – a practice in which organizations made performance claims based on internal benchmarks. The goal of running tailored benchmarks was simply to make one specific company's solution look far superior to that of the competition, with the objective of increasing sales. Companies created configurations specifically designed to maximize performance, called "benchmark specials," to force comparisons between non-comparable systems.

In response to this growing practice, a small group of individuals became determined to find a fair and neutral means to compare performance across database systems. Both

R. Nambiar and M. Poess (Eds.): TPCTC 2012, LNCS 7755, pp. 1–20, 2013.
© Springer-Verlag Berlin Heidelberg 2013

influential academic database experts and well-known industry leaders contributed to this effort. Their important work eventually led to the creation of the TPC.

Founded in 1988, the Transaction Processing Performance Council (TPC) is a non-profit corporation dedicated to creating and maintaining benchmark standards, which measure database performance in a standardized, objective and verifiable manner. The TPC's goal is to create, manage and maintain a set of fair and comprehensive benchmarks that enable end-users and vendors to objectively evaluate system performance under well-defined, consistent and comparable workloads. As technology and end-customer solutions evolve, the TPC continuously reviews its benchmarks to ensure they reflect changing industry and marketplace requirements.

The TPC draws on its long history and experience to create meaningful benchmarks. The organization recently introduced the TPC-DS benchmark standard [4] [6][7][12][17], which represents a modern, decision support workload. The TPC has also developed a TPC-Energy standard [1][15] designed to augment existing TPC benchmarks with energy metrics, so that end-users can understand the energy costs associated with a specific benchmark result. The organization is working on several new benchmarks for virtualized database environments.

Before the release of any new benchmark standard, the TPC creates a lengthy and detailed definition of the new benchmark. The resulting specifications are dense documents with stringent requirements; these very complete specifications help ensure that all published benchmark results are comparable. TPC members also constantly work to update and improve specifications to help them stay current and complete.

Unique to the TPC is the requirement that all published benchmarks be audited by an independent third party, which has been certified by the organization. This requirement ensures that published results adhere to all of the very specific benchmark requirements, and that results are accurate so any comparison across vendors or systems is, in fact, comparing "apples to apples."

The end result is that the TPC creates benchmark standards that reflect typical database workloads. The process of producing a benchmark is highly structured and audited so that valid assessments can be made across systems and vendors for any given benchmark. Reported results include performance, price/performance, and energy/performance, which help customers identify systems that deliver the highest level of performance, using the least amount of energy.

To date the TPC has approved a total of ten independent benchmark standards. Of these TPC-C [16], TPC-H [5], TPC-E [18][20] and TPC-DS are currently active standards. TPC-C and TPC-E are Online Transaction Processing (OLTP) benchmarks. Both benchmarks simulate a complete computing environment where a population of users executes transactions against a database. TPC-C is centered around the principal activities (transactions) of an order-entry environment, while TPC-E simulates the OLTP workload of a brokerage firm. TPC-H and TPC-DS are benchmarks that model several generally applicable aspects of a decision support system, including queries and continuous data maintenance. Both simulate the business model of a retail product supplier. TPC-DI, TPC-VMS and TPC-V are under development. The TPC-Pricing Specification and TPC-Energy Specification are common across all the benchmark standards. The timelines are shown in Figure 1.

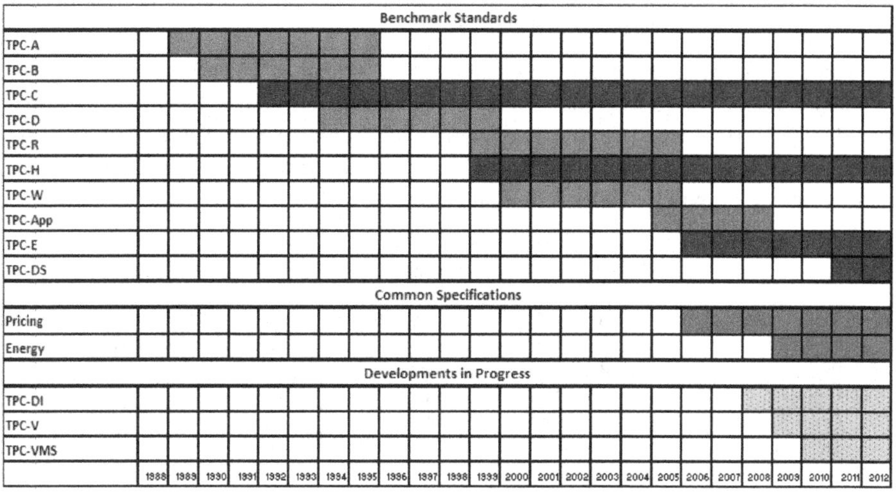

| Benchmark Standards | | | | | | | | | | | | | | | | | | | | | | | | | |
|---|---|---|---|---|---|---|---|---|---|---|---|---|---|---|---|---|---|---|---|---|---|---|---|---|---|
| TPC-A | | | | | | | | | | | | | | | | | | | | | | | | | |
| TPC-B | | | | | | | | | | | | | | | | | | | | | | | | | |
| TPC-C | | | | | | | | | | | | | | | | | | | | | | | | | |
| TPC-D | | | | | | | | | | | | | | | | | | | | | | | | | |
| TPC-R | | | | | | | | | | | | | | | | | | | | | | | | | |
| TPC-H | | | | | | | | | | | | | | | | | | | | | | | | | |
| TPC-W | | | | | | | | | | | | | | | | | | | | | | | | | |
| TPC-App | | | | | | | | | | | | | | | | | | | | | | | | | |
| TPC-E | | | | | | | | | | | | | | | | | | | | | | | | | |
| TPC-DS | | | | | | | | | | | | | | | | | | | | | | | | | |
| Common Specifications | | | | | | | | | | | | | | | | | | | | | | | | | |
| Pricing | | | | | | | | | | | | | | | | | | | | | | | | | |
| Energy | | | | | | | | | | | | | | | | | | | | | | | | | |
| Developments in Progress | | | | | | | | | | | | | | | | | | | | | | | | | |
| TPC-DI | | | | | | | | | | | | | | | | | | | | | | | | | |
| TPC-V | | | | | | | | | | | | | | | | | | | | | | | | | |
| TPC-VMS | | | | | | | | | | | | | | | | | | | | | | | | | |
| | 1988 | 1989 | 1990 | 1991 | 1992 | 1993 | 1994 | 1995 | 1996 | 1997 | 1998 | 1999 | 2000 | 2001 | 2002 | 2003 | 2004 | 2005 | 2006 | 2007 | 2008 | 2009 | 2010 | 2011 | 2012 |

**Fig. 1.** TPC Benchmark Standards Timeline

The TPC continues to explore developments of new standards and enhancements to existing standards, and the TPC Technology Conference Series on Performance Evaluation and Benchmarking (TPCTC) initiative brings industry experts and researchers together to discuss novel ideas and methodologies in performance evaluation, measurement, and characterization [9][10][11].

The remainder of this paper is divided into five sections. The first section focuses on the benefits of TPC-E - the modern OLTP benchmark, the second section gives a historical perspective of benchmarks in the decision support space, the third section provides a high level overview of benchmark developments in the virtualization area, the fourth section summarizes the development of a new data integration benchmark, followed by a summary of the TPC Technology Conference Series on Performance Evaluation and Benchmarking.

## 2  OLTP Benchmarks

The TPC has developed and maintained a number of OLTP (Online Transaction Processing) benchmark standards over the course of its history. TPC-A (1989-1995) and TPC-B (1990-1995) were early attempts to create meaningful OLTP benchmarks but were quickly found lacking in various areas. TPC-C (1992-present) was the first comprehensive OLTP benchmark standard, which was designed around the order-entry model. The TPC-C benchmark is often referred to as TPC's flagship benchmark, with over 750 publications across a wide range of hardware and software platforms representing the evolution of transaction processing systems [16]. TPC-E (2007-present) was designed around a stock-trading model, and sought to be more representative of modern OLTP environments, and to address the high costs associated with constructing and operating large TPC-C benchmark environments [16][20].

## 2.1    A Comparison of TPC-C and TPC-E

The typical enterprise computing environment has changed considerably during the 15 years between the first releases of TPC-C and TPC-E. As a result there are some considerable differences in these two workloads. Tables 1 and Table 2 outline the business transactions found in each workload, along with some properties of each transaction, which will be expanded upon below.

**Table 1.** Business Transactions of TPC-C

| Transaction | Mix | Access | ANSI Isolation | Type | Notes |
|---|---|---|---|---|---|
| New-Order | 45% | Read-Write | Serializable | Core | Primary Metric |
| Payment | 43% | Read-Write | Repeatable Read | Core | |
| Delivery | 4% | Read-Write | Repeatable Read | Core | |
| Order-Status | 4% | Read-Only | Repeatable Read | Lookup | |
| Stock-Level | 4% | Read-Only | Read Committed | Lookup | |

**Table 2.** Business Transactions of TPC-E

| Transaction | Mix | Access | ANSI Isolation | Type | Notes |
|---|---|---|---|---|---|
| Trade-Order | 10.1% | Read-Write | Repeatable Read | Core | |
| Market-Feed | 1% | Read-Write | Repeatable Read | Core | Dependency on Trade-Order |
| Trade-Result | 10% | Read-Write | Serializable | Core | Dependency on Trade-Order and Market-Feed Primary Metric |
| Broker-Volume | 4.9% | Read-Only | Read Committed | Reporting | |
| Customer-Position | 13% | Read-Only | Read Committed | Lookup | |
| Security-Detail | 14% | Read-Only | Read Committed | Lookup | |
| Market-Watch | 18% | Read-Only | Read Committed | Reporting | |
| Trade-Lookup | 8% | Read-Only | Read Committed | Lookup | |
| Trade-Update | 2% | Read-Write | Repeatable Read | Update | |
| Trade-Status | 19% | Read-Only | Read Committed | Lookup | |

The primary metric of both TPC-C and TPC-E is the transaction rate of a specific business transaction that is relevant to the workload. What is notable is that the primary metric of TPC-E (the Trade-Result transaction) has functional dependencies on other transactions (Trade-Order and Market-Feed), which makes attaining a higher performance score more challenging.

The workload composition by and large determines the complexity of the workload and the effort required to optimize the workload as a whole. In TPC-C, 92% of the workload is read-write and covers the core business transactions of an order-entry workload, with the remaining 8% covering supplemental lookup transactions. However, in TPC-E 21.1% of the workload is read-write and covers the core business transactions of a stock-trading workload. The remaining 78.9% is distributed among supplemental lookup (54%), reporting (22.9%) and update (2%) transactions. While the core business transactions still play an essential part in the workload, more attention must be given to the read-only operations on the system.

The data domains which a workload is designed around are a byproduct of the target audience of the workload. In TPC-C, the data is based around a single domain – the warehouse. In TPC-E, the data is arranged around two domains – customers and securities. By having data arranged around multiple domains, it becomes more difficult to partition data in order to take advantage of data locality.

The transaction isolation used when implementing the business transactions of the workload determine the amount of concurrency that the workload can exhibit. A workload with a larger number of heavily-isolated business transactions will exhibit less concurrency and lower performance. In TPC-C, 45% of the business transactions are at the highest isolation level, and 96% of the transactions are at the two highest isolation levels. In TPC-E, 10% of the business transactions are at the highest isolation level, and 23.1% of the transactions are at the two highest isolation levels. In both cases, the business transactions at the highest isolation level are also the primary metrics of the workloads. In addition, TPC-E has a much smaller proportion of business transactions at the highest isolation levels, which allows for greater concurrency.

The durability of a database and the redundancy of the storage subsystem supporting the database play an important role in the performance of the environment and relevance of the environment to a typical customer. In TPC-C, there are no specific durability or redundancy requirements, aside from the requirement that the database must be durable. Typically, this is validated by restoring from a backup and doing a roll-forward recovery through the transaction logs. In TPC-E, there are specific durability requirements (Business Recovery) and redundancy requirements (Data Accessibility). In the case of durability, the task of recovering from a system failure is measured and reported; it behooves test sponsors to implement hardware and software solutions that provide quick recovery while ensuring durability. In the case of redundancy, it is required that all storage devices are protected by some level of redundancy. This ensures that critical data is always protected and accessible, even in the face of component failures.

All of these differences stem from a desire to reflect changes in real-world OLTP workloads, which are based around complex and highly-integrated business processes. While it is still true that these workloads are built around a set of core OLTP business transactions, the successful implementation of the entire workload relies on a variety of factors, including the interaction of multiple business transactions with each other, co-existence with many other light-weight lookup and reporting transactions, the need to operate on different domains of data, increased concurrency due to reduced isolation levels, and the requirement for redundant storage to minimize the impact of outages.

## 2.2    The Relevance of TPC-C and TPC-E Today

With the advent of any new standard, it is always tempting to deprecate and discontinue older standards. However, there are benefits in keeping the standards active as they appeal to different audiences. TPC-C has a long history. It is a well-understood workload, is simple to implement and execute, and the order-entry model is easy to conceptualize. This makes it a great choice for simple performance measurement and analysis purposes, by both test sponsors and academia.

TPC-E, on the other hand, is relatively new. It is a complex workload, which is more difficult to implement. The larger number of transactions, their explicit and implicit dependencies, the use of multiple data domains and increased concurrency rates make it more challenging to understand how everything operates – but customers face these problems every day with their production OLTP workloads. This makes TPC-E a very useful engineering tool, as test sponsors can better understand how their hardware and software behaves in such an environment, and use that knowledge to improve the adaptability, scalability and performance of their products to better serve their customers.

## 2.3    Why a Stock Trading Workload?

When most people think of OLTP, they think of retail or financial applications, as these are quite central to our everyday lives. This is part of the reason why the TPC-C order-entry model has become entrenched as the standard for OLTP benchmarking.

When the TPC released TPC-E designed around a stock-trading model, there was some initial confusion. While stock-trading does combine many aspects of retail and financial OLTP workloads, it is very much an outlier. While the TPC has always maintained that the TPC-E workload is quite relevant to today's OLTP environments, a demonstration will make this much clearer.

**Table 3.** Transformation of TPC-E into an Order-Entry Workload

|  | TPC-E (Stock-Trading) | Transformed (Order-Entry) |
|---|---|---|
| Business    Model Description | A brokerage firm, where the brokerage accepts trades from customers which are then fulfilled by the market. | A web-based retailer, where the retailer accepts orders from customers which are then fulfilled directly by suppliers. |
| Business    Model Components | Broker<br>Market | Retailer<br>Supplier |
| Schema | Trade<br>Security<br>Exchange | Order<br>Item<br>DistributionCenter |
| Transactions | Trade-Order<br>Market-Feed<br>Trade-Result<br>Broker-Volume<br>Customer-Position<br>Market-Watch<br>Security-Detail<br>Trade-Lookup<br>Trade-Update<br>Trade-Status | Order-Entry<br>Supplier-Feed<br>Order-Completion<br>Retailer-Volume<br>Customer-Status<br>Supplier-Watch<br>Item-Detail<br>Order-Lookup<br>Order-Update<br>Order-Status |

For ease of comprehension, it is not very hard to transform TPC-E from a stock-trading model into an order-entry model. While this is not a perfect transformation, it is sufficient to understand how the complex TPC-E stock-trading workload adequately represents a complex order-entry workload that is relevant to today's real-world applications. Under this transformation, the new workload has:

- multiple data domains – customers and items
- core OLTP queries
- customers who purchase items from a retailer (Order-Entry)
- retailers who pass on those orders to a supplier in batches (Supplier-Feed)
- suppliers who fulfill the orders (Order-Completion)
- reporting queries (Retailer-Volume, Supplier-Watch)
- lookup queries (Order-Lookup, Order-Status, Customer-Position, Item-Detail)
- update queries (Order-Update)

This transformation demonstrates that the core OLTP transactions are present, the reporting and lookup transactions serve meaningful purposes and the data domains are relevant to the order-entry model. Hence, the choice of the stock-trading model is quite valid for an OLTP workload, as it mirrors the complexity of today's order-entry workloads.

In summary, the TPC-E workload presents a very relevant, complex, OLTP workload that brings the challenges of customer environments into the engineering departments of test sponsors. TPC-E will continue to push the boundaries of effective optimization and performance tunings, ultimately for the benefit of customers. However, this does not diminish the position of TPC-C in this area, which is still a useful workload for academic and engineering analysis.

## 3     Decision Support Benchmarks

For the last decade, the research community and the industry have used TPC-D and its successor TPC-H to evaluate the performance of decision support (DSS) technology. Recognizing the paradigm shifts that happened in the industry over the last fifteen years, the TPC has developed a new decision support benchmark, TPC-DS, which was released in February 2012. The ideas and tools of TPC-DS stem from an early papers in SIGMOD [4], VLDB [6] and WOSP [2]. From an ease of benchmarking perspective it is similar to TPC-D and TPC-H. However, it adjusts for new technology and new approaches the industry has embarked upon over the fifteen years.

### 3.1    History of Decision Support Benchmarks

The roots of TPC-H date back to April 1994 when the TPC's first decision support benchmark, TPC-D, was released. For the technology available at that time, TPC-D imposed many challenges on both hardware and DBMS systems. Although the development of aggregate/summary structures, originally spurred by TPC-D (e.g. join indices, summary tables, materialized views, etc.) benefitted the industry, they effectively broke the benchmark because the decrease of query elapsed times resulted in an over proportional increase in the main performance metric. As a consequence the TPC spun off two modified versions of TPC-D: TPC-H and TPC-R. The main difference between TPC-H and TPC-R was that TPC-R allowed the use of aggregate/summary structures, where TPC-H prohibited their use. As a result, TPC-H posed a more challenging workload that was more customer-relevant and garnered the support of the industry.

## 3.2    Overview of the TPC-H Workload

TPC-H implements an ad-hoc decision support benchmark. The ad-hoc nature of the benchmark is intended to simulate a real-life scenario where database administrators (DBAs) do not know which queries will be executed against the database system; hence, knowledge about its queries and data may not be used to optimize the DBMS system. It uses a 3rd Normal Form (3NF) schema consisting of eight tables, which can be populated with up to 100 terabytes (TB) of raw data with mostly uniform distributions. It contains 22 complex and long running queries combined with 2 data maintenance functions (insert and delete). Six of the eight tables grow linearly with the scale factor.

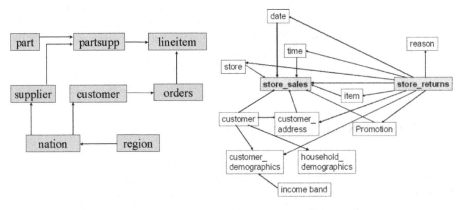

**Fig. 2.** TPC-H ER-Diagram              **Fig. 3.** TPC-DS ER-Diagram

The differences between today's decision support systems and the TPC-H benchmark specification are manifold. The TPC-H schema, although sufficiently complex to test the early systems, is not representative of all of today's more complex DSS implementations, where schemas are typically composed of a larger number of tables and columns. Furthermore, the industry's choice of schema implementation appears to have shifted from pure 3NF schemas to variations of the star schema, such as snowflake schemas.

The purity of TPC-H's 3NF schema and the low number of tables and columns may not fully reveal the differences in indexing techniques and query optimizers. Because the main tables scale linearly with the database size (scale factor), the cardinalities of some tables reach unrealistic proportions at large scale factors.

For instance, at scale factor 100,000 the database models a retailer selling 20 billion distinct parts to 15 billion customers at a transaction rate of 150 billion per year.

The database population, consisting of mostly un-skewed and synthetic data, imposes little challenges on statistic collection and optimal plan generation by the query optimizer.

The TPC-H data maintenance functions (rf1, rf2) merely constrain a potential excessive use of indices rather than testing the DBMS' capability of performing realistic data maintenance operations, common during Extraction Transformation Load (ETL) processes, also known as Data Integration (DI) processes. The data maintenance functions insert and delete orders randomly rather than ordered by time. The inserted data is assumed to be clean so that no data transformations are necessary. Data is loaded and deleted from 2 out of 8 tables.

There are relatively few distinct queries in TPC-H, and because they are known before benchmark execution, engineers can tune optimizers and execution paths to artificially increase performance of the system under test. Also, actual data warehouses are not subject to the TPC-H benchmark constraints and will define indices on non-date and non-key columns as well as contain summary tables.

### 3.3    Overview of the TPC-DS Workload

While TPC-DS [17] may be applied to any industry that must transform operational and external data into business intelligence, the workload has been granted a realistic context. It models the decision support tasks of a typical retail product supplier. The goal of selecting a retail business model is to assist the reader in relating intuitively to the components of the benchmark, without tracking that industry segment so tightly as to minimize the relevance of the benchmark. TPC-DS takes the marvels of TPC-H and TPC-R and fuses them into a modern DSS benchmark. Its main focus areas include

i)    Realistic benchmark context;

ii)   Multiple snowflake schemas (also known as a Snowstorm schema) with shared dimensions;

iii)  24 tables with an average of 18 columns;

iv)   Realistic table content and scaling

v)    Representative skewed database content;

vi)   Realistic workload;

vii)  99 distinct SQL 99 queries with random substitutions;

viii) Ad-hoc, reporting, iterative and extraction queries;

viiii) Continuous ETL (data integration process) and

x)    Easy to understand, yet meaningful and un-breakable metric.

## 3.4　Benchmark Schema and Data Population

The schema, an aggregate of multiple star schemas, contains essential business information such as detailed customer, order, and product data for the classic sales channels: store, catalog and Internet. Wherever possible, real world data are used to populate each table with common data skews such as seasonal sales and frequent names. In order to realistically scale the benchmark from small to large datasets, fact tables scale linearly while dimensions scale sub-linearly [7][12].

The design of the data set is motivated by the need to challenge the statistic gathering algorithms used for deciding the optimal query plan and the data placement algorithms, such as clustering and partitioning. TPC-DS uses a hybrid approach of data domain and data scaling. While pure synthetic data generators have great advantages, TPC-DS uses a mixture of both synthetic and real world based data domains. Synthetic data sets are well understood, easy to define and implement. However, following the TPC's paradigm to create benchmarks that businesses can relate to, a hybrid approach to data set design scores many advantages over both pure synthetic and pure real world data. This approach allows both realistically skewed data distributions yet still a predictable workload.

Compared to previous TPC decision support benchmarks, TPC-DS uses much wider tables (up to 39 columns), with domains ranging from integer, float (with various precisions), char, varchar (of various lengths) and date. Combined with a large number of tables (total of 25 tables and 429 columns) the schema gives both the opportunity to develop realistic and challenging queries as well as the opportunity for innovative data placement algorithms and other schema optimizations, such as complex auxiliary data structures. The number of times columns are referenced in the dataset varies between 0 and 189.

Of those columns accessed, the largest numbers of columns are referenced between 5 and 49 times. The large column set and diverse query set of TPC-DS also protects its metric from unrealistic tuning and artificial inflations of the metric, a problem which rapidly destroyed the usefulness of TPC-D in the late 1990s. That, combined with the complex data maintenance functions and load time participating in the primary performance metric, creates the need for fast and efficient algorithms to create and maintain auxiliary data structures and the invention of new algorithms.

The introduction of NULL values into any column except the primary keys opens yet another dimension of challenges for the query optimizer compared to prior TPC decision support benchmarks. The percent of NULL values in each non-primary key column varies from 4 to 100 percent based on the column. Most columns have 4 percent NULL values. The important rec_end_date columns have 50 percent NULL values. Some columns were unused (total of 236) or intentionally left entirely NULL for future enhancements of the query set.

## 3.5　Benchmark Workload

The benchmark abstracts the diversity of operations found in an information analysis application, while retaining essential performance characteristics. As it is necessary to execute a great number of queries and data transformations to completely manage any business analysis environment, TPC-DS defines 99 distinct SQL-99 queries –with Online Analytical Processing (OLAP) amendment –and 12 data maintenance operations covering typical DSS-like query types such as ad-hoc, reporting, iterative (drill down/up) and extraction queries and periodic refresh of the database.

Due to strict implementation rules it is possible to amalgamate ad-hoc and reporting queries into the same benchmark; it is possible to use sophisticated auxiliary data structures for reporting queries while prohibiting them for ad-hoc queries. Although the emphasis is on information analysis, the benchmark recognizes the need to periodically refresh the database (ETL). The database is not a one-time snapshot of a business operations database, nor is it a database where OLTP applications are running concurrently. The database must be able to support queries and data maintenance operations against all tables. Some TPC benchmarks (e.g., TPC-C and TPC-App) model the operational aspect of the business environment where transactions are executed on a real time basis; other benchmarks (e.g. TPC-H) address the simpler, more static model of decision support. The TPC-DS benchmark, however, models the challenges of business intelligence systems where operational data is used both to support sound business decisions in near real-time and to direct long-range planning and exploration. The TPC-DS operations address complex business problems using a variety of access patterns, query phrasings, operators and answer set constraints.

## 3.6    Metric

The TPC-DS workload consists of three distinct disciplines: Database Load, Power Run and Throughput Run. The power run executes 99 templates using random bind variables. Each throughput run executes multiple sessions each executing the same 99 query templates with different bind variables in permutated order, thereby simulating a workload of multiple concurrent users accessing the system.

- SF is the scale factor used for a benchmark
- S is the number of concurrent streams, i.e. the number of concurrent users
- Q is the total number of weighted queries: Q=3* S*99, with S being the number of streams executed in a throughput run
- TPT=TPower*S, where TPT is the total elapsed time to complete the Power Test
- TTT= TTT1+TTT2, where TTT1 is the total elapsed time of Throughput Test 1 and TTT2 is the total elapsed time of Throughput Test 2
- TLD is the load factor TLD=0.01*S*TLoad, and TLoad is the actual load time
- TPT, TTT and TLD quantities are in units of decimal hours with a resolution of at least 1/3600th of an hour (i.e., 1 second)

The Performance Metric reflects the effective query throughput per second. The numerator represents the total number of queries executed on the system "198 * S", where 198 is the 99 individual queries times two query runs and S is the number of concurrent simulated users. The denominator represents the total elapsed time as the sum of Query Run1, Data Maintenance Run, Query Run 2 and a fraction of the Load Time. Note that the elapsed time of the data maintenance run is the aggregate of S executions of all data maintenance functions. By dividing the total number of queries by the total elapsed time, this metric represents queries executed per time period. Using an arithmetic mean to compute the primary benchmark metric should cause DBMS developers to concentrate primarily on long-running queries first, and then progressively continue with shorter queries. This generally matches the normal business case, where customers spend most of their tuning resources on the slowest queries. For a complete specification, please refer to [17].

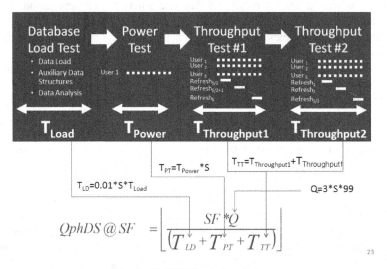

**Fig. 4.** TPC-DS Execution Order

## 4      Virtualization Benchmarks

Virtualization on x86 systems started out as a means of allowing multiple Linux and Windows operating systems to execute simultaneously on a single PC, but it has since become a foundation of enterprise data centers. It enables:

- Consolidation of multiple operating environments onto one server
- Migration of a VM to a new physical server while the applications on the VM continue to be in use, freeing the original server for maintenance operations
- Live migration of VMs between hosts allows for a rich set of load balancing and resource management features. Virtualization is the fundamental enabling technology behind cloud computing.
- High-Availability after a server failure by allowing its VMs to restart on a new server
- Fault-tolerance on generic servers without hardware fault-tolerance features

Databases are the last frontier to be conquered by virtualization. Only recently have virtualized servers been able to offer the level of throughput, predictable performance, scaling, storage and networking load, and reliability that databases demand. This in turn has led to customer demands for better metrics to compare virtualization technologies under database workloads. TPCTC 2009 and TPCTC 2010 papers outlined this need, and presented proposals for developing a benchmark for virtualized databases [14][8].

## 4.1   The Evolution of Two Virtualization Benchmark Endeavors

In response to this demand, the TPC formed a Development Subcommittee[1] in 2010 with the goal of developing a new benchmark called TPC-V. During the development phase of TPC-V, it became obvious that a second, simpler benchmark would be useful because:

- TPC-V is a complex benchmark which will take a few years to develop.
- The development of a new workload necessitates system and database vendors to develop new benchmark kits, for use during prototyping.
- It represents a complex, cloud-inspired workload but there is also demand for a simpler configuration of small numbers of databases virtualized on one server.

These reasons led to the formation of a second Development Subcommittee to develop a TPC-VMS (TPC Virtual Measurement Single System) benchmark. The TPC-VMS Specification leverages the existing TPC benchmarks, TPC-C, TPC-E, TPC-H and TPC-DS, by adding the methodology and requirements for running and reporting virtualization metrics. A major driving force behind TPC-VMS was defining the specification in such a way as to make it possible for benchmark sponsors to run an existing TPC benchmark on a virtual server without the need for modification to the existing benchmarking kit for that benchmark. Hence, it is expected that the TPC-VMS specification will be completed quickly, and will lead to a large number of publications using existing benchmarking kits.

TPC-VMS and TPC-V fulfill the demands of two different market segments. TPC-VMS emulates a simple consolidation scenario of three identical databases running the same workload on the same OS, DBMS, etc. TPC-V emulates a complex cloud computing environment with varying numbers of VMs, two different workloads (with OLTP and DSS properties), dynamic increases and decreases of the load presented to each VM, etc.

## 4.2   TPC-VMS Benchmark

The goals for TPC-VMS are to measure TPC benchmarks in a virtualized environment as follows:

---

[1] A TPC Development Subcommittee is the working forum within the TPC for the development of a Specification.

- Provide the virtualization measurements that a typical customer of the particular systems benchmarked would consume.
- Provide virtualization metrics that are comparable between systems under test for a particular TPC Benchmark Standard.
- Provide for repeatable and documented measurements.
- Leverage existing TPC Benchmark Standards without requiring any implementation changes.

The TPC Benchmark Standard Database Servers are consolidated onto the Consolidated Database Server as depicted by Figure 5. As shown the Database Server's Operating Systems and DBMSs are consolidated onto the Consolidated Database Server each in a separate Virtual Machine.

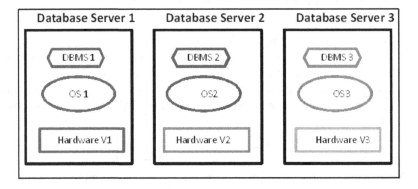

**Fig. 5.** TPC-VMS Consolidation Configuration

Aggregating the results of three different benchmark runs into a single metric can be daunting, given the potential for gaming the results by boosting the performance of one VM at the expense of another. TPC-VMS avoids the aggregation problem by defining the metric as the lowest metric reported by any of the three VMs.

Early prototyping results with the TPC-E and TPC-H benchmarks have shown that TPC-VMS will meet its goals with a quick development schedule. The benchmark specification is nearing completion, and TPC-VMS is expected to be approved in late 2012.

### 4.3    TPC-VMC Benchmark Proposal

The TPC has formed a Working Group to investigate a TPC-VMC (TPC Virtual Measurement Complex Systems) benchmark. The idea is to extend TPC-VMS into a more complex benchmark. The Working Group is considering the following functions:

- Elasticity: the load presented to the VMs will vary with time
- Live migrations: Due to increase in load, VMs will migrate from one server to a second, idle server

- Deployment: this important property of cloud computing datacenters will be emulated by the creation of a VM from a template, and subsequent deployment and booting up of the VM before it starts running transactions

TPC-VMC is still in the definition stage. Since it can be run using existing TPC benchmarking kits, it is a good alternative to TPC-V should TPC-V development be delayed due to its dependence on a new benchmarking kit.

### 4.4    TPC-V Benchmark

The TPC-V Development Subcommittee chose to base TPC-V upon the existing TPC-E [18] benchmark to speed the development process. Using the TPC-E transactions as a base, the working group has defined 3 VMs that together form a *Set* for the TPC-V benchmark. The functionality of the Tier B component of the TPC-E System Under Test (SUT) has been divided into two separate VMs. One VM handles the Trade-Lookup and Trade-Update transactions, simulating the high storage I/O load of a decision support environment. The second VM services all other transactions, which have a CPU-heavy profile and represent an OLTP environment.

Tier A in TPC-V functions similarly to a TPC-E Tier A with one major difference: based on the transaction type, it routes the transaction to one of the two Tier B VMs. In Figure 6, notations TL, TU, etc. under the VMs are the 2-letter abbreviations of TPC E transactions.

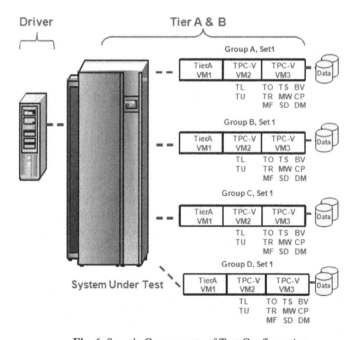

**Fig. 6.** Sample Components of Test Configuration

The Subcommittee has devised a Set architecture whereby both the number of Sets, and the load placed on each Set grow as the performance of the system increases. The advantage here is that the benchmark will emulate the behavior of real-world servers: more powerful servers host more VMs, but also VMs that handle more load.

Another major feature of TPC-V is varying the load to the many VMs during the measurement interval to emulate the elasticity that is ubiquitous in cloud computing environments. The overall load will remain constant, but the portion directed to each Set will vary. An expected side effect is configuring the VMs with oversubscribed resources that are typical of virtualized servers. For example, a server with 64 physical CPUs might need to run with 24 VMs whose virtual CPUs total 150 in order to handle the elastic nature of the load. The chart below depicts how the load to four Sets might vary over the 2-hour Measurement Interval.

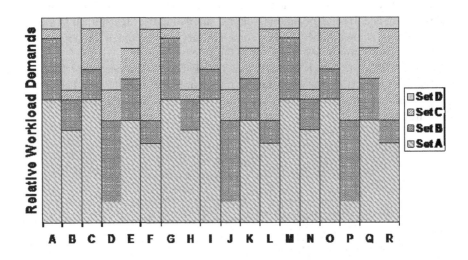

**Fig. 7.** TPC V elastic load variation

### 4.5    A Reference Kit for TPC-V Benchmark

The Development Subcommittee has taken on the task of developing a publicly-available, end-to-end reference kit for the benchmark. The reference kit is being developed in Java and C++ and will use the PostgreSQL open source database. This is the first TPC benchmark that will be available with an end-to-end kit, making it possible for anyone to download the kit and immediately run a very complex benchmark using an open source database. Furthermore, the availability of the kit with its driver, which will take care of apportioning the load among the VMs as well as varying the load from period to period, will mean the test sponsors are relieved from dealing with all the complex features of the benchmark. If a sponsor chooses to run the benchmark against a commercial DBMS, they can replace PostgreSQL with a commercial DBMS and publish results.

### 4.6    Status of TPC-V Benchmark

The TPC-V Development Subcommittee has focused much of its effort on developing the end-to-end reference kit, as it will be highly useful when prototyping the workload and evaluating changes. The kit is now mostly functional, as it is able to drive both the TPC-E and TPC-V workloads, and runs all but 2 of the transactions. Early prototyping results indicate that while PostgreSQL performance might not match that of a highly-tuned commercial database, it will be more than sufficient to evaluate a heavily-virtualized database benchmark.

## 5    Data Integration Benchmark

The TPC-DI benchmark originated from the TPC-ETL initiative, outlined in [3]. It is designed to be a performance test for systems that move and integrate data from various data sources, so called Data Integration (DI) systems (a.k.a. Extract, Transform and Load, or ETL systems). As these systems perform an intricate part in building data warehouse systems, they have been around for quite some time and are available from a number of vendors. However, until now there has been no standard to compare them in a fair and accurate way.

The benchmark workload transforms data extracted from an On-Line Transaction Processing (OTLP) system and loads it along with data from ancillary data sources (including tabular and hierarchical structures) into a data warehouse. The source and destination schemas, data transformations and implementation rules have been designed to be broadly representative of modern data integration requirements. No single benchmark can reflect the entire range of possible DI requirements. However, using data and operation models of a retail brokerage the TPC-DI benchmark exercises a breadth of system components associated with DI environments, which are characterized by:

- The manipulation and loading of large volumes of data
- A mixture of transformation types including error checking, surrogate key lookups, data type conversions, aggregation operations, data updates, etc.
- Historical loading and incremental updates of a destination Data Warehouse using the transformed data
- Consistency requirements ensuring that the integration process results in reliable and accurate data
- Multiple data sources having different formats
- Multiple data tables with varied data types, attributes and inter-table relationships

**Fig. 8.** TPC-DI Benchmark Phases

The Performance Metric reported by TPC-DI is a throughput measure, the number of source rows processed per second. Conceptually, it is calculated by dividing the total rows processed by the elapsed time of the run. Each benchmark run consists of the following phases, which are performed in the following sequence:

The primary performance metric is defined as: GeoMean($T_H$, min($T_{I1}$ , $T_{I2}$) ) with:

- $T_H$ being the historical load performance: $T_H = \dfrac{R_G}{E_H}$
- $T_{Ii}$ i$\in${1,2} being the incremental load performance: $T_H = \dfrac{R_{Ii}}{\max{(E_{Ii}, 1800)}}$

TPC-DI is still under development and, therefore, the specification may change until its planned release in 2013.

# 6    TPC Technology Conference Initiative

Over the past quarter-century, the Transaction Processing Performance Council (TPC) has developed several industry standards for performance benchmarking, which have been a significant driving force behind the development of faster, less expensive, and more energy efficient systems.

To keep pace with the rapidly changing information technology landscape, four years ago the TPC initiated the international conference series on Performance Evaluation and Benchmarking (TPCTC). The objective of this conference series is to bring industry experts and research community together in developing new standards and enhancing existing standards in performance evaluation and benchmarking.

The first TPC Technology Conference on Performance Evaluation and Benchmarking (TPCTC 2009) was held in conjunction with the 35th International Conference on Very Large Data Bases (VLDB 2009) in Lyon, France from August 24th to August 28th, 2009 [9]. The second conference (TPCTC 2010) was held in conjunction with the 36th International Conference on Very Large Data Bases (VLDB 2010) in Singapore from September 13th to September 17th, 2010 [10], while the third (TPCTC 2011) was held in conjunction with the 37th International Conference on Very Large Data Bases (VLDB 2011) in Seattle from August 29th to September 3rd, 2011 [11]. This conference series has been a tremendous success. The initiation of the development of benchmarks in virtualization and data integration has been a direct result.

The areas of focus of the fourth TPC Technology Conference on Performance Evaluation and Benchmarking (TPCTC 2012) include:

- Big Data analytics and infrastructure
- Database Appliances
- Cloud Computing
- In-memory databases
- Social media infrastructure
- Business intelligence
- Complex event processing
- Database optimizations

- Green computing
- Disaster tolerance and recovery
- Energy and space efficiency
- Hardware innovations
- Data Integration
- Hybrid workloads
- Virtualization

**Acknowledgements.** The authors thank the past and present members of the TPC for their contribution to the specifications and documents referenced in this paper.

TPC Benchmark$^{TM}$ and TPC-C$^{TM}$ are trademarks of the Transaction Processing Performance Council.

# References

1. Young, E., Cao, P., Nikolaiev, M.: First TPC-Energy Benchmark: Lessons Learned in Practice. In: Nambiar, R., Poess, M. (eds.) TPCTC 2010. LNCS, vol. 6417, pp. 136–152. Springer, Heidelberg (2011)
2. Stephens, J.M., Poess, M.: MUDD: a multi-dimensional data generator. In: WOSP 2004, pp. 104–109 (2004)
3. Wyatt, L., Caufield, B., Pol, D.: Principles for an ETL Benchmark. In: Nambiar, R., Poess, M. (eds.) TPCTC 2009. LNCS, vol. 5895, pp. 183–198. Springer, Heidelberg (2009)
4. Poess, M., Smith, B., Kollár, L., Larson, P.-Å.: TPC-DS, taking decision support benchmarking to the next level. In: SIGMOD Conference 2002, pp. 582–587 (2002)
5. Poess, M., Floyd, C.: New TPC Benchmarks for Decision Support and We-Commerce. SIGMOD 2000 Record 29(4), 64–71 (2000)
6. Poess, M., Stephens, J.M.: Generating Thousand Benchmark Queries in Seconds. In: VLDB 2004, pp. 1045–1053 (2004)
7. Poess, M., Nambiar, R., Walrath, D.: Why You Should Run TPC-DS: A Workload Analysis. In: VLDB 2007, pp. 1138–1149 (2007)
8. Sethuraman, P., Taheri, H.R.: TPC-V: A Benchmark for Evaluating the Performance of Database Applications in Virtual Environments. In: Nambiar, R., Poess, M. (eds.) TPCTC 2010. LNCS, vol. 6417, pp. 121–135. Springer, Heidelberg (2011)
9. Nambiar, R., Poess, M. (eds.): Topics in Performance Evaluation, Measurement and Characterization. Springer (2012) ISBN 978-3-642-32626-4
10. Nambiar, R., Poess, M. (eds.): Performance Evaluation, Measurement and Characterization of Complex Systems. Springer (2011) ISBN 978-3-642-18205-1
11. Nambiar, R., Poess, M. (eds.): Performance Evaluation and Benchmarking. Springer (2009) ISBN 978-3-642-10423-7
12. Nambiar, R., Poess, M.: The Making of TPC-DS. In: VLDB 2006, pp. 1049–1058 (2006)
13. Nambiar, R., Poess, M.: Transaction Performance vs. Moore's Law: A Trend Analysis. In: Nambiar, R., Poess, M. (eds.) TPCTC 2010. LNCS, vol. 6417, pp. 110–120. Springer, Heidelberg (2011)

14. Bose, S., Mishra, P., Sethuraman, P., Taheri, R.: Benchmarking Database Performance in a Virtual Environment. In: Nambiar, R., Poess, M. (eds.) TPCTC 2009. LNCS, vol. 5895, pp. 167–182. Springer, Heidelberg (2009)
15. TPC Energy Specification, http://www.tpc.org/tpc_energy/spec/TPC-Energy_Specification_1.2.0.pdf
16. TPC: TPC Benchmark C Specification, http://www.tpc.org/tpcc/spec/tpcc_current.pdf
17. TPC: TPC Benchmark DS Specification, http://www.tpc.org/tpcds/spec/tpcds_1.1.0.pdf
18. TPC: TPC-Pricing Specification, http://www.tpc.org/tpce/spec/v1.12.0/TPCE-v1.12.0.pdf
19. TPC: TPC Benchmark H Specification, http://www.tpc.org/tpch/spec/tpch2.14.4.pdf
20. Hogan, T.: Overview of TPC Benchmark E: The Next Generation of OLTP Benchmarks. In: Nambiar, R., Poess, M. (eds.) TPCTC 2009. LNCS, vol. 5895, pp. 84–98. Springer, Heidelberg (2009)

# Incorporating Recovery from Failures into a Data Integration Benchmark

Len Wyatt[1], Brian Caufield[2], Marco Vieira[3], and Meikel Poess[4]

[1] Microsoft Corporation, USA
lenwy@microsoft.com
[2] IBM, USA
bcaufiel@us.ibm.com
[3] CISUC - Department of Informatics Engineering, University of Coimbra, Portugal
mvieira@dei.uc.pt
[4] Oracle Corporation, 500 Oracle Pkwy, Redwood Shores, CA 94065, USA
meikel.poess@oracle.com

**Abstract.** The proposed TPC-DI benchmark measures the performance of Data Integration systems (a.k.a. ETL systems) given the task of integrating data from an OLTP system and other data sources to create a data warehouse. This paper describes the scenario, structure and timing principles used in TPC-DI. Although failure recovery is very important in real deployments of Data Integration systems, certain complexities made it difficult to specify in the benchmark. Hence failure recovery aspects have been scoped out of the current version of TPC-DI. The issues around failure recovery are discussed in detail and some options are described. Finally the audience is invited to offer additional suggestions.

**Keywords:** Industry Standard Benchmarks, Data Integration, ETL, ACID properties, Durability, Dependability, Reliability, Recovery, Data Warehouse, Decision Support.

## 1 Introduction

A data integration (DI) tool is software whose purpose is to provide a way to specify the steps to be taken in moving and transforming data from different sources to specific destinations. Such tools typically aid in the parsing and processing of input data, performing data type transformations, looking up data in other data sets or joining data sets, performing certain operations conditionally depending on data values, aggregating data, cleansing data, and writing data to a destination location which is often a data warehouse. Despite the long list of common functions, there is no standard definition of a data integration tool and available tools follow a variety of conceptual models. What unites them is that such tools increase the productivity of a developer of DI applications.

While productivity is a difficult aspect to measure, it is possible to measure the performance of the resulting implementation. Just like benchmarks for relational

R. Nambiar and M. Poess (Eds.): TPCTC 2012, LNCS 7755, pp. 21–33, 2013.
© Springer-Verlag Berlin Heidelberg 2013

databases focus on the performance of the databases while ignoring other important evaluation criteria, the TPC-DI benchmark focuses on the performance of the implementation. The metric measures throughput, effectively the number of data rows per second that the DI system processes, for the workload defined.

At the TPC Technical Conference in 2009, the paper "Principles for an ETL Benchmark" [1] noted marketplace conditions that suggested a need for a data integration benchmark. It outlined key characteristics of such a benchmark, discussed some key decision points, and noted that a TPC committee (TPC-ETL development subcommittee) had been formed to pursue the effort. Since then the benchmark has evolved. The first obvious difference between the ETL benchmark proposed in 2009 and the work discussed here is a name change, from TPC-ETL (for Extract-Transform-Load) to TPC-DI (for Data Integration). This does not represent a change in the focus of the benchmark, but is intended both to reflect more current nomenclature and to emphasize the idea that truly disparate data sources are being integrated into one data warehouse. As will be discussed later, the benchmark models Change Data Capture (CDC) data from a relational data source being combined with XML data from another system and with variable-format records from a third system. In all, there are five distinct data sources and 19 file definitions.

Data integration problems and tools can be divided in two classes: batch-oriented and "real-time." Batch-oriented systems are quite common, with the canonical case involving businesses that update a data warehouse from the OLTP system on a daily basis, usually after the close of business. Each batch covers a time period, and while daily batches are exceedingly common, the time periods can be from minutes to months. There are even cases where the data warehouse is created once and never updated. At the other end of the spectrum, there are organizations that want the data warehouse updated on a "real-time" basis. ("Real-time" is placed in quotes because there is always some lag in processing the data.) Such systems require very different tools, and many organizations will instead emulate "real-time" updates by running batches on short cycles, perhaps every few minutes. The TPC-DI benchmark focuses on batch data integration, and models daily updates.

As noted in "Principles for an ETL Benchmark", reliability in situations where the system is degraded (such as failed disk drives) is an important aspect of DI systems. Furthermore, despite the best efforts of system designers and software developers, failures that terminate data processing (such as a power loss) will eventually occur. In practice, a well-designed DI system should have provisions for these situations and be able to recover expediently. The authors of the benchmark intended from the beginning to include some measure of the performance of the DI system in recovery circumstances. However, this has proven intractable so far as it is not trivial to incorporate the complexities of reliably and recovery into this benchmark which is otherwise focused on performance.

Various questions arose during discussions, including: What types of failures to include? What is the tradeoff between failure prevention versus failure recovery? How can failure recovery be included in the primary performance metric? This paper puts forward some ideas on how to address such questions in a future version of TPC-DI.

The remainder of the paper is organized as follows: Section 2 gives a brief overview of TPC-DI focusing on the key differences between the early draft of TPC-ETL and the current version, TPC-DI. Section 3.2 outlines the principles for scaling and measurements in the benchmark. Section 4 addresses some reasons why the decision to integrate failure recovery has been difficult for the TPC-DI development subcommittee. Finally, Section 5 discusses how recovery and dependability aspects might be integrated into the benchmark metric.

## 2     Overview of TPC-DI

Each TPC benchmark is modeled after a specific business, which helps the reader understand the benchmark and relate real world business and their workloads to the benchmark. The TPC-DI benchmark models the loading of data into the data warehouse of a brokerage company. The data is modeled as coming from multiple sources, including the brokerage OLTP system, a human resources (HR) database, a customer management system, a market data "newswire" feed, and an external source with marketing information on prospective clients. This scenario was chosen because integrating and loading data from operational systems into a data warehouse is a very common usage pattern for DI tools. Data from these sources is initially stored in a staging area, and from the staging area it must be integrated together, transformed according to defined business rules, and loaded into the data warehouse. Figure 1 illustrates the model conceptually.

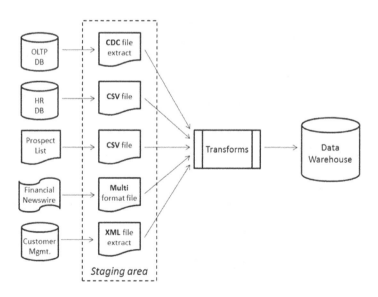

**Fig. 1.** DI Data Sources

## 2.1    Scope of the SUT

The source systems shown on the left side of Figure 1, i.e. OLTP DB, HR DB, Prospect List, Financial Newswire and Customer Management, are not physically present in the benchmark; rather, a data generator creates data that represents the output of those systems. Figure 2 illustrates the benchmarked system, which is referred to in TPC as the System under Test (SUT).

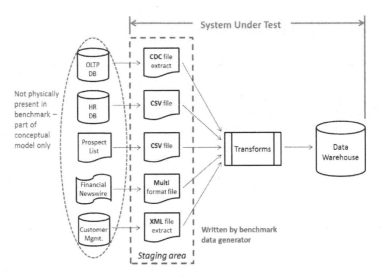

**Fig. 2.** The System Under Test (SUT)

The data generator writes data into a staging area, which represents a common feature of DI systems. Staging areas are used to allow DI processing to be done asynchronously from data extraction, and also to provide safe-keeping for data that can be referenced again in case of future needs. The staging area is also valuable for the benchmark, because actually requiring access to the source systems would make the benchmark intractable to perform. The other boundary of the SUT includes the target data warehouse because of the tight coupling that is common between DI systems and data warehouses.

The implementation can include separate servers for the staging area, transformations and data warehouse, or all three functions can be combined on a single server, or any of the roles distributed over clusters of machines. Regardless of the topology, all hardware, software and communication facilities used to perform the benchmark are part of the SUT.

## 2.2    Data Warehouse Model

A dimensional design approach [2] is used for the TPC-DI data warehouse. In a dimensional model, dimension tables describe entities of interest to the business.

Examples include the broker dimension table, which lists all the brokers and their attributes of interest, the customer dimension, the security dimension, etc. Fact tables describe events of interest, such as a trades table recording all stock purchases and sales, or a security history table which lists the closing prices and trade volumes of all the securities. Foreign key relationships provide the connection between the events in fact tables and the entities in dimension tables. For example, a trade is executed by a particular broker on behalf of a particular customer, involving a particular security.

The TPC-DI schema involves several dimension tables and fact tables, some reference tables that remain static after they are initially populated, and one table that records the status of the data integration work itself (see **Error! Reference source not found.**). There are some tables that can play multiple roles, depending on the context in which they are used.

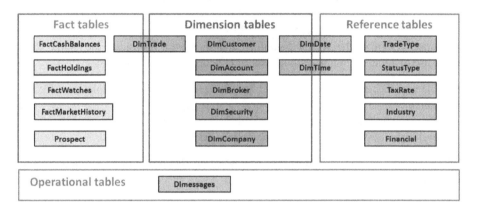

**Fig. 3.** Pictorial overview of the Data Warehouse Tables

## 2.3    Historical Load and Incremental Updates

Most data warehouses are initially created from a large volume of existing data, then are maintained by incrementally adding more data. TPC-DI defines the initial creation as the Historical Load and the update operations as Incremental Updates. The model defines the updates as occurring on a daily basis, which is a natural fit for the brokerage business model. In practice, the financial markets have daily closings, and portfolios are given valuations corresponding to the daily market closings.

The Historical Load and Incremental Updates have some different properties:

- The Historical Load includes a large data volume, representing a significant amount of historical data being transformed and loaded at the initial creation of the data warehouse.
- During Incremental Updates, which have generally have a smaller data set and a limited time window, the data warehouse must remain readable for users.

Because the work involved in a Historical Load is different from an Incremental Update, the benchmark allows two implementations to be used. Furthermore, two incremental updates are required for the benchmark, but the same implementation must be used for each incremental update. This ensures that all actions needed to prepare for another batch are included in the benchmark implementation.

## 2.4   ACID versus OPEN Data Warehouse Systems

The destination of the transformed data is a data warehouse system. Whether or not full ACID database properties are required in the data warehouse is a choice unique to each customer organization. Some have reasons to require ACID properties, but for others those properties impose unnecessary overhead. To reflect the variety of systems used to implement data warehouses, TPC-DI defines two data warehouse classes, called ACID and OPEN. The use of the OPEN class is analogous to many sporting events, where there are classes that restrict the potential contestants by age or equipment, while the OPEN class allows all contestants meeting the basic criteria for the sport. As the names suggest, the ACID data warehouse class requires the data warehouse system to be ACID compliant, while the OPEN class allows the data warehouse to adhere to a more relaxed set of concurrency requirements:

1. Data in the data warehouse needs to be consistent upon completion of each batch,
2. Data in the data warehouse can be queried at any time after the completion of each batch, even during execution of a successive batch.

Benchmark results from different classes are not considered comparable and will be listed separately on the TPC website.

## 2.5   Transformations Summary

Transformations, generally speaking, are everything that must be done to prepare data for loading into the Data Warehouse. The benchmark operations model activities that are common in DI systems, including:

- Conversion of data from raw characters (from the flat files) to data types compatible with the Data Warehouse implementation
- Lookups of business keys to obtain surrogate keys for the data warehouse
- Merging or formatting multiple fields into one, or splitting one field into multiple
- Determining the interpretation of a field with multiple possible meanings
- Checking data for errors or for adherence to business rules
- Detecting changes in dimension data, and applying appropriate tracking mechanisms
- Adding new data for fact tables

It is not uncommon for the rules governing a historical load to be different from those governing an incremental update. This is also true in the TPC-DI benchmark: some properties of the Historical Load data are different than the Incremental Update data, and in fact there are data sources that are used only in the Historical Load.

## 3    Measurement and Scaling Principles for TPC-DI

### 3.1    Metrics

TPC-DI, as any other TPC benchmarks, defines three metrics: primary performance, price-performance, and availability. The primary performance metric chosen for TPC-DI is a throughput measurement. Clearly this metric is highly dependent on the workload, so a throughput result from the benchmark should not be compared to any particular real-world environment.

The performance result is stated in terms of rows per second. Given that there are multiple data sets in the benchmark and varying amounts of work-per-record, this is an indicative result only – it does not measure the speed of any single operation. A result in terms of bytes per second would be possible, but that was avoided to discourage comparisons to I/O systems, which clearly do not have the computational complexity of a DI system. Despite those caveats, rows-per-second is a simple concept to understand and allows easy comparison of different benchmark executions. The performance result is computed as follows:

- The data generator provides in its output the total number of "rows" in each batch of data generated.
- The time to execute the historical load is measured, and a throughput $T_H$ is calculated using the row count for that batch.
- The time to execute each of two incremental updates is measured, and throughputs $T_{I1}$ and $T_{I2}$ are calculated using the row counts for those batches.
- The overall metric is defined as the geometric mean of the historical load speed and the slower of the two incremental updates:

$$T = \sqrt[2]{T_H * \min\left(T_{I1}, T_{I2}\right)} \text{ , with } T_H = \frac{R_H}{E_H} \text{, } T_{I1} = \frac{R_{I1}}{\max\left(E_{I1}, 1800\right)} \text{ and } T_{I2} = \frac{R_{I2}}{\max\left(E_{I2}, 1800\right)}$$

Where:

$R_H$ denotes the number of rows processed during the historical load

$R_{I1}$, $R_{I2}$ denote the number of rows processed during the two incremental updates

$E_H$ denotes the elapsed time of historical load

$E_{I1}$, $E_{I2}$ denote the elapsed times of the two incremental updates

The price-performance metric is computed by dividing the performance metric by the cost of the system, using standard rules that apply to all TPC benchmarks. The availability metric gives the date when a similar system could be purchased, and also follows standard TPC rules.

Production DI systems tend to have time between batches: a batch might run one night and another batch won't start until the next night. In a benchmarking context this is not acceptable, because it could allow useful work to be performed between batches ("off the clock," so to speak). For example, data might be inserted into a data warehouse table and the batch could be declared finished because the data is committed and available. Then indexes might be created on the table after the batch completes but before the next batch is started. If the DI system benefits from that index, then some of the work for the benchmark has been omitted from the timing. To prevent such situations, TPC-DI is designed to have the batches run sequentially with each immediately following the prior batch. There is no available time between batches.

## 3.2    Data Set Scaling

The size of the data set is determined by a Scale Factor (SF). The SF is input to the data generator, which generates and writes all data for the staging area. With the exception of a few small files of fixed size, files scale linearly with the SF. The Scale Factor is chosen at the discretion of the test sponsor, but must result in a run time for the first incremental update that is less than 60 minutes. If the incremental update run time exceeds 60 minutes, the run is considered invalid and a smaller SF should be chosen. If the incremental update run time is less than 30 minutes, the run will be assigned a value of 30 minutes. This is not in the best interest of the test sponsor, so they should choose a larger SF.

The reason for setting the SF based on the incremental update time is that many real-world DI implementations are constrained to a "batch window" – the time available for the DI system to work. For systems that run on a daily basis, the batch window often occurs at night. A goal of TPC-DI is to model the time constraint while also making the batch window small enough so that overall execution of the benchmark can be done in a reasonable time. Furthermore, as the metric for TPC-DI is a throughput metric and the batch window is limited, it will be necessary for implementations to use a larger data set in order to report higher results. At the same time, a reasonable range of times is acceptable so that test sponsors can find a workable SF without too much trouble.

# 4    Issues When Including Failure Recovery

A system failure occurs when the service delivered by the system deviates from fulfilling the system's goal [4]. An error is a perturbation of the system state, which is prone to lead to a failure. The cause for an error is called a fault that can be active or latent (an active fault leads to an error, otherwise the fault is latent). In the context of this benchmark we are particularly interested in failures that cause the data integration processing to be interrupted unexpectedly. In fact, the data integration process should be capable of restarting the processing (by performing the required recovery tasks) whenever there is a failure, in particular during the incremental loads. In practice, the final result, in terms of the data loaded into the data warehouse, has to be the same as if there was no failure.

## 4.1    Possible Points of Failure

As explained in Section 2.1, TPC-DI defines the SUT to contain three logical components, the Staging Area, the Data Integration Server, and the Data Warehouse. The physical deployment topology is allowed to range anywhere from a single system containing all components to dedicated systems for each component (which may in turn be made up of multiple physical systems). The benchmark also defines three phases of execution and the transformations that must be performed in each, but each implementation is free to define when, where, and how the processing of the transformations occur within each phase. This creates a wide variety of possible points of failure and recovery scenarios that may be considered.

Failures that occur as a result of a hardware problem could be considered. These include power failures, disk failures, memory faults, and loss of network connectivity. Since the benchmark allows for many configurations, the software components running on any particular hardware component may differ, and therefore the nature of the recovery scenario will differ. For example, if a configuration uses a single server, a power failure on the server will cause an immediate interruption of all software components. On the other hand, in a configuration that uses multiple servers, a power failure in a server may only cause the Data Warehouse component to become unavailable.

Other failures can occur which are not necessarily caused by hardware faults, but due to software faults or user mistakes. Example of these include the Staging Area or Data Warehouse becoming unavailable, a process being killed by a user or the OS, and resource limits being reached, e.g. running out of memory. However, the resulting recovery scenario for these types of failures is also dependent on which software component the failure occurs in, and the hardware topology used.

## 4.2    Defining Failure Scenarios

Due to the variety of failures and variability of deployment topologies, defining the failure scenarios is a difficult task. In fact, the number and type of failures that may impact a complex computer system is immense. Thus, the *failure-load* should comprise the minimum set of representative failures that are deemed relevant for the characterization of the existing recovery features.

In a benchmarking context, a failure is characterized by three attributes: the type, the trigger, and the duration. The *type* defines the kind of failure being emulated (e.g. disk failure, power failure). The *trigger* defines how the failure is activated and can be time-based (e.g. the failure is emulated some time after starting an incremental load) or event-based (e.g. synchronized with an event of the workload). Finally, the *duration* specifies for how long the failure is active. In practice, a failure may be transient (i.e. the failure is active for a limited period of time; an example may be a power failure) or permanent (i.e. fixing the problem may require human intervention; an example is a disk failure, where the disk has to be replaced).

Table 1 presents some examples of failures that could be included in the benchmark, considering the different benchmark components. It is important to emphasize that instantiation of these failures involves additional information and may require understanding the specific SUT configuration. For example, for the "File Corrupted" failure we need to specify which file. Also, the "OS Reboot" failure would affect the entire system if the system is based on a single machine, while it would affect only one component if the staging area, the transforms, and the data warehouse run in different machines.

**Table 1.** Failure Examples

| Benchmark Component | Type of Failure | Comments |
|---|---|---|
| Staging Area | File Inaccessible | Simulates a problem in the storage device (e.g. transient disk failure). |
| | File Corrupted | Simulates a problem in the disks or file system (may be transient or permanent). |
| Transforms | OS Restart | Clean operating system restart while the transforms are running. Simulates an operator mistake. |
| | OS Reboot | Abrupt operating system reboots. Simulates a problem in the operating system or other component that causes the system to crash. |
| Warehouse DB | DB Connection Drops | Connection from the transforms to the data warehouse drops. Simulates a problem in the communication (e.g. a network problem) |
| | DB crash | The database server crashes and must be restarted (database recovery may happen during restart) |
| SUT | Power Failure | All the system goes down due to a failure in the power source. |

Another aspect that needs to be taken into account when defining failure scenarios is failure distribution. In order to accurately characterize the impact of failures in the data integration process, multiple failures should be injected in different moments (i.e. the trigger should be distributed over time). This is particularly relevant, as a given failure happening in the beginning of an incremental load may have a different impact from happening close to the end of the same load.

## 5    Integrating Recovery into the Benchmark Metric: Prevention vs. Recovery

There is an old adage, 'An ounce of prevention is worth a pound of cure'. So perhaps the benchmark should be focusing more on preventing failures than recovering from them? The committee has considered this, but felt that no system can be 100% failure proof, and so it was still important to address recovery. However, there is still the question of the relative importance of recovery. If running in a system that is highly fault tolerant, the potential for a failure to occur is greatly diminished and so the recovery mechanisms are much less likely to need to be exercised. In contrast, a system with many potential points of failure will be more susceptible to failures, and much more likely to exercise recovery mechanisms. Also, a system that is highly fault tolerant is most likely more expensive and might perform worse, e.g. RAID systems need more disks, which make them more expensive and they occur an overhead for writing data.

So, several questions may be raised: how much weight should be given to recovery? Is it fair to place a high amount of significance on recovery in a highly fault tolerant system? Is it fair to place little significance on a system that is high susceptible to failures? Is it fair to place an equal amount of significance on recovery for all systems? Responding these questions is not an easy task, but answers deeply affect the benchmark definition:

- Characterizing only prevention mechanisms: the benchmark performance metric should portray the impact of the prevention mechanisms in the performance of the system. Also, the effectiveness of those mechanisms (i.e., the degree to which they prevent failures) needs to be verified. This may consist of injecting failures and then simply verify if there is impact in the data integration process (i.e. if the process is interrupted), or include the definition of an additional metric that quantifies the degree of protection.
- Characterizing only recovery mechanisms: the goal is to characterize the system while recovering from failures that somehow interrupted the data integration process and, consequently, triggered recovery. Again, this may consist of the simple verification of the success of the recovery actions (e.g. check that the data in the data warehouse is the same that would be there if no failure happened), or included in the primary performance metric, which would then characterize the impact of recovery in the system performance.
- Characterizing both prevention and recovery mechanisms: a mix of the two approaches presented above. A key problem here is that representing the effectiveness of the prevention and of the recovery mechanisms in the same performance metric may not be possible.

The following sections address some aspects that are orthogonal to the approach described above, namely the calculation of the performance metric and the verification of the effectiveness of the prevention and recovery mechanisms. Despite some differences both performance metrics and "system implementation properties" apply when prevention or recovery mechanisms are addressed. For example, prevention mechanisms impact performance. The same applies to recovery mechanisms. But the meaning may be different: while prevention mechanisms impact performance in "normal conditions", i.e. in the absence of failures to prevent failures, recovery mechanisms impact performance not only in "normal conditions" but also when recovery is being performed (the faster the recovery is, the higher is the overall performance of the system - as the impact of the failure is lower - assuming that measurement is not stopped).

## 5.1    Performance Metric

The committee would like to include a recovery component in the primary performance metric. However, there are some challenges on how to accomplish this.

First, well defined starting and stopping points need to be defined. Should the time it takes to reboot the system be included or excluded? What about the time it takes to change a part? What if the part is not on hand? A typical approach in the dependability benchmarking area regarding the measurement interval is never to stop measuring. In other words, the time needed to reboot the system is included in the measurement (and systems that recover faster perform better) and impact the primary performance metric. As failures are emulated (and not physically inducted), the definition of the time it takes to change a part is facilitated. One approach is to postulate a typical replacement time (that may vary according to the component targeted). This is an acceptable approach if the replacement of parts is typically a human activity, and not a characteristic of the system being benchmarked. What matters here is that all SUT are benchmarked in similar conditions. However, a system vendor may want to highlight their ability to react quicker to failures than its competitor as part of a service plan. The swifter failure response time may be reflected in the maintenance cost of the system. In that case, postulating a typical replacement time based on the component targeted may not be acceptable. To reflect varying failure response times, the benchmark could define a typical failure response time for each targeted system part based on a defined service plan (i.e. 24h) that any system has to provide as a minimal requirement. Depending on the failure response time listed in the maintenance cost of a system, the vendor may reduce the typical replacement time with its own replacement time.

Second, how can a recovery scenario be defined such that it is fair, but also not so predictable that benchmark implementations could make special accommodations for it? Depending on what an implementation has already completed and what it is currently processing, the recovery that will need to be performed can be drastically different. Due to the variability allowed in implementations, time-based methods of failure injection will not result in equivalent recovery scenarios between implementations, i.e. a failure at time N in one implementation may not result in the same recovery scenario as another implementation. Similarly, some event-based methods (e.g. fail on the 100th row) may also not ensure the same recovery scenario between two implementations, and in addition are not desirable because they are too predictable. A potential approach is somehow combining event-based and time-based activation. For example, a failure is injected a random amount of time (different statistical distributions may be considered) after processing the 100th row.

## 5.2    System and Implementation Property

The committee has also considered making recovery a property of the system that must be demonstrated, rather than including it in the primary performance metric. While this does eliminate some of the challenges associated with measuring performance, there are still some important aspects to consider.

Any implementation can be 'recoverable'. In the worse case, one can completely recreate the system and start again from scratch. In a sense, recovery solutions simply make it possible to reduce the time and effort required by this worse case. So in order make recovery a meaningful property that can be demonstrated, there must be some minimum bar establish as to the time and effort required to recover. However, establishing this minimum bar is not straight-forward. It is not clear how to determine how much time and effort to recover is too much. In addition, if the requirement is only to demonstrate the ability of the implementation to recover, it would be desirable to do this on the smallest set of data needed. However, recovery times and techniques can be greatly influenced by the amount of data involved, so it may not be meaningful to use only a very small set of data for this test. This could result in an additional large scale run needing to be executed, which can add significant amount of additional time and effort for those executing the benchmark.

**Acknowledgements.** The authors would like to thank the past and present members of the TPC for their contribution to specifications and documents referenced in this paper.

# References

1. Transaction Performance Council website (TPC), http://www.tpc.org
2. Wyatt, L., Caufield, B., Pol, D.: Principles for an ETL Benchmark. In: Nambiar, R., Poess, M. (eds.) TPCTC 2009. LNCS, vol. 5895, pp. 183–198. Springer, Heidelberg (2009)
3. Kimball, R.: The Data Warehouse Toolkit: Practical Techniques for Building Dimensional Data Warehouses. John Wiley (1996)
4. Laprie, J.C.: Dependable Computing: Concepts, Limits, Challenges. In: Proceedings of the 25th International Symposium on Fault-Tolerant Computing, FTCS-25, Special Issue, Pasadena, CA, USA, pp. 42–54 (1995)

# Two Firsts for the TPC: A Benchmark to Characterize Databases Virtualized in the Cloud, and a Publicly-Available, Complete End-to-End Reference Kit

Andrew Bond[1], Greg Kopczynski[2], and H. Reza Taheri[2]

[1] Red Hat, Inc.
[2] VMware, Inc.
abond@redhat.com, {gregwk,rtaheri}@vmware.com

**Abstract.** The TPC formed a subcommittee in 2010 to develop TPC-V, a benchmark for virtualized databases. We soon discovered two major issues. First, a database benchmark running in a VM, or even a consolidation scenario of a few database VMs, is no longer adequate. There is demand for a benchmark that emulates cloud computing, e.g., a mix of heterogeneous VMs, and dynamic load elasticity for each VM. Secondly, waiting for system or database vendors to develop benchmarking kits to run such a benchmark is problematic. Hence, we are developing a publicly-available, end-to-end reference kit that will run against the open source PostgreSQL DBMS. This paper describes TPC-V and the proposed architecture of its reference kit; provides a progress report; and presents results from prototyping experiments with the reference kit.

**Keywords:** Database performance, virtualization, PostgreSQL, cloud computing.

## 1 Introduction

Gartner Group has again placed Cloud Computing on its list of top strategic technologies for 2012 [5]. Today, virtualization is a common component of enterprise data centers, and is the foundational technology of cloud computing. But databases are the last frontier to be conquered by virtualization. Not surprisingly, there is strong demand for a performance benchmark for enterprise-level virtualized servers that run database workloads. In this paper, we will briefly introduce virtualization, discuss existing benchmarks, describe the evolution of TPC-V benchmark, provide details of the architecture of a reference kit for TPC-V, and present results of prototyping experiments with this kit. The intent is not to pre-announce a benchmark specification. This is a status report of where the benchmark development stands at this point in time.

## 2 Virtualization

In the late 1960s, IBM's VM operating system [2] permitted the execution of a variety of IBM operating systems in multiple virtual machines on a single hardware platform.

R. Nambiar and M. Poess (Eds.): TPCTC 2012, LNCS 7755, pp. 34–50, 2013.

Virtualization on the Intel x86 architecture was introduced in the late 1990s [4, 6, 8]. What started out as a means of simultaneously running multiple Linux and Windows operating systems on a single PC has evolved into the availability of enterprise-class *hypervisor* operating systems from multiple vendors, including Microsoft, Oracle, Red Hat, VMware, etc., enabling users to serve multiple operating environments on a single enterprise-class server. The first foray for virtualization into the enterprise data center was to enable *server consolidation*, followed by what we now call cloud computing. In a nutshell, without live migration [7] of VMs between servers in the cloud, and without the ability to dynamically expand or shrink the resources allocated to a VM, cloud computing would have remained an abstract concept.

### 2.1    What Is a Virtual Machine?

A virtual machine (VM) is a software computer that, like a physical computer, runs an operating system and applications. An operating system installed on a virtual machine is called a guest operating system. Virtual machines run on host servers. The same server can run many virtual machines. Every VM runs in an isolated environment. So one VM may be running a Windows-based web server application while another runs a Linux-based database application, all on the same hardware platform. In the example in Figure 1, a server that ran a single OS and single application can run 6 different applications on 3 different operating systems using virtualization.

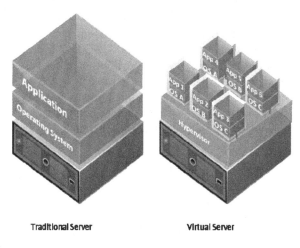

Traditional Server                    Virtual Server

**Fig. 1.** A virtualized server

## 3    Other Virtualization Benchmarks

### 3.1    VMmark

VMmark [17] was the first industry standard benchmark for server consolidations. It was developed by VMware for its vSphere hypervisor operating system although it is possible to run VMmark on other hypervisors. VMmark versions 1.0 and 1.1 have been retired. The current version 2.0 adds platform-level workloads such as dynamic VM relocation (vMotion) and dynamic datastore relocation (storage vMotion) to traditional application-level workloads. VMmark 1.x retired with 138 published results from 11 vendors. As of now, 6 vendors have published 34 VMmark 2.0 results.

## 3.2    SPECvirt_sc2010

In July, 2010, Standard Performance Evaluation Corporation (SPEC) released the SPECvirt_sc2010 [10] industry-standard benchmark. It incorporates modified versions of three SPEC workloads (SPECweb2005_Support, SPECjAppServer2004 and SPECmail2008) and drives them simultaneously to emulate virtualized server consolidation environments, much like VMmark 1.0 did. The key differentiators of this server consolidation benchmark compared to VMmark 1.0 are the use of a dynamic load for the SPECjAppServer2004 workload, a QOS metric, and an optional power metric. To date, there have been 26 SPECvirt_sc2010 publications from 3 vendors.

## 3.3    TPC-VMS

TPC-V has a rich, dynamic database virtualization workload, which results in a complex benchmark that will take time to develop. Hence the TPC decided to develop a second, simpler benchmark: TPC-VMS (TPC Virtual Measurement Single System), which emulates a simple consolidation scenario of 3 identical databases, and leverages the existing TPC benchmarks by adding the methodology for running and reporting virtualization metrics using TPC-C [11], TPC-E [12], TPC-H [14], and TPC-DS [16] as workloads. The key to TPC-VMS is that it does not need new benchmarking kits. If one has a TPC-E kit, one can also run TPC-VMS with the TPC-E workload. We expect this property to lead to a timely release of TPC-VMS in 2012. However, even though existing TPC benchmarks are being used, publications using the TPC-VMS methodology will not be comparable to publications without the methodology.

# 4    TPC-V Architecture

## 4.1    Genesis of TPC-V

We presented a paper at the 2009 TPCTC [2], advocating the need for a benchmark to measure the performance of virtual environments under a database-centric workload. The TPC then formed a Working Group of 14 companies to scope a virtualization benchmark. The Working Group evolved into a Development Subcommittee in June, 2010 with charter to develop a benchmark [9] that:

- Satisfies the industry need for a benchmark that:
    1. Has a database-centric workload
    2. Stresses the virtualization layer
    3. Has a moderate number of VMs, exercising enterprise applications
    4. Has a healthy storage and networking I/O content
    5. Does not contain many non-database application environments in an application consolidation scenario
- TPC-V results will not be comparable to other TPC benchmarks
- TPC-V generates information not covered by other benchmarks

- The benchmark has to have a timely development cycle (1-2 years) to satisfy the demand that member companies get from their customers
  - TPC-V will be based on the TPC-E benchmark and borrows a lot from it
  - But is a different workload mix and its results cannot be compared to TPC-E.

## 4.2    TPC-E as a Starting Point

An early decision reached by the Working Group was to utilize TPC-E [12] as the basis of TPC-V to speed up its development, and to provide a meaningful application environment with database components and transactions that are relevant and understandable. TPC-E is altered to provide the desired read-intensive and update-intensive environments. While TPC-E uses a business model of a brokerage house with transactions driven from multiple sources, the deployment of the adjusted application in TPC-V is intended to represent a wider variety of OLTP-based applications that could be employed in a virtualized computing environment.

TPC-V has the same basic schema, DDL, and even much of the DML of TPC-E. It has the same 33 tables and 12 transactions. The differences are few, yet fundamental, and make the two benchmarks non-comparable, which was one of our starting goals:

- The frequencies of transactions in the overall mix are different.
- Eight tables that were *scaled* in TPC-E, i.e., their cardinalities were tied to the number of Load Units (a set of 1000 customers is known as a Load Unit), are *fixed* in TPC-V. The main reason is ease of benchmarking. Often, the test sponsor cannot predict the eventual throughput at the time of building and populating the database. Throughput dictates the number of Load Units, in turn dictating the size of all Scaling and Growing tables. So test sponsors often build a database sized for the maximum expected throughput, but run the benchmark against fewer Load Units if needed. The complex TPC-E schema makes this technique impractical, except for very small deviations from the initial throughput goal. Thus, test sponsors are forced to repopulate the database if the performance is not what the database was sized for. This may be OK for a single database, but becomes a major issue for TPC-V with multiple database instances to populate. By fixing the cardinalities of these 8 tables, we make it practical for the test sponsor to run the benchmark with fewer Load Units than the Load Unit count chosen during the database population phase. The 8 tables are:

1. COMPANY
2. COMPANY_COMPETITOR
3. DAILY_MARKET
4. FINANCIAL
5. LAST_TRADE
6. NEWS_ITEM
7. NEWS_XREF
8. SECURITY

- The Market-Feed transaction made up 1% of the TPC-E transaction mix. In TPC-V, the functionality of Market-Feed has been reduced (mostly transferred to a Frame 7 of Trade-Result), and it runs at a fixed rate of twice per second.
- A TPC-E database is populated with 300 Initial Trade Days. The database size and the I/O rate produced by the benchmark are proportional to the ITD value. We believe a lower I/O rate is appropriate for TPC-V, and chose an ITD value of 125.

TPC provides a C++ *EGen* module that is required to be used to populate a TPC-E database, and to generate the run time transaction mix. TPC-V has a similar module, *VGen*, which is based on EGen but modified due to the differences listed above.

We believe we have achieved the two seemingly conflicting goals: TPC-V borrows substantially from TPC-E, and its development phase is accelerated as a result, by as much as 2-3 years, judging by the earlier TPC benchmarks. Yet the benchmark profiles are so different that comparing TPC-E and TPC-V results will be meaningless.

### 4.3    Performance Metric

The TPC-V performance metric is transactions-per-second-V (tpsV), a business throughput measure of the number of Trade-Result transactions processed per second. The reported tpsV is the aggregate of throughput values for all Sets (see sections 4.4 and 4.5). All transactions are subject to a response time constraint.  To be compliant, all references to tpsV must include the tpsV rate, the associated price-per-tpsV, and the availability date of the priced configuration. To be compliant with the optional TPC-Energy standard, the additional primary metric watts-per-tpsV must be reported.

### 4.4    Set Architecture in TPC-V

Existing virtualization benchmarks, such as VMmark and SPECvirt_sc2010, rely on the *tile* concept, where a tile contains a constant number of VMs with static workloads. As the power of the server grows, the number of tiles it can support grows as well. The issue with this architecture is the static workload of each VM in the tile, leading to hundreds of VMs on today's high-end servers. This may make sense in a simple consolidation scenario of, say, web servers, but is not applicable to enterprise database servers. We posit that more powerful database servers host more VMs, but also VMs that handle more load. The Subcommittee has devised a *Set* architecture whereby both the number of Sets, and the load placed on each Set, grow as the performance of the system increases.

### 4.5    Multiple Sets of Heterogeneous Load Levels

Furthermore, we believe it is important for a realistic database virtualization benchmark to emulate the load of a heterogeneous collection of VMs. A TPC-V configuration is made up of 4 database *Groups*. Groups A, B, C, and D contribute an average of 10%, 20%, 30%, and 40% of the total throughput, respectively. Each Group has 1, 2, or more Sets depending on the overall performance of the server. Table 1 shows the number of Sets and VMs for a variety of server classes. To put the values in Table 1 in perspective, we believe results in the 400-6,400 tpsV range are likely to be disclosed at the benchmark introduction time. The last 3 columns represent what one can expect to be the high-end systems of 5-10 years after the introduction of the benchmark. So the number of VMs in TPC-V configurations will grow with time and with the increase in processing power of servers, but at a slower pace, and we will test servers with a reasonable number of databases.

**Table 1.** An Example of TPC-V Groups and Sets

| SUT Target tpsV=> | | 100 | 400 | 1600 | 6400 | 25600 | 102400 | 409600 |
|---|---|---|---|---|---|---|---|---|
| Avg Group A Contribution | | 10% | 10% | 10% | 10% | 10% | 10% | 10% |
| Avg Group B Contribution | | 20% | 20% | 20% | 20% | 20% | 20% | 20% |
| Avg Group C Contribution | | 30% | 30% | 30% | 30% | 30% | 30% | 30% |
| Avg Group D Contribution | | 40% | 40% | 40% | 40% | 40% | 40% | 40% |
| Min # of Sets in each Group | | 1 | 1 | 2 | 2 | 3 | 3 | 4 |
| Max # of Sets in each Group | | 1 | 2 | 2 | 3 | 3 | 4 | 4 |
| tpsV of each Set at Max # of Sets per Group | Group A | 10 | 20 | 80 | 213 | 853 | 2560 | 10240 |
| | Group B | 20 | 40 | 160 | 427 | 1707 | 5120 | 20480 |
| | Group C | 30 | 60 | 240 | 640 | 2560 | 7680 | 30720 |
| | Group D | 40 | 80 | 320 | 853 | 3413 | 10240 | 40960 |
| Tier A VMs per Set | | 1 | 1 | 1 | 1 | 1 | 1 | 1 |
| Tier B VMs per Set | | 2 | 2 | 2 | 2 | 2 | 2 | 2 |
| Min Total Sets | | 4 | 4 | 8 | 8 | 12 | 12 | 16 |
| Max Total Sets | | 4 | 8 | 8 | 12 | 12 | 16 | 16 |
| Min Total VMs | | 12 | 12 | 24 | 24 | 36 | 36 | 48 |
| Max Total VMs | | 12 | 24 | 24 | 36 | 36 | 48 | 48 |

## 4.6     Tier A VM and Two Tier B VMs.

Figure 2 depicts the Set architecture of TPC-V. Starting with TPC-E transactions as a base, we have defined 3 VMs that together form a Set for the TPC-V benchmark. To emulate databases virtualized in the cloud, the functionality of the Tier B component of a TPC-E SUT has been divided into two separate TPC-V VMs with heterogonous workloads. One VM handles the Trade-Lookup and Trade-Update transactions, simulating the high storage I/O load of a decision support environment. The second VM services all other transactions, which have a CPU-heavy profile and represent OLTP applications. This emulates the diversity of workloads on cloud databases. In Figure 2, notations TL, TU, etc. under the VMs are the 2-letter abbreviations of TPC-V transactions.

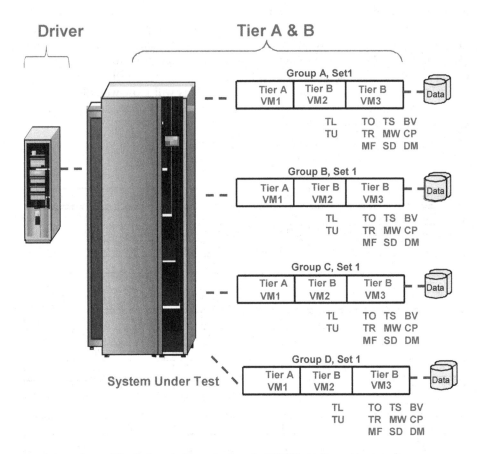

**Fig. 2.** Sample Components of a TPC-V configuration

Tier A in TPC-V functions similarly to a TPC-E Tier A with one major difference: Based on the transaction type, it routes the transaction to one of the two Tier B VMs.

### 4.7    Elasticity

A cloud computing benchmark has to emulate the elastic nature of the load placed on servers. We want a benchmark that places a challenge on the hypervisor to react to unexpected changes to the load placed on each VM, and allocate just the right amount of resources to each VM. The benchmark maintains a constant overall tpsV load level, but the proportion directed to each VM changes every 12 minutes. The chart in Figure 3 shows the variation of the load offered to each of the 4 Groups.

An expected side effect is configuring the VMs with oversubscribed resources that are typical of virtualized servers. For example, a server with 64 physical CPUs might

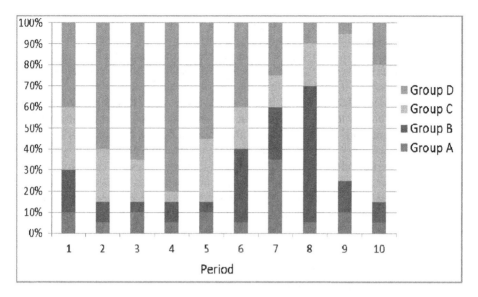

**Fig. 3.** TPC-V elastic load variation

need to run with 24 VMs whose virtual CPUs total 150 in order to handle the elastic nature of the load. The chart below depicts how the load to 4 Groups will vary over the 2-hour Measurement Interval.

### 4.8    Benchmark Development Schedule

Originally, the benchmark was scheduled for completion in 2012. This schedule relied on one or more owners of existing TPC-E benchmarking kits to allocate resources to modify their kits to execute the TPC-V transactions, and supply this kit to subcommittee members for prototyping. This did not happen, so the subcommittee moved forward with developing a reference kit. The current schedule calls for a beta kit to be available by Q3 2012. We expect prototyping and finishing the functional specification to move the overall TPC-V completion date to the second half of 2013.

## 5    Reference Kit

The decision to develop a complete, end-to-end reference benchmarking kit from scratch is a first for the TPC. Early TPC benchmarks were released as paper functional specifications with pseudo-SQL code included as development aids. Later, TPC provided a small amount of code for some benchmarks. For example, TPC-H comes with a DBGEN program [15] that is required to generate the data used by the benchmark. TPC-E went one step further by providing a C++ EGen [13] module that not only generates the flat-file data used to populate the database, but it also generates the run-time transactions with the prescribed frequency mix and numerical parameters.

However, the benchmark developer still has to write the DDL to create the schema and load the flat file data into the database. And while EGen will generate the correct transaction calls, that is simply because those calls have been predefined by EGen. But the benchmark developer still has to write the content of these calls, along with the actual database DML code, multiple threads of execution, timing of transactions, etc. In short, EGen offers code and a framework that assures consistent and correct execution of its part of the transaction request process, but leaves most of the benchmark development work still to be done by the intended user of the benchmark.

The TPC-V subcommittee decided an end-to-end kit would be a good way to enable company participation in the TPC-V development process. This type of kit would remove each company's cost of developing their own TPC-V kit. Also if everyone was testing with the same code, a more collaborative development environment would be created. Since this kit will be used by multiple companies during benchmark development, it would be very robust by the time the benchmark was released and could be provided outside of the TPC.

### 5.1   Origins of the Reference Kit

Once the subcommittee decided a kit was needed, it investigated various sources.

- TPC-E subcommittee: The TPC-E subcommittee only provides the EGen component and not an entire kit, and no general purpose kit was available.
- Companies with TPC-E kits: The companies that publish TPC-E benchmarks do not make their kits available for general use. So these kits could not be used as basis for a TPC-V kit especially since the goal was to eventually release the TPC-V kit outside the TPC.
- DBT-5: This option was intriguing since it is an open source TPC-E based driver for PostgreSQL [3]. It matched many of the needs of the subcommittee. However, it was decided that the work required to get DBT-5 into the form the subcommittee was seeking is better spent building a kit from scratch. While DBT-5 was not used as the basis for the kit, it provided a valuable reference on what can be done.

Given the absence of an existing kit to adopt, the subcommittee formed a coding team to develop a kit. The kit was to have the following properties:

1. Use an open source database
2. Use the ODBC library for portability
3. Use Java for the driver harness where appropriate for portability
4. Develop to TPC-E version 1.12.0   since it is a known working environment

### 5.2   Open Source PostgreSQL Database

An end-to-end kit requires the use of a DBMS. The subcommittee decided to base the kit on open source PostgreSQL. PostgreSQL has a strong following in academia, but is also in widespread use in the industry. Most importantly, since it is open source, the subcommittee does not have to deal with the DeWitt Clauses or competitive pressures that accompany the use of commercial database products. Admittedly, we expect performance of PostgreSQL to be much lower than commercial databases, which have the advantage of years of tuning for TPC benchmarks, as well as other DBMS benchmarks. However, we feel that PostgreSQL performance is good enough to place a heavy, database-centric load on the lower levels, especially the virtualization management system and the hypervisor, which are the focus of this benchmark.

## 5.3    Public Availability

The TPC-V end-to-end benchmarking kit will be released to the public as a reference kit. The details are yet to be worked out. But we expect the following properties:

- The kit will be available to anyone, possibly with a minimal charge similar to SPEC benchmarks.
- The kit will likely not be open source. The TPC will retain the rights, and make the kit available under an End-User License Agreement, similar to the EULA for other TPC-provided code, such as the EGen module for TPC-E.
- Since the DML is written at the ODBC API level, it is expected that a test sponsor can install the kit, take out the PostgreSQL DDL and DML, insert the DDL and DML of their favorite DBMS, and run the benchmark. The kit has all the necessary code to deal with the complexity of the benchmark in driving different loads to different VMs, and in dynamically changing the loads to VMs. A test sponsor, or a researcher who wants to test a new DBMS, can take the reference kit, and with simple modifications, measure the performance of any DBMS, including commercial products.
- A proposal we are considering is requiring any publication with a non-PostgreSQL DBMS to be accompanied by results using the reference kit intact on PostgreSQL. This proposal mimics SPEC's *base* and *peak* result publications rule. So the consumer of benchmark results can see, in rough terms, how much of the difference between the two systems is inherent in H/W, OS, and the virtualization layer, and how much is due to the difference between the database management systems.

## 5.4    Reference Kit Architecture

The TPC-V reference driver was developed using a combination of Java and C++ code, with the Java Native Interface (JNI) used for inter-language communication. Transaction-specific and frame-specific executions are handled solely in the C++ code while other bench-mark execution-related tasks are handled in Java.

The key processes in the reference driver are the prime client, the Customer Emulator (CE) drivers, the Market Exchange Emulators (MEEs), and the Tier A Connectors. The CE drivers, MEEs, and Tier A Connectors are all started manually at the beginning of a test, and each of them opens a listening port for Remote Method Invocation (RMI) commands from the prime client. Once these processes are started and listening on their respective ports, the prime client is started. Similarly, the prime

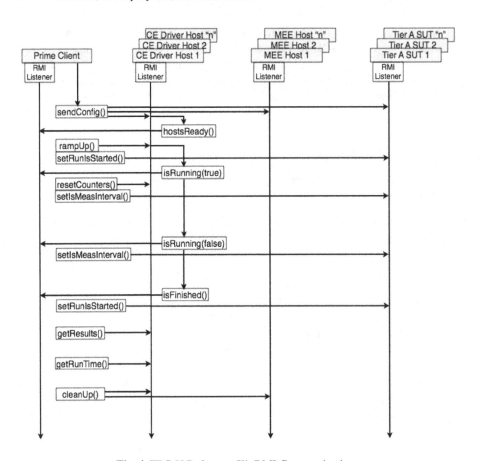

**Fig. 4.** TPC-V Reference Kit RMI Communication

client opens its own RMI listening port, where it will listen for RMI commands from the CE drivers, MEE drivers, and Tier A Connectors. The flow diagram in Figure 4 illustrates the RMI communication sequence between processes:

The reference kit uses a single configuration file located on the prime client. When the prime client is started, it reads the benchmark configuration from that file and determines which CE drivers, MEEs, and Tier A Connectors will be used in the benchmark run. It then sends this configuration information to each of these processes on their RMI listening ports before beginning the run.

After receiving the configuration information, the CE drivers, MEEs, and Tier A Connectors use JNI calls to instantiate the C++ classes required to interact with the TPC-provided VGen code. Once these classes are instantiated for the MEEs, all benchmark interaction with the MEEs happens within the C++ classes. There is no longer any interaction with the Java side unless a benchmark abort occurs. For the Tier A Connectors, this is also mostly the case, except that they also receive synchro-nization-specific RMI commands during the run.

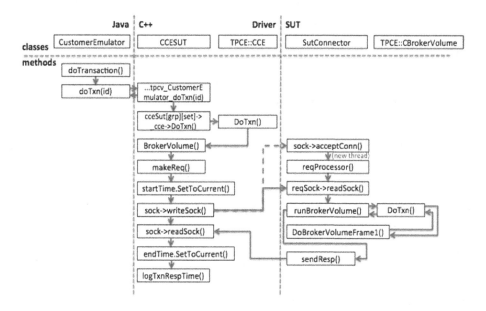

**Fig. 5.** Sample Transaction Execution Path

Regular transitions between Java and C++ through the JNI interface occur only in the CE drivers, because every transaction request is initiated on the Java side. Figure 5 illustrates a typical transaction execution path.

One of the key challenges in the driver design is how to support the elastic load variation in the reference driver. Due to the limited number of VM sets, we instantiate a CE class for each database group and VM set. By doing so, each CE driver thread is capable of driving load against any of the Tier A VMs. One can allocate, for example, 10% of the driver threads to send transactions to a Set that is to receive 10% of transactions. But in practice, if that Set is bottlenecked, it will be impossible to guarantee it received 10% of the load. If fact, even absent bottlenecks, this scheme is impractical since there is no way to tie the loads of different driver threads together. It would require a complex synchronization scheme to slow down or speed up the threads. It might have worked for a benchmark, such as TPC-C, where the threads of execution have think times and a cycle time. But since each TPC-V driver thread goes as fast as it can (pacing is optional), it is hard to maintain a proper ratio between threads.

In our reference kit, all threads can issue transactions to all VMs. On each transaction, the thread consults a deck of cards to see which Set will get the transaction. This way, we are guaranteed a proper distribution of transactions over Sets.

### 5.5    TPC-E Functionality

As mentioned in section 4.2, the TPC-E benchmark was the starting point for TPC-V. So we decided to start with a kit integrated with EGen, populating a database with TPC-E cardinalities (except that we still used 125 for Initial Trade Days), and generating the TPC-E transaction mix. Our end goal was not a TPC-E benchmarking kit. But since TPC-E is a well-understood benchmark, we can analyze our kit by studying published TPC-E results, and draw on the experience of subcommittee members who have experimented with TPC-E for the past 5 years. Of course, a byproduct of this process is that once the TPC-V reference kit is complete, it should be easy to replace VGen with EGen, and produce a TPC-E reference kit if the TPC desires so.

# 6 Current Status of the Benchmark and the Reference Kit

The key to producing a successful TPC-V is completing a reference kit that produces the variability and elasticity behavior that we have described in sections 4.5 and 4.7. Hence, the completion of the kit is currently the single focus of the subcommittee. The results described in section show that the kit is running, and is running well. The push now is to complete the MEE component of the kit. We have a draft specification, which is currently on revision 0.12.

## 6.1 Status of the Reference Kit

The TPC-V Reference Kit has three key components: the VGen framework, the PostgreSQL stored procedures, and the driver component. The VGen framework will likely be a lightly modified version of the existing EGen framework. Modifications have been proposed and implemented, but still require testing and acceptance from the subcommittee (and are therefore still subject to change). The PostgreSQL stored procedures are also functional and being used for ongoing benchmark prototyping.

The reference driver has four separate components: the Tier A Connectors, the CE drivers, the MEEs, and the prime client component that controls and coordinates with the other three. All of these components are implemented though some are not yet fully functional. All of the CE-driven transactions are currently functional, but the two MEE transactions remain to be coded. (The MEE transactions are currently stubbed out in order to allow reference kit testing with all of the CE-driven transactions.) The code that supports the CE drivers dynamically changing the Tier A Connector to which they drive load is also coded but as yet untested.

Another way to look at the reference driver's progress would be to say that in terms of a driver capable of running the TPC-E benchmark from which TPC-V was derived, only the two MEE transactions prevent us from having a functionally complete TPC-E driver (though there is a still more to do to move from a functional driver to an auditable one). So with the exception of those two transactions, what remains, fundamentally, is some additional development and testing of code that makes this a TPC-V benchmark reference kit, as well as any code needed to turn a functional kit into a TPC-auditable one.

The DDL for creating and populating a PostgreSQL database is complete and functional. Of the 12 transactions, DML has been written and extensively tested for 9.

Data-Maintenance and Market-Feed are relatively easy to code, and do not affect the throughput very much. So both in terms of development cost and impact on run time performance, the Trade-Result transaction is the major missing piece.

# 7    Results from Prototyping Experiments

Although the kit is missing a major component of the benchmark (the MEE transactions), we feel that the results obtained using it are quite instructive as to whether it can handle the load we want from it, whether PostgreSQL can provide good enough performance, etc. The two sets of results outlined here are with a kit that still does not have the variability and elasticity features described in sections 4.5 and 4.7. It runs all the transactions against a single database, very much in the mode of TPC-E.

## 7.1    Benchmarking Configuration

We ran our tests on the following system configuration:

- Two blades of an HP BladeSystem c-Class c7000 with 2-socket Intel E5520 (Nehalem-EP) processors and 48GB of memory per blade
- 8 cores, 16 threads per blade
- 48GB of RAM per blade
- Storage was an EMC VNX5700 with 14 SSDs fronting 32 15K RPM drives
- The Tier B database VM was alone on a blade with 16 vCPUs, 40GB of memory, 4 virtual drives with various RAID levels
- The driver and Tier A VMs were on the second blade
- RHEL 6.1
- PostgreSQL 8.4
- unixODBC 2.3.2

## 7.2    First Experiment

For this experiment, we integrated EGen with our kit, and populated the database with 300 Load Units. This is a large database (nearly 1TB, too large for our 40GB of memory). It is also much larger than the databases that were used during the TPC-E prototyping. But we felt that we wanted to put the kit and PostgreSQL through their paces to make sure they would hold up. Table 2 has the output of a 15-minute run.

The Tier B database server was around 59% idle. The database disk buffer cache is too small for such a large database, causing an I/O rate that exceeded 27,000 IOPS. This overwhelmed our storage, causing the idle. Nonetheless, the fact that the kit was running with 130 threads of execution (users in benchmarkers parlance) error-free on a strained server was one of the outcomes the team was looking for.

**Table 2.** Results from a 300-LU database using EGen

| Transaction | Tx rate/sec | Resp Time in seconds |
|---|---|---|
| Trade-Order | 71.4 | 0.04 |
| Trade-Lookup | 56.3 | 1.21 |
| Trade-Update | 13.9 | 1.64 |
| Trade-Status | 133.3 | 0.09 |
| Customer-Position | 91.7 | 0.05 |
| Broker-Volume | 34.5 | 0.01 |
| Security-Detail | 98.6 | 0.02 |
| Market-Watch | 126.8 | 0.14 |

## 7.3     Second Experiment

For this experiment in Table 3, we integrated VGen with our kit, and populated the database with 30 Load Units to reduce the I/O rate and saturate the CPUs. This 140GB database is still large for early prototyping phase. Below is the output of a 30-minute run. Note that the transaction mix is now the TPC-V transaction mix.

With this smaller database, the Tier B server was over 90% utilized. At around 18,000 IOPS, the I/O rate is still too high for this size system. The Trade-Lookup and Trade-Update transactions are the two I/O-bound transactions in the mix, and will be directed to the DSS VM in a TPC-V Set (see section 4.6). Yet, the I/O rate is still high, causing some idle, and heavier than expected CPU cost per transaction. We plan to investigate the source of the high I/O rate, and expect that a solution will improve the bottom line performance.

**Table 3.** Results from a 30-LU database using VGen

| Transaction | Tx rate/sec | Resp Time in seconds |
|---|---|---|
| Trade-Order | 183 | 0.02 |
| Trade-Lookup | 145 | 0.17 |
| Trade-Update | 36 | 0.20 |
| Trade-Status | 343 | 0.01 |
| Customer-Position | 235 | 0.01 |
| Broker-Volume | 89 | 0.08 |
| Security-Detail | 253 | 0.02 |
| Market-Watch | 325 | 0.03 |

To put this performance in perspective, let us look at the CPU cost per transaction. Let us assume that when we add Trade-Result, the weighted average CPU cost of the 9 transactions will remain roughly the same as the cost for today's 8 functioning transactions. With that, the CPU cost per transaction is around 8.6ms/tran. Based on published TPC-E results on a similar server, and allowing for the differences in hardware, virtualization overhead, etc., we estimate that the CPU costs for a commercial database would be around 3.2 ms/tran. Furthermore, the commercial database results were obtained using its native access interface, rather than the more expensive ODBC interface we used.

Our results were measured with little tuning. So we believe being 35-40% of the performance of a highly-tuned commercial database at this point of the project is more than adequate. With further tuning, and possibly even engaging the open source PostgreSQL community to optimize the base code for TPC-V the way commercial databases have used TPC benchmarks as tuning guides in the past, we should reach the point where the performance difference is between 2X and 1.5X. That would mean the reference kit on open source PostgreSQL has reached its goal.

**Acknowledgements.** Cecil Reames modified EGen to create the VGen module that the team is currently using. Doug Johnson, Matt Emmerton, and Jamie Reding have been invaluable with sharing their vast knowledge of the TPC-E benchmark. Karl Huppler and Wayne Smith have contributed many of the conceptual properties of the benchmark. Matthew Lanken designed the original Set architecture, and answered many TPC-E questions. Jignesh Shah has been our PostgreSQL guru.

# References

1. Bose, S., Mishra, P., Sethuraman, P., Taheri, R.: Benchmarking Database Performance in a Virtual Environment. In: Nambiar, R., Poess, M. (eds.) TPCTC 2009. LNCS, vol. 5895, pp. 167–182. Springer, Heidelberg (2009)
2. Creasy, R.J.: The Origin of the VM/370 Time-Sharing System. IBM Journal of Research and Development 25(5), 483
3. Database Test 5 (DBT-5TM), http://sourceforge.net/apps/mediawiki/osdldbt/index.php
4. Figueiredo, R., Dinda, P.A., Fortes, J.A.B.: Guest Editors' Introduction: Resource Virtualization Renaissance. Computer 38(5), 28–31 (2005), http://www2.computer.org/portal/web/csdl/doi/10.1109/MC.2005.159
5. Gartner Identifies the Top 10 Strategic Technologies for (2012), http://www.gartner.com/it/page.jsp?id=1826214
6. Nanda, S., Chiueh, T.-C.: A Survey on Virtualization Technologies. Technical Report ECSL-TR-179, SUNY at Stony Brook (2005), http://www.ecsl.cs.sunysb.edu/tr/TR179.pdf
7. Nelson, M., Lim, B.-H., Hutchins, G.: Fast Transparent Migration for Virtual Machines. In: USENIX 2005, pp. 391–394 (April 2005)
8. Rosenblum, M., Garfinkel, T.: Virtual Machine Monitors: Current Technology and Future Trends. Computer 38(5), 39–47 (2005)
9. Sethuraman, P., Taheri, R.: TPC-V: A Benchmark for Evaluating the Performance of Database Applications in Virtual Environments. In: Nambiar, R., Poess, M. (eds.) TPCTC 2010. LNCS, vol. 6417, pp. 121–135. Springer, Heidelberg (2011)
10. SPEC Virtualization Committee, http://www.spec.org/virt_sc2010/
11. TPC: Detailed TPC-C description, http://www.tpc.org/tpcc/detail.asp
12. TPC: Detailed TPC-E Description, http://www.tpc.org/tpce/spec/TPCEDetailed.doc

13. TPC: EGen software package, `http://www.tpc.org/tpce/egen-download-request.asp`

14. TPC: TPC Benchmark H Specification, `http://www.tpc.org/tpch/spec/tpch2.14.4.pdf`

15. TPC: DBGen and Reference Data Set,
    `http://www.tpc.org/tpch/spec/tpch_2_14_3.zip`

16. TPC: TPC Benchmark DS Specification, `http://www.tpc.org/tpcds/spec/tpcds_1.1.0.pdf`

17. VMware, Inc.,
    `http://www.vmware.com/products/vmmark/overview.html`

# Adding a Temporal Dimension to the TPC-H Benchmark

Mohammed Al-Kateb, Alain Crolotte, Ahmad Ghazal, and Linda Rose

Teradata Corporation
100 N. Sepulveda Blvd. El Segundo, CA, 90245
{mohammed.al-kateb,alain.crolotte,ahmad.ghazal,
linda.rose}@teradata.com

**Abstract.** The importance of time in decision-support is widely recognized and has been addressed through temporal applications or through native temporal features by major DBMS vendors. In this paper we propose a framework for adding a new temporal component to the TPC-H benchmark. Our proposal includes temporal DDL, procedures to populate the temporal tables via insert-select thereby providing history, and temporal queries based on a workload that covers the temporal dimension broken down as current, history, and both. The queries we define as part of this benchmark include the typical SQL operators involved in scans, joins and aggregations. The paper concludes with experimental results. While in this paper we consider adding temporal history to a subset of the TPC-H benchmark tables namely Part/ Supplier/Partsupp, our proposed framework addresses a need and uses, as a starting point, a benchmark that is widely successful and well-understood.

## 1    Introduction

Most decision support applications are temporal in nature. For that reason, most DBMS vendors have eventually added temporal features to their products. While the basic temporal elements are well-understood and agreed upon, there is no definite standard for temporal database implementation. For this reason we have made a choice and used the Snodgrass proposal ([1] and [2]) in our benchmark model definition. Also, rather than proposing a completely new model we use an existing benchmark as a basis. The TPC-H benchmark represents a very well-known and understood model widely used in research and industry. Yet it does not include a temporal element. In this paper we propose an approach that could be fill the gap. In section 2, we describe the general temporal model used, provide a brief description of the TPC-H benchmark, and finally we describe the general approach taken. In section 3, we describe the specific tables selected and show how these tables can be populated using the original TPC-H tables. In section 4, we propose queries that can be used to benchmark a temporal DBMS implementation. Finally, we provide experimental results in section 5.

## 2    Problem Definition

Temporal databases add the time dimension to traditional database models allowing keeping track of the history of data. It makes it possible to capture and record database contents before and after modifications over time.

R. Nambiar and M. Poess (Eds.): TPCTC 2012, LNCS 7755, pp. 51–59, 2013.
© Springer-Verlag Berlin Heidelberg 2013

In the temporal data model, two time dimensions are typically considered – valid time and transaction time. The valid time dimension concerns the time period during which the associated attribute values are genuine in reality. The transaction time dimension pertains to the time period during which attribute values are actually stored and present in the database. Valid time and transaction time are orthogonal dimensions. In other words, the structure of a temporal table can contain either or both of these dimensions. A temporal table with only valid time is referred to as a valid-time table. A temporal table with only transaction time referred to as a transaction-time table. A temporal table with both valid time and transaction time is referred to as a bi-temporal table.

In addition, the temporal data model may support either row time-stamping or column time-stamping. Row time-stamping associates a temporal dimension to an entire row – handling updates in data values of a single column (or multiple columns) as a modification to the row. Column time-stamping associates a temporal dimension to a single column - keeping track of updates in data values of that column without taking into considerations updates on other columns.

Extending a database design with temporal data model offers an opportunity to issue queries of richer semantics, running after either the history of data, current data, or both. Such queries normally involve temporal predicates and functions. Temporal predicates are temporal constructs for comparing two time periods. Examples of temporal predicates include *overlaps* (which returns true if the two periods intersect), *precedes* (which returns true if the first period ends before the second period starts), *succeeds* (which returns true if the first period starts after the second period ends), *meets* (which returns true if the first period ends when the second period starts or if the first period starts when the second period ends), and *contains* (which returns true if the first period starts before the second period starts and ends after the second period ends). Temporal functions apply to a time period and return a value extracted from that period. Examples of temporal functions include *begin* (which returns the beginning of a time period) and *end* (which returns the end of a time period).

Snodgrass presented a case study on temporal data [1], [2]. This case study examines specifics of implementing a temporal data model that supports bi-temporal spectrum, automated time handling, and time-slicing queries. The specifics of this model are as follows. The temporal model keeps track of row time-stamping by associating a temporal dimension to the entire row, and supports both temporal dimensions – valid time and transaction time. Valid time dimension and transaction time dimension are stored as a period data type in a single column if that column is defined using the AS VALIDTIME construct and the AS TRANSACTIONTIME construct, respectively. A row in a temporal table is classified as follows. In a valid-time table, a temporal row can be either a history row, a current row, or a future row. A *history* row has a valid time which ends before the current time. A *current* row has a valid time which overlaps (i.e., intersects) current time. A *future* row has a valid time which begins after current time. Current and future rows can be assigned an open-ended value of UNTIL CHANGED for the end of their valid time column in case such a value is not known beforehand. In a transaction-time table, a temporal row can be either a closed row or an open row. A *closed* row has a transaction time that ends before the current time. An *open* row has a transaction time that overlaps (i.e., intersects) current time, and it is automatically assigned an open-ended value of UNTIL CLOSED for the end of its transaction time column. Following Snodgrass's case study, query processing over temporal tables can be in the form of non-sequenced, current, or sequenced mode. The *non-sequenced* mode discards the temporal semantics and handles rows in a way similar to regular query processing. The *current* mode retrieves data from, and applies updates to, current rows (recall that current rows are those with a valid time which overlaps with current time). The *sequenced* mode pertains to rows whose valid time overlaps with a given time period defined in the user query. In the absence of a user defined time period, sequenced mode applies to all history, current, and future rows.

Benchmarking temporal databases is not a new problem. Several approaches have been already proposed whether the problem is attacked generally as in [3] and [4] , semantically as in [5] or as a tool to decide between two types of implementation [6]. The problem that we are attempting to solve here is somewhat different in the sense that we want to add a temporal component to an existing benchmark with an existing schema rather than producing a brand new benchmark. As such the issues we face are different because all or some of the existing tables need to be modified to make them temporal and these tables will need to be populated. The TPC-H business model represents a retail company operating internationally. The company receives orders and each order has a number of line items. The company has customers and suppliers (Supplier table) that supply parts (Part table). The part-supplier association i.e. which supplier supplies what part(s) is contained in the Partsupp table. Suppliers and customers are located in nations themselves located in regions. The TPC-H schema is defined as a relational 3rd normal form fully described in [7]. Part, Supplier, Partsupp taken together constitute a relatively isolated and predictable subset of tables that we selected for introducing the temporal element. In the next section we proceed to define the temporal DDL for these tables and the procedure to populate them. The DDL is compliant with the proposal of Snodgrass et al. [1,2].

# 3    Workload Tables and Populations

In order to make the Part, Supplier and Partsupp tables temporal we added two columns to each table, a VT column for valid time and a TT column for transaction time. Since the TT column is filled by the system at the time of the table update or insert or delete we will not be able to make any *a posteriori* changes to create a history. Instead the history will be created by updating the valid time column VT for all tables while the TT column will reflect the current time i.e. the time when the update to the tale is done. As a result the DDL will be that of a bi-temporal table because we are creating history after the fact – the TT column will receive the system at the time we update the tables.

```
PART: CREATE MULTISET TABLE PART_t
(P_PARTKEY INTEGER NOT NULL,P_NAME VARCHAR(55),P_MFGR VARCHAR(25),
P_BRAND VARCHAR(10),P_TYPE VARCHAR(25),P_SIZE INTEGER,
P_CONTAINER VARCHAR(10),P_RETAILPRICE DECIMAL(15,2),
P_COMMENT VARCHAR(101) CASESPECIFIC,
P_VT PERIOD(DATE) NOT NULL AS VALIDTIME,
P_TT PERIOD(TIMESTAMP(6) WITH TIME ZONE) NOT NULL AS TRANSACTIONTIME)
PRIMARY INDEX ( P_PARTKEY );


SUPPLIER: CREATE MULTISET TABLE SUPPLIER_t
(S_SUPPKEY INTEGER NOT NULL, S_NAME VARCHAR(25),S_ADDRESS VARCHAR(40),
S_NATIONKEY INTEGER, S_PHONE VARCHAR(15),S_ACCTBAL DECIMAL(15,2),
S_COMMENT VARCHAR(101) CASESPECIFIC,
S_SUPPLIER_VT PERIOD(DATE) NOT NULL AS VALIDTIME,
S_TT PERIOD(TIMESTAMP(6) WITH TIME ZONE) NOT NULL AS TRANSACTIONTIME)
PRIMARY INDEX ( S_SUPPKEY );


PARTSUPP: CREATE MULTISET TABLE PARTSUPP_t
(PS_PARTKEY INTEGER NOT NULL,PS_SUPPKEY INTEGER NOT NULL,
PS_AVAILQTY INTEGER,PS_SUPPLYCOST DECIMAL(15,2),
PS_COMMENT VARCHAR(199) CASESPECIFIC,
PS_VT PERIOD(DATE) NOT NULL AS VALIDTIME,
PS_TT PERIOD(TIMESTAMP(6) WITH TIME ZONE)NOT NULL AS TRANSACTIONTIME)
PRIMARY INDEX ( PS_PARTKEY );
```

After the tables have been created, we need to create a history. The first step in doing so is to initialize the valid time for all the tables which is performed via insert-select using the corresponding original tables . For example, to start the history of Partsupp on January 1$^{st}$ 2012 we submit the following SQL utilizing the original Partsupp table as a basis (note that the history of the other two tables will be initiated in exactly the same way):

```
NONSEQUENCED VALIDTIME INSERT INTO PARTSUPP_t (ps_partkey, ps_suppkey,
ps_availqty, ps_supplycost, ps_comment, ps_VT)
SELECT PS_PARTKEY, PS_SUPPKEY, PS_AVAILQTY, PS_SUPPLYCOST, 'initial
load', PERIOD (DATE '2012-01-01', DATE '9999-12-31') FROM PARTSUPP;
```

Next we populate the history table using updates based on assumptions that keep the database size predictable regardless of the scale factor. We have made choices in this benchmark definition that need to be regarded as examples. We kept the supplier and part identifiers constant and we modified field values in Part and Supplier but modified the associations between parts and suppliers. For the Partsupp  table for example we would like parts to be supplied by different suppliers for 50% of the parts. We also keep track of the updated rows using ps_comment:

```
SEQUENCED VALIDTIME PERIOD (DATE '2012-02-01', DATE '9999-12-31')
UPDATE PARTSUPP_t SET ps_suppkey = ps_suppkey + 1 ,
ps_comment = 'upd ps' WHERE ps_suppkey MOD 2 = 1;
```

This effectively updates all the rows and increases the size of the Partsupp table by 50% making of size 800000*SF*1.5 where SF is the scale factor. Next we proceed in updating the Part table by adding 10 to p_retailprice each 10<sup>th</sup> of the month for February through May. For each of the four updates we also modify p_comment by replacing it with a description of the change performed at the same time. This will help us keep track of the operations performed. The update for February for example looks like this:

```
SEQUENCED VALIDTIME PERIOD (DATE '2012-02-10', DATE '9999-12-31')
UPDATE PARTTBL_t SET p_retailprice = p_retailprice + 10,
p_comment='2/10: p_retailprice+10';
```

As a result the Part table size becomes 200000*SF*5. Similarly we update the Supplier table for the months February to May on the 20<sup>th</sup> of the month (as entered in the VALIDTIME parameter), by applying a multiplication factor to the supplier balance depending on the nation the supplier belongs to. The update statement will be the same for the four months with only the month changing so we show only February:

```
SEQUENCED VALIDTIME PERIOD (DATE '2012-02-20', DATE '9999-12-31')
UPDATE supplier_t SET s_acctbal = CASE
  WHEN s_nationkey MOD 5 = 0 THEN  s_acctbal * 2
  WHEN s_nationkey MOD 5 = 1 THEN  s_acctbal * 2.5
  WHEN s_nationkey MOD 5 = 2 THEN  s_acctbal * 3
  WHEN s_nationkey MOD 5 = 3 THEN  s_acctbal * 3.5
  WHEN s_nationkey MOD 5 = 4 THEN  s_acctbal * 4    END;
```

As a result of this update the size of the supplier table will be 10000*SF*5. It should be noted that the methods selected to add a temporal element to the three chosen tables are just examples. One could chose different fields and different update methods perhaps using fields that do not change often such as the part name or the supplier address. Instead of multiplying supplier balances by a factor we could chose to add or subtract a large or small number.

## 4    Workload Queries

There are several types of queries one could provide and this could depend on factors such as the type of implementation (DBMS native or special application) or the method selected for updating the temporal component. In all cases it is good to first have queries to verify the correct implementation of the updates. These queries must include row counts but also could involve averages of quantities modified. For example as scale factor 1 we could use the following query and associated answer set to verify the correct load of the Supplier table:

```
nonsequenced validtime sel s_vt, average(s_acctbal), count(*)
from supplier_t group by 1 order by 1;
S_VT                         Average(S_ACCTBAL)     Count(*)
--------------------------   ------------------     -----------
('12/01/01', '12/02/20')              4510.35         10000
('12/02/20', '12/03/20')             13528.38         10000
('12/03/20', '12/04/20')             42826.02         10000
('12/04/20', '12/05/20')            141948.84         10000
('12/05/20', '99/12/31')            488417.91         10000
```

Another example would be to trace the history of particular items answering questions such as "what is the history of ps_partkey=1" which can be expressed as follows:

```
SEQUENCED VALIDTIME SELECT ps_suppkey ,ps_partkey, ps_comment,
p_comment s_comment, p_retailprice, s_acctbal FROM PARTSUPP_t,
SUPPLIER_t, PART_t WHERE ps_suppkey=s_suppkey AND ps_partkey =
p_partkey AND ps_partkey=1 ORDER BY ps_partkey, ps_suppkey, VALIDTIME;
```

Yet another example could be "what is the status of the suppliers of partkey=1 on March 1$^{st}$, 2012?" expressed as the previous query but replacing SEQUENCED VALIDTIME with VALIDTIME AS OF DATE '2012-03-01'.

The second set of queries consists of the TPC-H queries involving any of the Part, Supplier, Partsupp tables. This set includes queries 2, 3, 5, 7, 8, 9, 11, 14, 15, 16, 17, 19 and 20. These queries are run two ways: (1) by replacing the original table names Part, Supplier and Partsupp with their temporal version and (2) with the original tables for Part, Supplier, Partsupp. The temporal version of the queries can be run as sequenced or using a particular date. For instance by adding the clause VALIDTIME AS OF DATE '2012-03-01' at the beginning of the query. Without the VALIDTIME statement in the query the default will be used i.e. the current time providing a snapshot of the data. In other words all the rows with a VALIDTIME period which intersects the system time will be used.

The last set of queries consists of temporal queries. This is a potentially very large set depending on what features are to be tested. A very simple example could be looking at the total part count, average retail price, and average balance for each supplier:

```
SELECT s.s_suppkey, s.s_name, count(p_partkey), avg(p_retailprice), avg(s_acctbal)
FROM SUPPLIER_t s ,PART_t p ,PARTSUPP_t ps
WHERE s.s_suppkey = ps.ps_suppkey AND p.p_partkey = ps.ps_partkey
GROUP BY 1,2 ORDER BY 4 desc;
```

Since the above query does not contain a VALIDTIME statement the default current time is used. Different VALIDTIME values can be used to create more variations of the query as is the case in the TPC-H benchmark. More sophisticated queries can be implemented such as the following query looking at the historical 3-day moving average of the retail price of a particular part by day. This query uses both historical and current values and it is provided only as an example as it uses interesting but specific temporal constructs, more specifically EXPAND.

```
NONSEQUENCED VALIDTIME
SELECT p_partkey, pricedate , AVG(p_retailprice)
OVER (PARTITION BY p_partkey ORDER BY pricedate ROWS 2 PRECEDING)
FROM ( SEQUENCED VALIDTIME
SELECT p_partkey, p_retailprice, BEGIN (Day_Dt_Tm) pricedate
FROM Part_t
WHERE p_partkey = 1
```

EXPAND ON p _vt AS Day_Dt_Tm
BY ANCHOR DAY FOR PERIOD (DATE '2012-01-01',DATE '2012-06-01')) dt;

A corresponding monthly version of this SQL can be defined in the same manner as above by replacing the Day_Dt_Tm parameter (standing for day) with the Month_Dt_Tm parameter (standing for month) as follows:

NONSEQUENCED VALIDTIME
SELECT p_partkey, pricedate , AVG(p_retailprice)
OVER (PARTITION BY p_partkey ORDER BY pricedate ROWS 2 PRECEDING)
FROM (
SEQUENCED VALIDTIME
SELECT p_partkey, p_retailprice, BEGIN(Month_Dt_Tm) pricedate
FROM Part_t
WHERE p_partkey = 1
EXPAND ON p _vt AS Day_Dt_Tm
BY ANCHOR DAY FOR PERIOD (DATE '2012-01-01',DATE '2012-06-01')) dt;

Many more queries can be defined depending on what types of temporal constructs need to be exercised. One example again very sophisticated, is the following using the P_NORMALIZE operator that returns a period value that is the combination of the two period expressions if the period expressions overlap or meet. If the period expressions neither meet nor overlap, P_NORMALIZE returns NULL. If either period expression is NULL, P_NORMALIZE also returns NULL. This historical query returns NULL for the value of the variable S_PS_normalized_vt if the PS and the S tables do not contain common time.

NONSEQUENCED VALIDTIME
SELECT ps_partkey ,ps_suppkey ,s_name ,n_name ,ps_vt ,s_vt
,s_vt P_NORMALIZE ps_vt S_PS_normalized_vt
,CASE WHEN s_vt OVERLAPS ps_vt THEN 'Y' ELSE 'N' END S_PS_overlapind
,SUM(s_acctbal) sumAcctBal
FROM
Partsupp_t, Supplier_t ,Nation
WHERE
ps_suppkey = s_suppkey AND s_nationkey = n_nationkey
AND n_name IN (SELECT n_name from nation where n_nationkey mod 5 = 0)
GROUP BY 1,2,3,4,5,6,7
ORDER BY 1,2,3,4,5,6,7;

Many queries can be constructed as seen before so many choices can be made. A fixed part of the benchmark though will be in the area of the TPC-H queries when run with temporal. We show some examples in the next section.

# 5     Experiments

The validity of the DDL and SQL proposed was determined on a small scale factor 1 database. We also ran a few experiments on a small Teradata appliance at scale factor 1000 to get an idea of the type of elapsed times involved in building the database and running the queries. The load itself i.e. the insert-select took close to half an hour. The TPC-H queries were run using three values for VALIDTIME, January $1^{st}$ 2012, March $1^{st}$, 2012 and no value specified which is equivalent to June $15^{th}$ 2012 which is around the time the experiments were run. To place things in somewhat of a perspective we also ran the equivalent TPC-H queries non optimized with the original non-temporal tables. The results are provided in seconds.

Execution time (sec) for TPC-H temporal queries

|  |  | VALIDTIME AS OF | | |
|---|---|---|---|---|
|  | original tables | 1/1/2012 | 3/1/2012 | current |
| Q02 | 6.2 | 12.4 | 12.1 | 29.0 |
| Q05 | 32.0 | 31.6 | 31.4 | 31.1 |
| Q07 | 54.4 | 43.8 | 44.0 | 44.0 |
| Q08 | 41.2 | 48.4 | 48.5 | 48.3 |
| Q09 | 501.0 | 272.8 | 272.7 | 269.9 |
| Q11 | 11.5 | 16.1 | 16.0 | 16.2 |
| Q14 | 9.8 | 16.8 | 16.5 | 16.6 |
| Q15 | 8.2 | 8.2 | 8.1 | 8.1 |
| Q16 | 11.5 | 21.9 | 21.4 | 22.6 |
| Q17 | 104.9 | 136.6 | 137.7 | 137.2 |
| Q19 | 30.4 | 34.9 | 36.6 | 36.0 |
| Q20 | 24.1 | 33.7 | 34.0 | 34.1 |

These elapsed times demonstrate that the model retained is adequate since the times are commensurate with the TPC-H elapsed times.

# 6     Conclusion

We have provided an approach to add a temporal component to the TPC-H benchmark. Our approach can be used as a model and be adapted *mutatis mutandis* to introduce a temporal component to any existing non-temporal benchmark. We have provided DDL, insert-select examples on how to populate the newly defined temporal tables and queries of various types that can be used to test the temporal implementation. Finally we have shown the adequacy of our approach by showing on a small example that the queries run in a reasonable time commensurate with their non-temporal counterparts.

# References

[1] Snodgrass, R.T., Böhlen, M.H., Jensen, C.S., Steiner, A.: Adding Valid Time toSQL/Temporal. Change Proposal, ANSI X3H2-96-501r2, ISO/IECJTC1/SC21/WG3 DBL MAD-146r2 (November 1996)

[2] Snodgrass, R.T., Böhlen, M.H., Jensen, C.S., Steiner, A.: Adding TransactionTime to SQL/Temporal. Change Proposal, ANSI X3H2- 96-502r2, ISO/IEC JTC1/SC21/WG3 DBL MAD-147r2 (November 1996)

[3] Jensen, C.S., et al.: The TSQL benchmark. In: International Workshop on an Infrastructure for Temporal Databases, Arlington, TX, pp. QQ-1 – QQ-28 (June 1993)

[4] Dunham, M., Elmasri, R., Nacimento, M., Sobol, M.: Benchmarking Temporal Databases A Research Agenda. Technical Report 95-CSE-20, Southern Methodist University (December 1995)

[5] Kalua, P., Rberson, E.: Benchmark queries for temporal databases. Technical report TR-379, Computer Science Department, Indiana University (1994)

[6] Noh, S.-Y., Gadia, S.K.: Benchmarking temporal database models with interval-based and temporal element-based timestamping. Journal of Systems and Software 81(11), 1931–1943 (2008)

[7] TPC-H specification – Transaction Performance Council, http://www.tpc.org

# Performance Per Watt - Benchmarking Ways to Get More for Less

Karl R. Huppler

IBM MS XQK, 3605 Highway 52 North, Rochester, MN 55901 USA
huppler@us.ibm.com

**Abstract.** The electrical cost of managing information systems has always been a concern for those investing in technology. However, in recent years the focus has increased, both because of increased costs of electricity and decreased costs of other components of the equation.

To understand the efficiency of a computing solution, one needs a measure of throughput per watt (or watts per unit of work) that employs a workload that is relevant to the target load on the system and that operates at a capacity that reflects the target throughput of the final application. The goal of this paper is to introduce the reader to some of the measures that are available and provide an explanation of the relative merits of each.

**Keywords:** Performance, Benchmark, Performance per Watt, Energy, Servers.

## 1    Introduction

The cost of information systems has always been a concern for those investing in technology. However, the components of that cost have not remained a constant. Over time, the costs of capital investment and personnel for computer management have dropped dramatically because of the rapid increase in compute power, the decrease in costs of manufacture and improvements in tools needed to manage systems.

At the same time, the average cost of electricity has increased, and the number of applications that rely on computer-based information (and therefore the number of actual computers) has increased. Couple this with the other increasing demands on electrical systems around the globe and it is easy to understand why the cost of electrical energy has become a significant part of the overall cost of computing.

The impact of this relative rise in cost has spawned

A) Consumer demand for more efficient solutions
B) Moves to establish efficiency incentive programs by several regulatory or voluntary efficiency organizations around the globe.
C) The creation of several benchmark and measurement methodologies.

To understand the energy costs of a computing solution, it is first important to understand the environment where the solution will be employed.

R. Nambiar and M. Poess (Eds.): TPCTC 2012, LNCS 7755, pp. 60–74, 2013.

As a common metaphor, consider the efficiency of a transportation vehicle:

- You would not base your entire evaluation on the amount of fuel that it consumed while idling in a parking lot. However, if the vehicle is used in heavy city traffic, you might base part of your evaluation on fuel use while the vehicle is at a stop sign.
- If your "application" involves transportation in very hilly country, you would not base your evaluation exclusively on the vehicle's ability to perform on a flat highway.
- You would likely not place a 2-person commuter automobile, a 20-person microbus, and a truck capable of hauling many tons of freight in the same comparison category.

The net is that you would not focus solely on fuel consumption, but rather on the fuel required to accomplish the work that is necessary. To accomplish this, you need to select a benchmark that matches both the type of work and the amount of work that the vehicle will be required to achieve.

Returning from the metaphor to the computing industry, the parallel is clear: To understand the efficiency of a computing solution, you need a measure of throughput per watt (or watts per unit of work) that employs a workload that is relevant to the target load on the system and that operates at a capacity that reflects the target throughput of the final application. The goal of this paper is to introduce the reader to some of the measures that are available and provide an explanation of the relative merits of each.

## 2    Benchmarks and Tools Ordered by Growing Configuration Complexity

For some computing solutions, the dominant requirement is efficient processor use with small requirements for memory, network, and storage. In this case, the main processor is likely the greatest single draw of electrical requirements, so there is some meaning for benchmarks that address this area, even for environments that require more robust configurations. In other cases, the requirements of the workload include storage, memory or network components that dwarf the contributions of the processor.

### 2.1    SPECpower_ssj2008

SPECpower_ssj2008 [1] has sometimes been called the first industry standard for performance per watt benchmarks. One could argue that distinction should go to the Green500 metric, discussed later in this paper. It is certain that SPECpower_ssj2008 is the first such benchmark to come from a benchmark standards consortium that is comprised of volunteer members of both industry and academic communities.

---

[1] http://www.spec.org/power_ssj2008/

Since the Standard Performance Evaluation Corporation (SPEC) introduced the benchmark in December 2007, there have been (as of August 1, 2012) 354 published results, demonstrating three key strengths of the benchmark:

1) It is relatively inexpensive and easy to run
2) It provides information that is of interest to the consumer
3) It has achieved sufficient popularity that it is often used as a comparison point in competitive sales situations that involve the kind of configuration that is benchmarked.

The benchmark requires the use of an externally attached power analyzer and the use of a probe to monitor temperature at the primary air inlet of the system under test. The use of physical, externally attached devices to measure computer functions is something that is foreign to the vast majority of computer performance analysts. This complicates the environment for the initial measurement of SPECpower_ssj2008. However, SPEC has provided a tool called the SPEC PTDaemon[2] (SPEC Power and Temperature Daemon) and a setup guide[3] to assist with this process. The SPEC PTDaemon has routines that adapt the generic actions that are required by the benchmark to the specific command and data interfaces of a variety of power analyzers that have been tested and accepted by SPEC as confidently delivering accurate power information to synchronize with the information that is being delivered by the performance benchmark driver.

A key innovation of SPECpower_ssj2008 is the concept of graduated workload levels. For performance benchmarks, the primary goal is to achieve the highest throughput possible on a given configuration. However, when examining energy efficiency, it is important to note that most computer systems are not operated at 100% of their capacity and so it is important to be efficient across a range of operational levels. And, while computers are not purchased with a purpose of standing idle, it is fairly certain that they will be idle for some fraction of time, so it is important to have a measure of energy requirements when no work is accomplished (the automobile idling at the Stop sign, in the introductory metaphor.) The figure below is taken from an early result[4] in the benchmark. Note that the throughput is measured at graduated load levels, from 100% of a calibration target that is established by the benchmark harness, down to an idle measure. The bars in the graph represent the performance per watt ratio for each of these measurement points, while the line graph is the actual power consumed at each point. Observe that although power requirements are much lower at smaller amounts of throughput, the optimal efficiency (highest performance per watt) is achieved at peak load.

---

[2] http://www.spec.org/power/docs/SPEC-PTDaemon_Design.pdf

[3] http://www.spec.org/power/docs/SPEC-Power_Measurement_Setup_Guide.pdf

[4] http://www.spec.org/power_ssj2008/results/res2008q1/power_ssj2008-20080311-00041.html

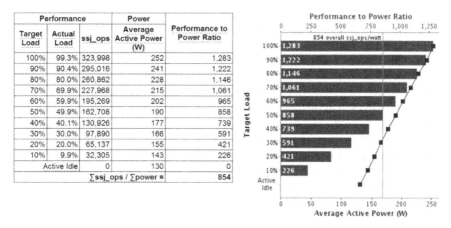

**Fig. 1.** An early SPECpower_ssj2008 result

The figure below is taken from a much more recent SPECpower_ssj2008 result.[5]

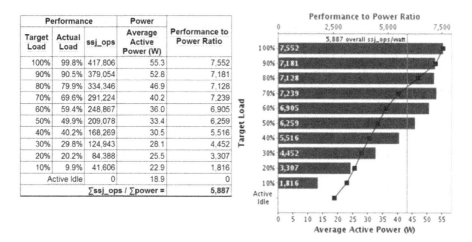

**Fig. 2.** A recent SPECpower_ssj2008 result

We can observe several changes in the four year span between the first result and this recent one:

1) The base technology has improved. The earlier result was a 2-socket server, requiring over 250 watts at high power and dropping to just 130 watts at idle, which was excellent for that time. The new result used a single processor

---

[5] http://www.spec.org/power_ssj2008/results/res2012q3/power_ssj20 08-20120625-00503.html

socket, delivered more throughput than the older result, and used less than 43% of the former's idle power when running at maximum capacity.

2) The characteristics of the power curve have changed. Instead of the near straight line of power reductions as throughput is reduced, the new curve demonstrates more aggressive power management that maintains a higher performance per watt ratio across more of the curve.

3) The overall result is almost 7 times as good, based on the metric formula chosen for the benchmark.

4) A benchmark is a benchmark. Although a substantial portion of the improved result is because of the improvements made in the base hardware technology and in power management firmware, the passage of time has also allowed the sponsor to fit the system to the benchmark. All of the following techniques that are employed are perfectly legitimate for the limited operational profile of the benchmark, but might not be appropriate for more general purposes:

a. The benchmark requires zero storage I/O, so the only disk is 5400 rpm SATA drive configured with controller options that allow for aggressive power management when the drive is idle.

b. In an era where 8, 10 and 12-core processors are commonplace, the processor configured has only 4 cores, with a nominal frequency of 2.5 GHz.

c. In an era where servers are often capable of supporting upwards of a terabyte of main memory, the maximum for this server is 32 GB and it was configured with 8 GB.

d. The system is a tower configuration, with potential space for expansion, but it is restricted to a single processor, a single PCI slot and a single PCIe slot.

e. Several firmware settings were altered to fit the very consistent, memory-resident nature of the benchmark.

f. Physical components such as USB ports and NIC ports that are not required for the benchmark are disabled

Note, again, that all of these techniques are legitimate consumer options. Essentially, they make the measured system a perfect match for the business model that is exemplified by the SPECpower_ssj2008 benchmark - - which is reflected in the outstanding score for this result. This also emphasizes the need to select a benchmark that is a reasonable match for the eventual use of the server.

## 2.2    SPEC Power and Performance Benchmark Methodology

Recognizing that the business model of the benchmark is a critical factor in evaluating computer server efficiency, the SPEC organization produced a guide for the inclusion of power measurements in a wide variety of performance benchmarks. Entitled the

SPEC Power and Performance Benchmark Methodology [6], this document is recommended reading for anyone who is interested in creating a measure of electrical efficiency for computer servers. It can also be useful for consumers wishing to better understand the challenges associated with performance per watt measurements and how they relate to benchmarks that are available today.

The methodology has been applied to the SPECweb2009[7] benchmark (now retired) and to the SPECvirt_sc2010[8] benchmark. Other SPEC benchmarks may follow. The methodology document can also be seen to have provided influence in the SAP Power benchmarks and TPC-Energy benchmarks, discussed later.

## 2.3   SPECweb2009

SPECweb2009 employed a graduated workload, similar to SPECpower_ssj2008, but with fewer measurement points, as exemplified by the performance per watt graphic from a result [9] published in January 2012, just prior to the retirement of the benchmark. The configuration required to measure the benchmark is somewhat more robust than that of SPECpower_ssj2008. The measurement in this example used 12 processor cores (2 processor chips), 96 GB of main memory, 8 storage devices and several network connections.

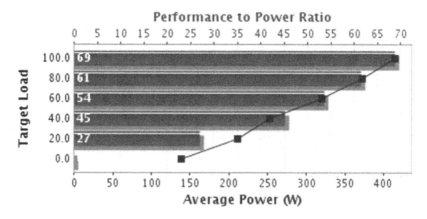

**Fig. 3.** A performance to power graphic from a published SPECweb2009 result

As a performance per watt benchmark, SPECweb2009 clearly satisfied a different set of system requirements than does SPECpower_ssj2008. However, it takes more than a unique set of hardware requirements to allow a benchmark to be relevant to

---

[6] http://www.spec.org/power/docs/SPEC-Power_and_Performance_Methodology.pdf

[7] http://www.spec.org/web2009/

[8] http://www.spec.org/virt_sc2010/

[9] http://www.spec.org/web2009/results/res2012q1/web2009-20120112-00010.html

specific consumer environments. While SPEC does not make their reasons for retiring a benchmark public, one might surmise that the zero publications in 2010 and 2011 may have had something to do with it.

## 2.4    SPECvirt_sc2010

SPECvirt_sc2010 also requires a somewhat more robust configuration than SPECpower_ssj2008. The virtualization benchmark targets a substantially different business model than the server-side JAVA benchmark used in SPECpower_ssj2008. It is substantially more complex to execute and achieve strong results, because it simulates an environment that may include dozens of virtual machines executing a variety of workloads.

The benchmark offers three publication options:

1) Performance only, without power measurement
2) Performance and power of the server system of the system under test
3) Performance and power of the server and storage used for the system under test.

Placing these three options in separate categories recognizes that a configuration that is optimized for performance per watt efficiency might not deliver as much performance as a system that is focused purely on delivering high performance. The split between server-only and full system recognizes that some configurations include storage in the processor enclosure, while others use external storage; and also that storage requirements vary from environment to environment, so that there may be more interest in the efficiency of the server enclosure.

While the benchmark brings the strengths of these publication options, the complexity of the benchmark made it difficult to construct graduated workload levels. As such, the power measurements are done only at full performance and at idle. In a virtualization environment there is likely to be more relatively high utilization computing than low, considering the deployment of many virtual machines on a single physical configuration. However, in a consumer environment, there will most likely be times when the server is not operating at 100%.

The following figure shows the power and performance/watt result of a sample publication[10] from SPECvirt_sc2010_PPW, which includes both server and storage power.

### SPECvirt_sc2010_PPW 0.6545 @ 102 VMs

...

| Run # | Power Consumption | | | | | |
|---|---|---|---|---|---|---|
| | System Power | | Ext. Storage Power | | Total Power | |
| | Avg. Power (W) | Avg. Perf/Power | Avg. Power (W) | Avg. Perf/Power | Avg. Power (W) | Avg. Perf/Power |
| 1 | 487.76 | 3.22 | 1911.61 | 0.82 | 2399.37 | 0.65 |
| 2 | 273.91 | 0.00 | 1803.34 | 0.00 | 2077.25 | 0.00 |

**Fig. 4.** Power information from a SPECvirt_2010_PPW publish

---

[10] http://www.spec.org/virt_sc2010/results/res2011q4/virt_sc2010-20111018-00038-ppw.html

One can surmise from the power listed that the configuration is significantly more robust than the configurations typically used for SPECpower_ssj2008. Clearly the benchmarks are not comparable and it would be inappropriate to use a SPECpower_ssj2008 result to project performance per watt efficiency in an environment such as one modeled by SPECvirt_sc2010. The server is 2 sockets, uses 16 cores and is configured with a quarter terabyte of main memory and with 6 active network ports.

The other clear point is that there are configurations where the computer server represents only a fraction of total power requirement of the complete configuration. In this case, the benchmark configuration included a total of 144 storage drives in 6 enclosures.

This emphasizes the need to match both the benchmark model (in this case, over 100 virtual servers performing a variety of workloads that each consumes a fraction of a processor core of compute capacity) and the benchmark configuration to the consumer environment being evaluated.

Since (as of August 1, 2012) its first publication in 3Q2010, there have been 26 total published in SPECvirt_2010. Of these, only two have been SPECvirt_2010_PPW (server and storage power) and two have been SPECvirt_2010_ServerPPW. A total of 26 is not unusual for a complex benchmark. It is possible that the limited number of performance per watt measurements may indicate that the general consumer is not sufficiently aware of the differences in power benchmarks.

## 2.5    EPA ENERGY STAR for Servers, Version 1 Specification

There are a great many energy efficiency initiatives in government and government-affiliated organizations across the globe. Programs are created, or efforts to create programs are underway in Japan, Australia, New Zealand, South Korea, China, India, Brazil, Israel, The European Union, Mexico, Canada, the United States and perhaps others. To describe each of these efforts would comprise more than a single paper. We have chosen to focus on the United States Environmental Protection Agency's Enterprise Servers ENERGY STAR program[11], because there is some evidence that other organizations may adopt or adapt the EPA's program over time. From the perspective of both computer manufacturers and consumers, there is an advantage to having some consistency in programs such as this.

ENERGY STAR programs have three key differences from typical benchmarks:

1) They are threshold achievement programs - - There is no fighting to get 1% higher than the competitor. If your product meets the required threshold, you are allowed to label your product as ENERGY STAR compliant. As product efficiency improves over time, the thresholds may be made more stringent, but the concept of meeting a threshold specification remains.

---

[11] http://www.energystar.gov/index.cfm?fuseaction=find_a_product. showProductGroup&pgw_code=DC

2) They tend to be closer to "out of the box" configurations, without the hyper-tuning of hardware, software and application that often occurs with benchmarks

3) To place an ENERGY STAR label on a specific configuration, it must be shown that the specific configuration satisfies the ENERGY STAR requirements, unlike benchmarks where a single superior result is often associated with a broad range of product in marketing literature.

The EPA has a strong history of energy efficiency programs for consumer goods, including electronics. Understandably, items such as televisions and personal computers tend to have intermittent use, so the energy requirements when the units are standing idle is a key factor in understanding their power efficiency. Indeed, as Version 1 of the Server program was being developed, statistics were available to show that a great many multi-user servers also stood idle for the majority of time, providing strong incentive for the EPA to base their Enterprise Server specification on the ability of systems to efficiently do nothing.

However, as shown in Figures 1, 2 and 3, above, if there is meaningful work to accomplish, there is clear evidence that computer servers achieve the highest efficiency in terms of energy consumed per unit of work produced when they are running at reasonably high utilization. In recognition of this, the EPA's ENERGY STAR® Program Requirements for Computer Servers[12] specification makes some adjustments that recognize the complexity of computer server configuration and the myriad of uses that different configurations may serve:

- An idle threshold is only required for 1-socket and 2-socket servers, whereas a default power-management deployment is required for 3-socket and 4-socket servers
- A separation is made between servers that include a service processor and those that do not
- All servers are required to show their power consumption when running at peak load for some benchmark
- For 1s and 2s servers, the idle threshold is adjusted by a set of "adders" that recognize the consumer requirements for more than minimum memory, disk, adapters, etc.

This last point shifts the ENERGY STAR program from the simplest of measures (idle only) to one that spans a range of computer configurations that exceeds that of most benchmarks. It presents some challenges, however, as shown in the figure, below, which is copied from the referenced specification.

The allowances were set using technology that was readily available in 2008. In the interim, technology improvements in memory density and in delivery of cost effective solid state storage devices has created a scenario where, to achieve ENERGY STAR qualification, all that is necessary is to configure the system with more memory and more solid state storage than might normally be needed.

---

[12] http://www.energystar.gov/ia/partners/product_specs/program_re qs/Computer_Servers_Program_Requirements.pdf

| System Characteristic | Applies To | Additional Idle Power Allowance |
|---|---|---|
| Additional Power Supplies | Power supplies installed explicitly for power redundancy | 20.0 watts per Power Supply |
| Additional Hard Drives (including solid state drives) | Installed hard drives greater than one | 8.0 watts per Hard Drive |
| Additional Memory | Installed memory greater than 4 GB | 2.0 watts per GB |
| Additional I/O Devices (single connection speed rounded to nearest Gbit) | Installed Devices greater than two ports of 1 Gbit, onboard Ethernet | < 1 Gbit: No Allowance<br>= 1 Gbit: 2.0 watts / Active Port<br>> 1 Gbit and < 10 Gbit: 4.0 watts / Active Port<br>≥ 10 Gbit: 8.0 watts / Active Port |

**Fig. 5.** Additional Power Allowances for Version One of EPA ENERGY STAR for Computer Servers

While the notion of increasing the configuration size to meet an energy efficiency specification might appear to be counter productive, in fact it demonstrates one of the EPA's main purposes. If they can incent the global use of more efficient technology to meet their thresholds, they are happy to award the ENERGY STAR label on a fairly broad basis. As they revise their specifications for subsequent versions of the program, they will likely restrict these allowances to reflect more modern technology and hopefully provide incentive for further improvements.

## 2.6    Server Efficiency Rating Tool (SERT)

As we have discussed, it is a substantial challenge to find any single measure or tool that fairly evaluates a wide variety of workload requirements and a wide variety of computer configurations. We've also looked at some of the differences between a competitive benchmark, such as SPECpower_ssj2008, and a qualification specification, such as ENERGY STAR.

The SPEC organization has been working with the EPA for several years to develop a tool that will address some of these challenges. Called the SERT[13], the SPEC committee that is creating the tool recognized the strengths and weaknesses of the SPECpower_ssj2008 benchmark, along with the EPA's goal of having a method for evaluating a broad range of configurations, and the need to have a large base of measurement information in order to set threshold levels for programs such as ENERGY STAR.

The SERT includes small workloads (worklets) that focus on small segments of the functions required for general purpose computing. Some focus on the processor (such as XML validation, Encryption, Sort, etc.) Some focus on storage (Sequential I/O, Random I/O.) Some focus on memory use. The overall tool is designed to allow additional worklets to be added, should valuable additions become available.

---

[13] http://www.spec.org/sert/

Key features of the SERT are:

- The inclusion of a variety of worklets, as discussed above
- Graduated workload intensity levels
- A set list of allowable parameters to simulate near out-of-box computing.
- A graphical interface that allows for relatively easy set up and execution of the tool
- A discovery process that helps to define the system under test in a consistent manner
- Automated validation of part of the overall load
- Assistance in setting parameters for many of the analyzers that are on SPEC's accepted list
- A proposed license requirement that the output for the tool may not be used for typical "benchmarking" purposes, but only as a means of either qualifying for a program such as ENERGY STAR or collecting data to help set criteria for such a program.

The SERT is also likely to be shown to be a very flexible tool for research, as new techniques for improvement of power management become available.

As of 1.August, 2012, the SERT had not been officially accepted as the tool of choice for any energy efficiency program. However, it is clearly an improvement on prior technology and one would expect it to be used in several such programs.

### 2.7 SAP Server Power Benchmark; SAP System Power Benchmark

Thus far, the majority of the benchmarks and tools discussed do not address database transaction processing environments. There is some amount of database activity associated with a fraction of the workloads in SPECvirt_sc2010. Some of the physical configurations needed for a database application environment can be tested using the SERT. We have also noted that it is difficult to include graduated levels of workload when measuring complex benchmark environments.

The SAP power benchmarks[14] satisfy both of these, delivering a benchmark that is strongly focused on both database transaction processing and the application processing that is typical for enterprise applications, and at the same time providing a series of different workload intensity periods for the evaluation of performance per watt at different levels.

SAP has defined two benchmark environments – one that focuses on the server power and one that includes the total system power. Both start from the base of the well-known SAP Sales and Distribution (SD)[15] performance benchmark, with adjustments put in place to measure power at the various throughput levels that are defined in the specification. As the figures, below, show, the SAP benchmark developers took the notion of graduated workload levels farther than SPEC, varying

---

[14] http://www.sap.com/solutions/benchmark/pdf/Specification_SAP_Power_Benchmarks_V12.pdf
[15] http://www.sap.com/solutions/benchmark/sd.epx

the workload intensity in a way that might be considered more "customer like" than the graduated step-down employed by other benchmarks and tools. Unlike other such benchmarks, the SAP team felt that realism was better achieved by requiring the ramp-up period for one measurement point to overlap the ramp-down period for the prior point, simulating a fairly smooth flow from point to point without artificial breaks.

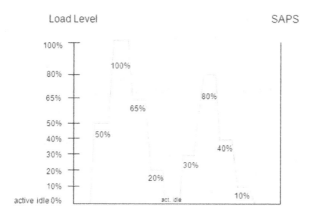

**Fig. 6.** Benchmark load profile from the SAP Power Benchmark specification

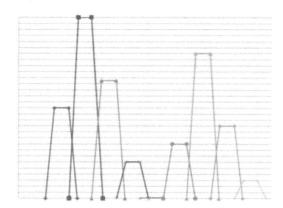

**Fig. 7.** SAP Power Benchmark specification, showing required load overlap

The SAP Power Benchmarks may be the most complete performance per watt benchmarks or tools discussed in this paper. They come as close to a "real" application as any benchmark might hope. They require robust system configurations. They include both database and application processing compute requirements. They demonstrate power efficiency and power management at a wide variety of load levels.

Unfortunately, the engineering strengths of the benchmarks may be considered practical weaknesses. The benchmark is more complex to execute than others. The benchmark requires a more robust configuration than many, but there has not been sufficient consumer demand for efficiency data on robust configurations. Although it is technically applicable to a wide range of similar applications, the inclination is to associate it only with SAP environments.

## 2.8     TPC-Energy for the Suite of TPC Benchmarks

Transaction Processing Performance Council (TPC) benchmarks are clearly focused on enterprise database environments. While the SAP SD benchmark that is the basis of the SAP Power Benchmarks focuses on a mix of database and application, the TPC suite of benchmarks (TPC Benchmark C, TPC Benchmark E, TPC Benchmark H and TPC Benchmark DS) focus almost entirely on database and data processing, with limited focus on the application server layer of a typical enterprise environment. This makes the TPC benchmarks unique among all of the benchmarks that currently have power measurements associated with them.

A unique characteristic of the TPC-Energy[16] Specification is that it applies to all active TPC benchmarks. The single specification is designed to apply to all four individual TPC performance benchmarks and can be adapted to work with any new benchmark that may be created. This is clearly a strength, since the individual benchmarks do not require adjustment. However, it also sacrifices the potential to adjust the benchmarks to show power requirements at less than full capacity.

Recognizing that consumers interests may be more localized than the entire configuration required to produce a TPC benchmark result, or that manufacturers may want to highlight a particular portion of the benchmark configuration, the TPC-Energy specification requires the power of the complete system under test, and offers the option to separate the power measurement into subsystems, including the primary processor subsystem, the storage subsystem, a possible middle-tier subsystem and a miscellaneous subsystem with other components. Primarily for this reason, the TPC chose to present the efficiency result in terms of watts per throughput, rather than throughput per watts. The sum of the watts per throughput for each subsystem yields the primary result of the total SUT watts per throughput.

In the slightly more than two year period that TPC-Energy results have been published, there have been 15 results published on three benchmarks. The benchmark with the largest collection of comparable results (TPC-E) has seen an improvement in watts/tpsE of nearly an order of magnitude in that period. This demonstrates improvement in not only processor technology, but also in storage, as the first TPC-Energy for TPC-E result[17] used 700 rotating storage drives and the current (as of

---

[16] http://www.tpc.org/tpc_energy/

[17] http://www.tpc.org/tpce/results/tpce_result_detail.asp?id=1100 62103; TPC-E Throughput: 1,400.14, Price/Performance: 330.00 USD, TPC-Energy Metric 6.72 Watts/TpsE, Availability Date: 06/21/10

August 1, 2012) leader[18] used just 8 rotating disks and 60 solid state devices, even while achieving a higher throughput score.

To understand the robust configurations used for TPC benchmarks, one need only look at the subsystem breakdown from this most recent TPC-Energy for TPC-E result, as shown in the next figure. There are significant contributions to the energy footprint from both the database server and storage subsystem. Compare this to the SPECpower_ssj2008 result shown in Figure 2, where the maximum power of the entire system under test was larger than the idle power of the application server subsystem in this TPC-E configuration.

**Subsystem Reporting:**

|  | Secondary Metrics | Additional Numerical Quantities | | | |
|---|---|---|---|---|---|
|  | watts/tpsE | Full Load Avg Watts | Full Load % of REC | Idle Avg Watts | Idle % of REC |
| Database Server *) | 0.32 | 592.41 | 45.97% | 239.56 | 28.39% |
| Storage *) | 0.31 | 578.42 | 44.88% | 544.80 | 64.56% |
| Application Server *) | 0.05 | 100.99 | 7.84% | 59.12 | 7.01% |
| Miscellaneous *) | 0.01 | 17.00 | 1.32% | 0.40 | 0.05% |
| Total REC | 0.69 | 1,288.82 | 100.00% | 843.88 | 100.00% |

*) see pricing for list of components

**Fig. 8.** Subsystem reporting from a recent TPC-Energy result

## 2.9    Green500

Any paper on computer server energy efficiency would be remiss in not including a few notes on the Green500[19]. The application environment for the Green500 list is greatly different from that of any other tool discussed in this paper - - - that of high performance computing within super computer centers. The kind of configurations that are measured for the Green500 and its counterpart the Top500 performance rating is of such a scope that it almost has to be a final product installation – Computer manufacturers could not afford to set one of these on the side, just for testing.

The first Green500 list was released in November 2007[20]. Updated lists have been created 2-3 times a year since then.

## 3    Summary

The importance of server energy efficiency is exemplified in the myriad of benchmarks, tools and programs that focus on performance per watt efficiency. SPEC made great strides in the development of SPECpower_ssj2008 and is furthering the art

---

[18] http://www.tpc.org/tpce/results/tpce_result_detail.asp?id=1120 70501; TPC-E Throughput: 1,871.81; Price/Performance: 175.57 USD; TPC-Energy Metric .69 Watts/TpsE; Availability Date: 08/17/12

[19] http://www.green500.org/

[20] http://www.green500.org/lists/2007/11/top/list.php

with the development of the SERT. However, the SPECpower_ssj2008 benchmark tends to focus on light weight configurations. The combination of the dominance of SPECpower_ssj2008 in this space and the relative lack of consumer interest in efficiency measures for more robust environments has tended to reduce the incentive for computer manufacturers to publish on more robust benchmarks like SPECvirt_sc2010, SAP Power Benchmarks and the suite of TPC benchmarks.

On the other hand, programs like the EPA's ENERGY STAR look to focus on a broad range of server configurations. If the SERT is adopted for such programs, the interest in more robust benchmarks should improve.

In the final analysis, it is clear that no single measure will fit every need, and the consumer will need to match their own requirements to the benchmarks and tools they chose to make investment and implementation decisions.

# References

Most references in this paper are included as footnotes associated with the text that directly references the material. Other useful and pertinent information may be found in the following articles:

1. Poess, M., Nambiar, R., Vaid, K., Stephens, J., Huppler, K., Haines, E.: Energy benchmarks: a detailed analysis. In: e-Energy, pp. 131–140 (2010)
2. Fanara, A., Haines, E., Howard, A.: The State of Energy and Performance Benchmarking for Enterprise Servers. In: Nambiar, R., Poess, M. (eds.) TPCTC 2009. LNCS, vol. 5895, pp. 52–66. Springer, Heidelberg (2009)
3. Young, E., Cao, P., Nikolaiev, M.: First TPC-Energy Benchmark: Lessons Learned in Practice. In: Nambiar, R., Poess, M. (eds.) TPCTC 2010. LNCS, vol. 6417, pp. 136–152. Springer, Heidelberg (2011)
4. Schall, D., Hoefner, V., Kern, M.: Towards an Enhanced Benchmark Advocating Energy-Efficient Systems. In: Nambiar, R., Poess, M. (eds.) TPCTC 2011. LNCS, vol. 7144, pp. 31–45. Springer, Heidelberg (2012)

# Revisiting ETL Benchmarking:
# The Case for Hybrid Flows

Alkis Simitsis and Kevin Wilkinson

HP Labs, Palo Alto, CA, USA
{firstname.lastname}@hp.com

**Abstract.** Modern business intelligence systems integrate a variety of
data sources using multiple data execution engines. A common example
is the use of Hadoop to analyze unstructured text and merging the results
with relational database queries over a data warehouse. These analytic
data flows are generalizations of ETL flows. We refer to multi-engine data
flows as hybrid flows. In this paper, we present our benchmark infrastructure for hybrid flows and illustrate its use with an example hybrid
flow. We then present a collection of parameters to describe hybrid flows.
Such parameters are needed to define and run a hybrid flows benchmark.
An inherent difficulty in benchmarking ETL flows is the diversity of operators offered by ETL engines. However, a commonality for all engines
is extract and load operations, operations which rely on data and function shipping. We propose that by focusing on these two operations for
hybrid flows, it may be feasible to revisit the ETL benchmark effort
and thus, enable comparison of flows for modern business intelligence
applications. We believe our framework may be a useful step toward an
industry standard benchmark for ETL flows.

## 1 The Emergence of Hybrid Flows

The practice of business intelligence is evolving. In the past, the focus of effort
was on ETL to populate a data warehouse. ETL data flows extract data from
a set of operational sources, cleanse and transform that data, and finally, load
it into the warehouse. Although there are common flow paradigms, there are no
industry standard languages or models for expressing ETL flows. Consequently,
a variety of techniques are used to design and implement the flows; e.g., custom
programs and scripts, SQL for the entire flow, the use of an ETL engine. Flow
designers must choose the most appropriate implementation for a given set of
objectives. Based on their level of expertise, their choice may be sub-optimal. The
industry lacks good tools such as standardized benchmarks and flow optimizers
to enable designers to compare flows and improve their performance.

The success of industry standard benchmarks such as the TPC suites led to
hope that similar benchmarks could be developed for ETL flows. An exploratory
committee was formed, but so far no results are publicly available. The various
ETL engines offer a diverse set of features and operators, so it is difficult to
choose a common set for a meaningful comparison. However, the need for an

R. Nambiar and M. Poess (Eds.): TPCTC 2012, LNCS 7755, pp. 75–91, 2013.

ETL benchmark, as envisioned, is less relevant now because the demands on business intelligence have changed. The traditional BI architecture used periodic, batch ETL flows that produced a relatively static, historical view of an enterprise on a centralized, back-end server. Enterprises now require a dynamic, real-time views of operations and processes. To enable these views, flows must integrate numerous, dispersed data sources in a variety of data formats. These flows may utilize multiple processing engines, some general-purpose and some special-purpose for a particular type of data. We refer to these multi-engine flows as *hybrid flows*. For hybrid flows, there is no single, most appropriate engine for the entire flow. Instead, the designer must choose how to partition the flow into sub-fragments that each run on different engines.

For an example of a hybrid flow, consider a hypothetical consumer product company that desires real-time feedback on new products. To do this, one flow might load product commentary from sources like Twitter and Facebook into a map-reduce cluster (e.g., Hadoop) and use text analytics to compute customer sentiments. Separately, a second flow might aggregate retail sales data from an operational data store. The results of these two flows would then be joined to correlate sales to product sentiment, and thus, evaluate product launches.

Designing and implementing a correct hybrid flow is difficult, because such flows involve many computing systems and data sources. Optimizing a hybrid flow is an even more difficult and challenging task. For example, there may be overlapping functionality among the execution engines, which presents a choice of engines for some operators. Also, the engine with the fastest operator implementations may not be the best choice since the design must consider the cost of shipping input data to that engine. On the other hand, some operators in the flow may run on multiple engines while other operators may require a specialized engine. Some operators have multiple implementations with different characteristics (e.g., sorted output, blocking or pipelined execution). Some engines provide fault-tolerance. Consequently, the number of alternative designs grows exponentially. In our view, the role of the (human) flow designer is to create a correct, logical hybrid flow. An optimization tool should then be used to find an alternative design (i.e., a partitioning of the flow such that different flow fragments may run on different engines) that meets the optimization objectives. Our research group has been developing the QoX optimizer to do this.

The cost of transferring large datasets is a critical factor in choosing the best partitioning for a hybrid flow. Hence, a key challenge for the optimizer is obtaining good cost estimates for *data* and *function shipping*, as we detail in Section 3. Poor estimation risks either pruning good designs or choosing designs with bad performance. The QoX optimizer derives its estimates from a set of microbenchmarks for data shipping and for function shipping. For a given pair of repositories, a series of data transfer experiments are run to extract data from the source repository and load it in the target repository. The optimizer can then interpolate over these results to estimate the data transfer time for an operator in a given flow. The microbenchmarks are effectively extract and load operations. As such, they could form the basis for an ETL benchmark suite.

In the next section, we present an example analytic, hybrid data flow and we discuss it through our optimizer. We show alternative hybrid designs, each with a different partitioning of the flow into subflows. We compare the execution times for the alternative designs and discuss performance factors. Section 3 discusses the optimizer microbenchmarks themselves including metrics for hybrid flows and infrastructure for data collection. Section 4 presents a collection of parameters to describe hybrid flows. Parameters like these would be required in any general framework to benchmark hybrid flows. Section 5 reviews related work and Section 6 concludes the paper.

## 2    QoX Optimizer for Hybrid Flows

The input to the QoX optimizer is a logically correct data flow, expressed as a directed graph of operators and source and target data stores, and a set of objectives. The optimizer generates alternative, functionally equivalent, flow graphs using graph transitions such as operator swap, flow parallelization, insert recovery point. The execution cost of each alternative is estimated and compared to the objectives. Heuristic search is used to prune the search space.

For each operator in the flow graph, the optimizer identifies all available implementations on all the execution engines. For example, filtering operators and scalar aggregation operators might be offered on all execution engines while some specialized operators, such as k-means clustering, might be available on just a single engine. The source and target datasets may be initially bound to specific repositories, e.g., HDFS (Hadoop file system), UFS (Unix file system), SQL engine. However, the optimizer will consider shipping the datasets to other repositories to improve the flow.

For a given a flow graph the optimizer must assign operators and datasets to execution engines. It performs an initial assignment using first-fit starting with the source datasets and traversing the flow graph. It then uses two graph transitions, data shipping and function shipping, to generate alternative feasible assignments. Function shipping reassigns the execution of some operator from one execution engine to another engine that supports the operator. Data shipping copies a dataset from one data repository to another. Note that function shipping may induce data shipping if the data is not local to the engine and that must be included in the cost of function shipping.

As an example of function shipping, consider a binary operator assigned to one execution engine, but with input datasets from two other engines. Moving the binary operator to execute on the engine with the largest input will minimize data movement and so, this may be a better plan. For data shipping, a common example is when an ETL engine extracts data from an SQL engine. As another example, suppose an operator can only read from a text file. If the operator input happens to be stored in a relational database, the optimizer must insert a data shipping operator to copy the table to the file system.

Hence, given a hybrid flow, the QoX optimizer partitions it into sub-flows that each run on separate engines. There are many possible cut points for partitioning

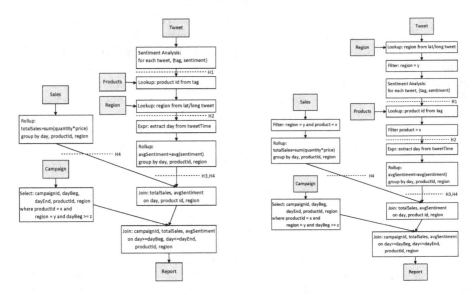

**Fig. 1.** Example flow combining structured and unstructured information (left) and an optimized variant of the flow (right) with each showing possible flow partition choices

a flow. The function shipping and data shipping transitions enable the optimizer to consider all feasible partitionings. The design with the lowest estimated cost relative to the objectives is chosen. The final graph is a collection of sub-flows, each assigned to execute on a single execution engine, and with data shipping operators used to connect the sub-flows.

**Example Flow.** The left side of Figure 1 shows a real-world, analytic flow that combines free-form text data with structured, historical data to populate a dynamic report on a dashboard. The report joins sales data for a product marketing campaign with sentiments about that product gleaned from tweets crawled from the Web. The report lists *total sales and average sentiment for each day of the campaign.* Campaigns promote a specific product and are targeted at non-overlapping, geographical regions. The sentiment analysis of a tweet yields a single metric, e.g., like or dislike the product over a range of -5 to +5.

Our example flow starts with text analysis that computes a sentiment value for a product mentioned in a tweet. Then, two lookup operators are performed, one that maps product references in the tweet (e.g., ENVY Spectre, TopShot LaserJet 3) to a specific product identifier and a second that maps latitude and longitude of the tweet to a geographical region. Then, the tweet timestamp is converted to a date and the sentiment values are averaged over each region, product, and date. On a parallel path, the sales data is rolled up to compute total sales of each product for each region and day (assume the sales table includes the region of the sale). Next, the rollups for sales and sentiment are joined and finally the specific campaign of interest is selected and used to filter the result. The right side of Figure 1 shows the optimized flow generated by the

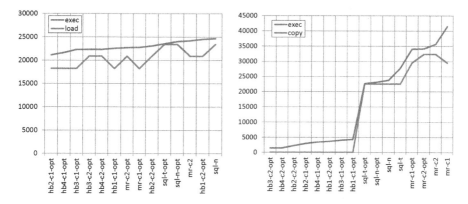

**Fig. 2.** Load (left) and Copy (right) times for 10G rows

QoX optimizer. The details of the flow restructuring are not described here (for details, see [11]) since our focus is on the flow partitioning.

In our example, we assume a system configuration comprising a map-reduce engine, MR, and a parallel database engine, pDB, each engine running on a separate set of nodes with no shared storage and all nodes connected with a single LAN. Each dataset is bound to a repository. Tweets are stored on the distributed file system of MR and the remaining four datasets are stored as relational tables distributed across all nodes of pDB. The sentiment analysis operator is only supported on MR while all other operators are supported on both engines.

We discuss four alternative assignments of sub-flows to execution engines for both flows of Figure 1. The first multi-engine flow (hybrid flow hb1) executes the sub-flow up to the sentiment analysis operator on MR and the remaining operators on pDB. This cut point is denoted by $H1$ in Figure 1. The second multi-engine flow (hb2) adds product lookup to the previous flow to be executed on MR. This cut point is denoted by $H2$. The third multi-engine flow (hb3) performs the sentiment rollup operator on MR and the cut point is denoted by $H3$. The fourth hybrid flow (hb4) performs two sub-flows in parallel, specifically, the MR rollup sub-flow and the rollup of sales data. Next, these two rollups are joined in pDB and then, joined with campaign data. This cut point is denoted by $H4$ in Figure 1.

The relative merits of the various partitionings depend on the dataset sizes as well as our assumptions about the initial bindings of datasets to repositories. Figure 2 shows the effect of load and copy times (in sec) in a 10G rows dataset for various flow configurations on two clusters, a smaller c1 (16 nodes) and a larger c2 (32 nodes) clusters. (In this experiment, 10 billion rows of tweet data occupy 1.22TB disk space, while for the other datasets the same amount of rows needs around 270GB of disk storage.) Load refers to the case where we load data from the file system to an engine; here from the filesystem to the MR and pDB according to the flow. Copy refers to the data shipping from one engine to another; here from MR to pDB. In the stacked lines of Figure 2, the execution times (exec) add up to the copy and load times, in order to get the total

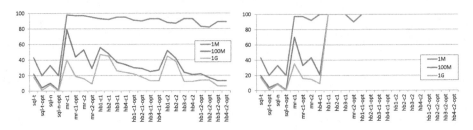

**Fig. 3.** Effect (%) of load (left) and copy (right) with varying sizes

processing time for a flow. The graphs show that the copy and load dominate the total times. However, we observe that single engine policies (mr for MR, sql for pDB) do not give the best results in both cases, while the hybrid flows (hb-x) perform much better. In particular, the sql-x cases (both the unoptimized sql-n, sql-t and the optimized sql-n-opt, sql-t-opt) although they perform really well in terms of execution time, their total performance suffers from the load/copy times, and thus, in total, these are not good solutions.

Similar observations may be made by looking how each flow variant performs for different input sizes. Figure 3 shows different flow configurations (both single engine and hybrid flows) for varying sizes of 1M, 100M, and 1G rows. These lines shows percentages: values below the lines show the percentage of load and copy times, and values above the lines show the percentage of execution times for the different data sizes. We observe that the negative effect of load and copy times in the total performance decreases with the data size and this in general, is in favor of the hybrid flows.

Both these experiments show the significance of data and function shipping, especially as the data size increases.

## 3   Metrics and Benchmarks for Data and Function Shipping

### 3.1   Benchmark Design for Data Shipping

We now formulate the problem of estimating data shipping costs for a computing system configuration. A computing system comprises a number of nodes and a set of execution engines. Some engines execute in parallel on a subset of nodes whereas others may be single node engines. A computing system has one or more storage repositories. As with execution engines, a repository may be local to a single node or be distributed, storing its data objects across a set of nodes. A repository provides a namespace to identify objects and, at a minimum, operations to create, destroy, read, and write objects. To simplify the discussion we assume a repository supports a single data representation/format (e.g., table, key-value pairs, XML). In practice, some engines support multiple data formats, but we consider them here as logically distinct repositories.

**Table 1.** Data Paths matrix

| src/tgt | repo$_1$ | repo$_2$ | ... | repo$_S$ | null |
|---------|----------|----------|-----|----------|------|
| repo$_1$ | - | p$_{12}$ | ... | p$_{1S}$ | x$_1$ |
| repo$_2$ | p$_{21a}$,p$_{21b}$ | - | ... | - | x$_2$ |
| ... | ... | ... | ... | ... | ... |
| repo$_S$ | - | p$_{S2}$ | ... | - | x$_S$ |
| null | l$_1$ | l$_2$ | ... | l$_S$ | - |

For each storage repository, we need cost estimates for shipping data to other repositories. We also need costs for loading data to the repository and for extracting data from the repository (e.g., to/from an application). We use the generic term *path* to refer to a direct data transfer method from one repository to another. Path also refers to methods to extract from or load to a repository. Each repository has its own storage format so a path handles data reformatting/transformation as needed.

Assume there are $s$ possible repositories. Then, we can represent the data shipping costs as an $s \times s$ matrix where each cell, $p_{ij}$, represents a path for data movement from a source repository $i$ to a target repository $j$ (see an example Data Paths matrix in Table 1). Each path has an associated method (executable program) to perform the data transfer. Note that there may be multiple paths from a source repository to a target, e.g., most SQL engines can store data to a text file either by using a "select into file" statement or by using an export tool. A null source or target signifies an unconstrained path, representing the highest possible data load rate or data extract rate; e.g., use of a high-speed, artificial data generator as the source in loading a target repository. Note that the matrix is not symmetric, i.e., a path in one direction does not imply an inverse path and, if there is one, the cost may differ.

A set of metrics is associated with each non-empty cell in the matrix. To simplify the discussion, we assume a single metric, elapsed time. But depending on the optimization objectives, other metrics may be relevant such as utilization, average throughput, and so on. In addition, each path has an associated set of properties that may be useful to the optimizer, e.g., is blocking or pipelined, output is ordered, is parallelizable, and so on.

The Data Paths matrix defines the feasible direct transfer paths for the optimizer to consider. For each path, the optimizer needs cost formulae to estimate data transfer costs. These are obtained by executing a series of microbenchmarks that exercise a transfer path for varying dataset sizes. The results can be used with a regression algorithm to derive a cost formula or else stored in a data structure for later lookup and interpolation by the optimizer. If there is no direct path between two repositories, the optimizer may consider multi-hop transfer paths by linking direct paths; e.g., in Table 1, to ship data from repo$_S$ to repo$_1$ the optimizer may use path $p_{S2}$ followed by $p_{21a}$ or $p_{21b}$.

Data shipping costs are not static. Data center infrastructure undergoes periodic change, e.g., software upgrades, replacement of compute racks, introduction and retirement of applications, and so on. Consequently, we must automate the

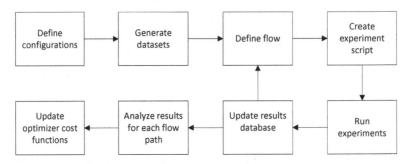

**Fig. 4.** Steps to create cost function for data transfer path

collection of metrics for data shipping to maintain accurate estimates. To do this, we adapted the technique used by database systems to calibrate query optimizers. When porting to a new platform, database engineers run a series of microbenchmarks to determine the resources required for each operator; e.g., scan a table, do an index lookup, compare two data values, copy a character string. These measurements are used to tune the query optimizer cost estimates for the various database operators.

Our QoX optimizer estimates costs for data transfer paths by following the steps illustrated in Figure 4. At a high level, the process can be summarized as follows. For a given data path, we define a base experiment to transfer data across the path and then run the experiment and measure its performance. We then vary the base experiment, e.g., by scaling the source dataset size, and run those experiments and repeat. Once we have sufficient data points, we derive a cost formula and add it to the QoX optimizer.

At a more detailed level, the initial step is to define the computing system configuration used by a path. A path configuration includes, for both the source and target, the physical nodes, the execution engines on those nodes and the storage repositories. For example, consider a path that copies a distributed file from a map-reduce engine and stores it as a text file on the file system of a single node. The path configuration includes the physical nodes for the map-reduce engine and for the single node, the engines are the map-reduce engine and the operating system of the single node, and the repositories are the distributed file system and the local file system of the node.

The second step is to identify the datasets used in the experiments. Then, we create a metadata description of the flow (see also Figure 5 as we explain below). This comprises an identifier and textual description, links to the source and target datasets, and the path configuration. This metadata is linked with the metrics in the results database to provide provenance. The next step is to define a script or program to execute the flow. At this point, we can now conduct experiments. To reduce random error, we run each experiment a number of times. Metrics are collected in the results database. Once we have sufficient data points, we may create a new flow by altering the flow in any number of ways, e.g., by scaling the datasets, by modifying the node counts or adjusting software

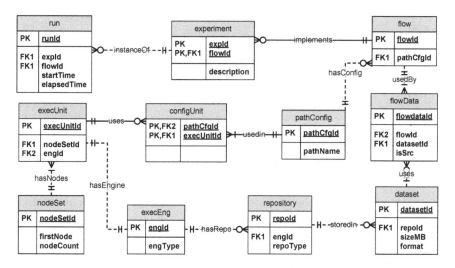

**Fig. 5.** Benchmark schema

configuration parameters such as replication level or block size. We then run more experiments with the new flow. Eventually, we break out of the loop and derive a cost formula for the path.

A synopsis of the schema used in the results database is shown in Figure 5. Each path is represented by a flow object. A flow has a number of associated experiments (e.g., at different scale factors) and, for each experiment, there are some number of runs. Each flow has a source and target dataset and each dataset is bound to some repository. Additionally, the flow is linked to its configuration that identifies the execution engines and nodes used by the path. The schema shown in Figure 5 is a simplified version of the actual schema used by the QoX optimizer. That schema is designed to support arbitrary hybrid flows, not just single source-target data transfers.

For a given flow, the metrics for a set of experiments can be extracted from the results database and graphed as in Figure 6. This first example (Figure 6, left) shows the time to load a dataset at different scaling factors for three repositories: the distributed file system of a map-reduce engine, a parallel database system, and the local file system for a node. The parallel systems outperform the single node for small datasets, but all systems converge to the same limiting performance for larger datasets.

The second example (Figure 6, right) shows the time to transfer the same datasets from the parallel database system to the distributed file system of the map-reduce engine. There are two transfer paths, a serial path that ships the data through a single node of each engine and a parallel path that ships data concurrently using all nodes of both engines. As can be seen, the serial path shows log-linear scalability and out-performs the parallel path for small datasets. This is because the parallel path has high initial overhead, e.g., it must start processes on each node. However, for large datasets, this overhead is a small fraction of

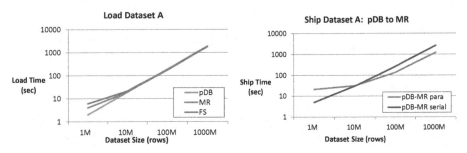

**Fig. 6.** Load results (left) and two data paths for shipping data from pDB to MR (right)

the total transfer time so the parallel path can leverage the additional resources to outperform the serial path.

### 3.2    Benchmark Design for Function Shipping

The Qox optimizer generates alternative flow graph designs using both data shipping and function shipping transitions. Section 3.1 describes how we derive cost estimates for data shipping. In this section, we propose a similar technique to estimate the cost of function shipping. For each flow operator $f$, we associate a set of pairs, $\{m_f\}$, where each pair specifies an implementation of $f$ on an execution engine; e.g., an operator to generate content-based keys using the SHA-1 hashing algorithm on a map-reduce engine.

Assume a flow has an operator $f$ assigned to an engine $e_x$. The optimizer will consider alternative flows in which $f$ is executed on all other implementations and engines in $\{m_f\}$. If there are $p$ execution engines, we can represent the cost of function shipping by a $p \times p$ matrix (see Table 2) where a cell entry, $c_{xi}$, is the cost of shipping the execution of $f$ from engine $e_x$ to engine $e_i$. Note that a cell may have multiple entries if the target engine supports multiple implementations for the operator; e.g., a database engine with more than one join method.

**Table 2.** Function shipping matrix

| src/trgt | $eng_1$ | $eng_2$ | ... | $eng_P$ |
|---|---|---|---|---|
| $eng_1$ | $c_1$ | $c_{12}$ | ... | $c_{1P}$ |
| $eng_2$ | $c_{21a}, c_{21b}$ | $c_2$ | ... | - |
| ... | ... | ... | ... | ... |
| $eng_P$ | - | $c_{P2}$ | ... | $c_P$ |

In Table 2, *src* is the execution engine with direct access to the storage repository for the input(s)[1] to operator $f$. The execution engine that actually executes

---

[1] Here, for the sake of presentation, we assume that all inputs of $f$ refer to the same repository. We assume specialized connectors to connect different repositories. But one may easily generalize our thoughts for hybrid n-ary operators that get their inputs from more than one repository.

| src/trgt | eng$_1$ | eng$_2$ |
|---|---|---|
| eng$_1$ | 1 | c$_{12}$ * 2 |
| eng$_2$ | c$_{21}$ | 2 |

| src/trgt | eng$_1$ | eng$_2$ |
|---|---|---|
| eng$_1$ | - | c$_{12}$ * 4 |
| eng$_2$ | - | 4 |

| src/trgt | eng$_1$ | eng$_2$ |
|---|---|---|
| eng$_1$ | - | min(c$_{12}$ * 4,c$_{12}$ * 8) |
| eng$_2$ | - | min(c$_{21}$*c$_{12}$ * 4, 8) |

**Fig. 7.** Shipping matrices for functions $f$, $g$, and $g(f)$

operator $f$ is *trgt*. The diagonal (*src* same as *trgt*) is the case where the data and operator are on the same engine so $c_i$ is just the operator cost (or null if the engine does not implement the operator). Of course, we may have more than one cost $c_i$ in the diagonal, if more than one implementation is supported on the engine $e_i$. If *src* differs from *trgt*, then the input data must be shipped to *trgt*. This shipping cost estimate should be added to $c_{xi}$.

A typical flow contains a sequence of operators, so the optimizer must compute function shipping costs for operator composition. This is accomplished with the function shipping matrix using the distance product matrix computation. In other words, to compose operators $f$ and $g$, the function shipping matrix for the composition is the distance product matrix multiplication of $\{m_f\}$ and $\{m_g\}$. As an example, suppose the function shipping matrices for $f$ and $g$ over two engines are given by the left and middle tables in Figure 7. Note that eng$_1$ does not implement $g$. Their composition $g(f)$ is given by the rightmost table in Figure 7.

In order to calibrate the optimizer, we conduct function shipping experiments similar to the data shipping experiments. For the various functions, we create simple flows and measure the performance over artificial datasets. Then, we scale the experiments and conduct more experiments to gather sufficient data to derive a cost formula. From the cost formula for single operators, the optimizer can compute costs for operator composition.

## 4    Benchmark Parameters for Hybrid Flows

Data shipping and function shipping are important aspects in the operation of hybrid flows. However, other parameters are of interest too. In this section, we provide a list of parameters and variants that should be considered for designing a benchmark for hybrid flows. We classify them into the following categories: flow, engine, operator, and data related variants.

### 4.1    Flow Related Variants

We create and measure flows with varying characteristics, as follows.

**Flow Size:** The number of operators (♯ops) and data stores (♯dst) contained in a flow.

**Engine Multiplicity:** The number of engines (♯eng) that can be used for the flow execution.

**Transition Likelihood:** A percentage tr% of possible transitions (e.g., swap, factorize, parallelize, function/data shipping) allowed for a flow. This parameter enables the creation of flows that can be further optimized. This will give us the flexibility to create equivalent variants of the flow produced.

The transition likehood may be further analyzed per transition, i.e., tr% may be read as X%, where:

*swapping factor*: X = swa          *data-shipping factor*: X = dsh
*factorization factor*: X = fac      *function-shipping factor*: X = fsh
*distribution factor*: X = dis       *add-replication factor*: X = rep
*add-partitioning factor*: X = par   *add-recovery-points factor*: X = rec

For example, in a flow of size ♯ops=50 with swa%=10, five operators may change their positions. In order to change the position of two operators (e.g., with swap), these two operators should be swapable. (We refer the interested reader to another paper for formal details on when swapping two operators is permitted [10].) So, the flow created in this example, should contain five operators that their schemata would allow a swap; e.g., one way to do this is to create operators that do not affect the schemata of nearby operators.

As another example, in the same flow and with rec%=5, we may add up to three recovery points, based on the following logic: a recovery point should be placed in a point where the cost of recovering from the closest existing recovery point (or from the beginning) is greater than the i/o cost for maintaining a new recovery point.

**P[fs]:** The probability of having function shipping for an operator $op$ in the same engine or across all applicable engines is related to the number of available implementations $imp$ for $op$ in the same engine and across all applicable engines, respectively. For example, if there is a single implementation for an operator in an engine, then the probability for function shipping on the same engine is zero. If there are multiple implementations for an operator, then we can either consider (a) a uniform probability for function shipping or as typically happens in practice, (b) a weighted probability of using a specific implementation –either in the same engine or in different engines– based on the cost for using that implementation. The lower this cost, the higher the probability of choosing that implementation. For example, assuming that all available implementations $imp_i$, $i = 1, ..., n$ have a cost $c_i$, then the possible outcomes are as follows:

$$\circlearrowright imp_i \ \rightarrow imp_j$$

That is, we either use the same implementation ($\circlearrowright$) or we do function shipping and use a different implementation ($\rightarrow$). The probability of having function shipping: $P(FS(imp_i \rightarrow imp_j)) = 0$, when $i = j$. If $i \neq j$ and assuming that for $k$ out of $n$ possible implementations $c_i > c_l$, $l = 1..k$, then:

$$P(FS(imp_i \rightarrow imp_j)) = \frac{1}{\sum_{l=1..k} \frac{1}{c_l}} \times \frac{1}{c_j} \tag{1}$$

Thus, we may vary the collection of operators used in a flow and their implementations as well, in order to test different scenarios for function shipping.

**P[*ds*]:** Following a similar logic, the probability of data shipping depends on the configuration of data stores. When a flow has data stores in two different engines, the probability of data shipping is high. (If the flows involving these data stores converge, then the probability is one). On the other hand, if all data stores are placed in a single engine, the probability of data shipping is low. For the latter case, the probability for data shipping is not zero, because sometimes, we may decide to execute part of the flow on another engine even if we do not have a related data store there for performance reasons –e.g., when the host engine is much slower than a remote engine or it does not support an implementation needed.

**Blocking/Pipeline Execution:** An operator may work on a tuple-by-tuple basis allowing data pipelining or it may need the entire dataset, which blocks the data flow. This not only affects the flow execution, but also flow optimization. A flow optimizer could group together pipeline operators (even if the local costs would not improve with a possible swap) in order to boost pipeline parallelism. Thus, we need to tune the number of pipeline ♯op-p and blocking operators ♯op-b in a flow.

### 4.2  Engine Related Variants

As hybrid flows involve more than one engine, we take into account this angle too.

**Operator Plurality:** The average number ♮eg-imp of different implementations per operator in an engine.

**Data Store Plurality:** The average number ♮eg-dst of data stores related to a flow in an engine.

**Engine Processing Type:** The processing nature of an engine eg-typ, e.g., streaming, in-memory, disk-based processing.

**Engine Storage Capability:** The variant eg-str shows whether a processing engine uses a disk-based storage layer too –e.g., files in a local filesystem, HDFS, and so on– or whether all data resides in memory.

**Engine Communication Capability:** The communication methods supported in an engine eg-con, like specialized connectors to exchange data with another engine or simple import/export functionality.

**Distributed Functionality:** The variant eg-par shows if an engine is a parallel engine –like a parallel database or a Map-Reduce engine– or it is installed on a single node.

**Node Plurality:** The number of nodes ♯eg-nds where the engine is installed.
**Threads:** The average number of threads an engine may assign to an operation ♮eg-thd-op or to a flow fragment ♮eg-thd-fl.

**CPU:** The average number of CPU's ♮eg-cpu per node that the engine may use.

**Memory:** The average memory size ♮eg-mem per node that the engine may use.

**Disk:** The average disk size ♮eg-mem per node that the engine may use.

**Disk Type:** The type of the disk eg-disk that the engine may use; e.g., SSD's.

**Failure Rate:** The average number of failures ♮eg-flr that may happen in an engine node. This variant helps is simulating an environment for measuring flow fault tolerance.

### 4.3    Operator Related Variants

We consider tuning capabilities for flow operators.

**Operator Type:** The operator type op-tp. A typical number of operators involved in hybrid flows, as those described in the previous sections, is in the order of hundreds. It is very hard to agreed on a common framework without a classification of operators. In a previous approach to flow benchmarking, we proposed a taxonomy for ETL operators based on several dimensions, like the arity of their schemata (unary, n-ary, n-1, 1-n, n-m, etc.) and the nature of their processing (row-level, holistic, routers, groupers, etc.) [9]. Here, we consider the same taxonomy augmented by one dimension: physical properties, as captured by the variants below.

**Parallelizable:** The variant op-par captures whether an operator can be parallelized.

**Code Flexibility:** The average number of implementations ♯op-imp per operator.

**Blocking/Pipeline:** The variant op-bl captures the blocking or pipeline nature of an operator implementation.

**In-Memory:** The variant op-mem shows whether the operator functionality can be performed solely in memory.

**CPU:** The average number of CPU's ♮op-cpu per node that the operator may use.

**Memory:** The average memory size ♮op-mem per node that the operator may use.

**Disk:** The average disk size ♮op-mem per node that the operator may use.

**Failure Rate:** The average number of failures ♮op-flr that may happen during the operator execution.

All operator related variants $V$ may be considered as flow related variants too, as an average number of $V$ represented as ♯$V$. For example, a flow related variant is the average number of parallelizable operators in a flow ♮op-par. With op-tp, at the flow level we may determine the distribution of operators in a flow based on their types.

## 4.4   Data Related Variants

Finally, we need to tune the input data sets for hybrid flows.

**Data Skew:** The skew of data skew.

**Data Size:** The average input data size size.

**Store Type:** The variant st-tp indicates the storage type for a data set; e.g., flat file, stream, key-value store, RDF, database table. This variant may also be detailed by setting an average number per store type per flow, like ♯st-X%, where $X$ takes any value from the domain: $X = \{$fixed-width file, delimited file, HDFS file, relational table, XML file, RDF file, document, image, spreadsheet, stream$\}$. For example, ♯st-file%=60 shows that 60% of the data stores involved in a flow will be delimited files (the default option for files). If there is no more information about store types, the remaining data stores are considered as database tables (this default value is tunable as fit).

**Structure:** The average structuredness of data as a percentage (str%); str%=0 shows unstructured data (like tweets) and str%=100 shows fully structured data (like tuples). Anything in between creates flows with mixed inputs; e.g., str%=$x$, where $x$<50, $x$% of ♯dst contain unstructured data and 100-$x$% of ♯dst contain structured data (if $x$>50, then the opposite percentage of ♯dst contain unstructured and structured data, respectively).

**Data Per Engine:** The average data size ♯eg-size stored per engine. We can also fine tune this at the node level: ♯eg-nd-size, the average data size residing per node of an engine.

**Data Rate:** The average rate in-rt that data arrive at the beginning of the flow.

# 5   Related Work

*Optimization of Hybrid Flows.* Previous work on hybrid flows has been done in two contexts: federated database systems and ETL engines. Research on federated database systems considered query optimization across multiple execution engines. But, this work was limited to traditional relational query operators and to performance as the only objective; for example, see query optimization in Garlic [8], Multibase [2], and Pegasus [3]. ETL flows are hybrid in the sense that they extract from and load to database engines. Most ETL engines provide pushdown of some operators, e.g., filter, to the database engines [6] but the pushdown is a fixed policy and is not driven by cost-based optimization.

*Optimizer Calibration.* In the past, several researchers have used synthetic data and specially-crafted benchmark queries to calibrate query optimizers (e.g., as in [4,5,7]). This approach is especially attractive for federated database systems because the database engines can be treated as black boxes without exposing internal details. In general, this technique is limited to execution engines in the same family, e.g., all relational stores or object stores. However, limited extensions to handle user-defined functions have been employed.

*Benchmark Frameworks.* For database systems, the suite of benchmarks devised by the Transaction Processing Performance Council are widely used in both industry and research. The benchmarks enable fair comparisons of systems due to the detailed specification of data and queries and the rules for conformance. Submitted results are audited for compliance. Because the benchmark is so well-understood, the associated datasets and queries are often used informally in research projects. The success of the database benchmarks inspired similar efforts in other domains. ETL benchmark efforts were begun [9,14], but to the best of our knowledge there has not been much progress. Several researchers have independently adapted TPC-H [13] or TPC-DS [12] for ETL benchmarks of their own design, but these are limited in scope and not designed for reuse.

An important requirement for benchmark frameworks is provenance and reproducibility. It must be possible to reproduce results and, to do this, a comprehensive accounting of the computing environment and input datasets used is needed. VisTrails [1] is a workflow management system for scientific computing that facilitates creation of workflows over scientific datasets and automatically tracks provenance. It is designed for change and tracks changes to workflows, including changes to operators and inputs. It also enable parameterized flow which makes it easy to scale a workflow to larger datasets. Such features are proving very useful to researchers and should be considered in the design of future benchmarks.

## 6   Conclusions

Enterprises are moving away from traditional back-end ETL flows that periodically integrate and transform operational data sources to populate a historical data warehouse. To remain competitive, enterprises are migrating to complex analytic data flows that provide near real-time views of data and processes and that integrate data from multiple execution engines and multiple persistent stores. We refer to these as multi-engine flows or hybrid flows. They are difficult to design and optimize due to the number of alternative, feasible designs; i.e., assignment of operators to execution engines. Our QoX optimizer is designed to optimize such hybrid flows. An important design factor is accurate estimation of data shipping and function shipping. This paper describes our approach to deriving cost formulae for the QoX optimizer. We have created a framework that utilizes microbenchmarks to collect metrics for data and function shipping, and we also list a set of interested variants. It is our hope that the emergence of hybrid flows may prompt reconsideration of work on industry standard benchmarks for analytic data flows. Our paper describes a step in this direction.

# References

1. Callahan, S.P., Freire, J., Santos, E., Scheidegger, C.E., Silva, C.T., Vo, H.T.: Managing the evolution of dataflows with VisTrails. In: ICDE Workshops, p. 71 (2006)
2. Dayal, U.: Processing queries over generalization hierarchies in a multidatabase system. In: VLDB, pp. 342–353 (1983)
3. Du, W., Krishnamurthy, R., Shan, M.C.: Query optimization in a heterogeneous DBMS. In: VLDB, pp. 277–291 (1992)
4. Ewen, S., Ortega-Binderberger, M., Markl, V.: A learning optimizer for a federated database management system. In: BTW, pp. 87–106 (2005)
5. Gardarin, G., Sha, F., Tang, Z.H.: Calibrating the query optimizer cost model of IRO-DB, an object-oriented federated database system. In: VLDB, pp. 378–389 (1996)
6. Informatica: PowerCenter Pushdown Optimization Option Datasheet (2011)
7. Naacke, H., Tomasic, A., Valduriez, P.: Validating mediator cost models with disco. Networking and Information Systems Journal 2(5) (2000)
8. Roth, M.T., Arya, M., Haas, L.M., Carey, M.J., Cody, W.F., Fagin, R., Schwarz, P.M., Thomas II, J., Wimmers, E.L.: The Garlic project. In: SIGMOD, p. 557 (1996)
9. Simitsis, A., Vassiliadis, P., Dayal, U., Karagiannis, A., Tziovara, V.: Benchmarking ETL Workflows. In: Nambiar, R., Poess, M. (eds.) TPCTC 2009. LNCS, vol. 5895, pp. 199–220. Springer, Heidelberg (2009)
10. Simitsis, A., Vassiliadis, P., Sellis, T.K.: State-space optimization of ETL workflows. IEEE Trans. Knowl. Data Eng. 17(10), 1404–1419 (2005)
11. Simitsis, A., Wilkinson, K., Castellanos, M., Dayal, U.: Optimizing analytic data flows for multiple execution engines. In: SIGMOD Conference, pp. 829–840 (2012)
12. TPC Council: TPC Benchmark DS (April 2012), http://www.tpc.org/tpcds/
13. TPC Council: TPC Benchmark H (April 2012), http://www.tpc.org/tpch/
14. Wyatt, L., Caufield, B., Pol, D.: Principles for an ETL Benchmark. In: Nambiar, R., Poess, M. (eds.) TPCTC 2009. LNCS, vol. 5895, pp. 183–198. Springer, Heidelberg (2009)

# MulTe: A Multi-Tenancy Database Benchmark Framework

Tim Kiefer, Benjamin Schlegel, and Wolfgang Lehner

Dresden University of Technology
Database Technology Group
Dresden, Germany
{tim.kiefer,benjamin.schlegel,wolfgang.lehner}@tu-dresden.de

**Abstract.** Multi-tenancy in relational databases has been a topic of interest for a couple of years. On the one hand, ever increasing capabilities and capacities of modern hardware easily allow for multiple database applications to share one system. On the other hand, cloud computing leads to outsourcing of many applications to service architectures, which in turn leads to offerings for relational databases in the cloud, as well.

The ability to benchmark multi-tenancy database systems (MT-DBMSs) is imperative to evaluate and compare systems and helps to reveal otherwise unnoticed shortcomings. With several tenants sharing a MT-DBMS, a benchmark is considerably different compared to classic database benchmarks and calls for new benchmarking methods and performance metrics. Unfortunately, there is no single, well-accepted multi-tenancy benchmark for MT-DBMSs available and few efforts have been made regarding the methodology and general tooling of the process.

We propose a method to benchmark MT-DBMSs and provide a framework for building such benchmarks. To support the cumbersome process of defining and generating tenants, loading and querying their data, and analyzing the results we propose and provide MULTE, an open-source framework that helps with all these steps.

## 1 Introduction

Academia and industry have shown increasing interest in multi-tenancy in relational databases for the last couple of years. Ever increasing capabilities and capacities of modern hardware easily allow for multiple database applications with moderate requirements to share one system. At the same time, cloud computing leads to outsourcing of many applications to service architectures (IaaS, SaaS), which in turn leads to offerings for relational databases hosted in the cloud as well [1, 2]. We refer to any database system that accommodates multiple tenants by means of virtualization and resource sharing, either on a single machine or on an infrastructure of machines, as a multi-tenancy database management system (MT-DBMS). All MT-DBMSs lead to interesting challenges like, (1) assigning logical resources to physical ones; (2) configuring physical systems

R. Nambiar and M. Poess (Eds.): TPCTC 2012, LNCS 7755, pp. 92–107, 2013.

(e.g., database design, tuning parameters); and (3) balancing load across physical resources, all of which require thorough testing to ensure scalability and system quality.

Although there have been several works on how to build multi-tenancy systems, little work has been done on how to benchmark and evaluate these systems—partly due to the diversity of the systems and the complexity of possible benchmark setups. There are many well-accepted database benchmarks, e.g., TPC benchmarks like TPC-C or TPC-H [3] or the XML benchmark TPoX [4]. These benchmarks concentrate on a certain scenario (e.g., OLTP or OLAP) and measure a system's peak performance with respect to the given scenario. The key challenge for multi-tenancy systems is usually not to provide the highest peak performance, but to scale well and deal with multiple changing workloads under additional requirements like performance isolation and fairness. A first attempt has been made to propose a benchmark for database-centric workloads in virtual machines (TPC-V) [5]. This benchmark is still under development and although it has the same goal as our work, i.e., to benchmark multi-tenancy systems, the means and priorities differ significantly. TPC-V, like all other TPC benchmarks, provides strict rules and conditions to ensure a comparable and long-lasting benchmark. At the same time, many implementation details and efforts are left to the benchmark sponsor. In contrast, our work provides a very flexible environment and tools for rapid developments and implementations of new multi-tenancy benchmarks. We will discuss our work's relation to TPC-V in more detail in Section 6.

In this work, we propose and provide methodology, workflow, and associated tools to benchmark MT-DBMSs. A great variety of MT-DBMSs exists and different systems are complex and diverse. Hence, we do not propose a single benchmark that fits all systems, but rather provide the framework MULTE[1] that allows for generating specific benchmarks quickly and easily. As shown in Figure 1, our approach is to re-use existing benchmarks, including their schemas, data, and queries/statements and to generate instances of these benchmarks to represent different tenants. Each tenant is given an individual, time-dependent workload that reflects a user's behavior. A workload driver is used to run all tenants' workloads against any multi-tenancy database system and to collect all execution statistics and benchmark metrics. All steps are supported with tools which together form our multi-tenancy benchmark framework MULTE.

**Fig. 1.** Multi-Tenancy Benchmark Workflow

---

[1] http://wwwdb.inf.tu-dresden.de/research-projects/projects/multe/

To demonstrate the ability to create meaningful benchmarks, we will sketch the process of building three different exemplary benchmarks throughout the paper. We will try to answer the following three questions related to MT-DBMSs:

1. SCALABILITYBENCHMARK: Does the system scale well with the number of tenants? How many tenants are able run in parallel? What is the individual performance? What is the overall performance?
2. FAIRNESSBENCHMARK: How fair is the system, i.e., are the available resources equally available to all tenants? If tenants have different priorities, how well are they implemented?
3. ISOLATIONBENCHMARK: How well are tenants isolated from one another with respect to performance? How do individual tenants influence other tenants' performance?

MULTE is flexible enough that many other aspects and components, e.g., for load balancing, of MT-DBMSs can be tested as well.

To summarize, our key contributions in this paper are:

– MULTE, an easy-to-use, extensible framework to build and run benchmarks for MT-DBMSs. MULTE comes with an example implementation for all components (e.g., TPC-H is supported as benchmark type), but is designed to allow for future extensions.
– The introduction of time-dependent workloads to allow for realistic, dynamic tenants and the analysis of effects caused by them. This includes a brief discussion of how time-dependent workloads should be defined.
– A new performance metric *relative execution time* for multi-tenancy benchmarks that considers time-dependent workloads.

The rest of the paper is organized as follows: In Section 2, we recapitulate the fundamentals of MT-DBMSs before we introduce our multi-tenancy benchmark concept in Section 3. Following in Section 4, we provide an overview of design and implementation decisions for MULTE. In Section 5, we describe the process of building and running exemplary benchmarks with MULTE before we reference related work and conclude in Sections 6 and 7, respectively.

## 2   Multi-Tenancy Database Management Systems

In this section, we briefly recap the fundamentals of MT-DBMSs for the interested reader. We further demonstrate the range of multi-tenancy systems that can be evaluated with MULTE by naming some examples.

The layered system stack of a DBMS—from the database schema to the operating system—allows for consolidation at different levels. Previous works have classified virtualization schemes, leading to classes like *private process*, *private database*, or *private schema* [6, 7]. A variety of specific MT-DBMSs can be built following this classification, all of which can be tested with MULTE. Figure 2 shows three possible Systems Under Test (SUT). The topmost two layers (Tenant Workload and Workload Driver) are provided by MULTE and are the same

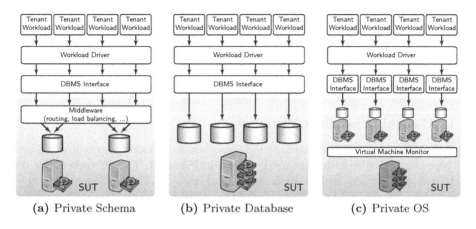

(a) Private Schema        (b) Private Database        (c) Private OS

**Fig. 2.** MT-DBMSs Under Test

for all systems, whereas the implementation of the multi-tenancy functionality differs significantly.

*Private Schema:* The system shown in Figure 2a is an example for a private schema virtualization. A middleware is responsible for the routing and load balancing of different tenants. Each tenant is implemented as a schema in any of a small number of physical databases. In this setup, MULTE can be used to test the performance of the middleware with respect to routing and load balancing as well as each backend DBMS. All three exemplary benchmarks—SCALABILITYBENCHMARK, FAIRNESSBENCHMARK, and ISOLATIONBENCHMARK—are of great interest in this scenario.

*Private Database:* The system shown in Figure 2b implements a private database virtualization. Here, a single large machine hosts a number of private databases— a common setup for many database servers. MULTE, especially the SCALABILITYBENCHMARK, can be used to test the system's ability to scale with the number of tenants and hence databases. The DBMS is the main focus for benchmarks in such MT-DBMSs.

*Private Operating System:* The system shown in Figure 2c implements a private OS virtualization where each tenant is implemented with a complete stack of virtual machine, operating system, and database management system. Consequently, MULTE can not only test DBMSs in virtualized environments, but also provide insights on the performance of the virtual machine monitor and its ability to balance and isolate multiple virtual machines that run database workloads (cf. Soror et al. [8]). Again, all three exemplary benchmarks are relevant for such systems.

## 3    Benchmark Framework Conception

To explain our concepts of multi-tenancy benchmarks, we introduce the general workflow first. The idea of time-dependent workloads is described in Section 3.2. Finally, the metric that we propose for multi-tenant benchmarks is presented in Section 3.3.

### 3.1    General Benchmark Workflow

Based on the idea to re-use existing database benchmarks, the general workflow of benchmarks built with MULTE is shown in Figure 3. The characteristics of a tenant are defined with a basic set of parameters. This includes, e.g., the benchmark type (like TPC-H), the size of the raw data, and the query mix. Based on these descriptions, instances of the benchmarks are generated and loaded as tenants into the MT-DBMS. All three steps are supported by a set of Python scripts. Once populated, a Java workload driver runs the tenants' workloads against the MT-DBMS and collects all relevant performance statistics. These statistics are analyzed, evaluated, and visualized with Python and R.

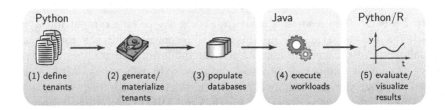

**Fig. 3.** MULTE—General Benchmark Workflow

### 3.2    Time Dependent Workloads—Activities

One approach to test MT-DBMSs is to let all tenants execute constant (peak) workload over a period of time. While this is perfectly valid to evaluate the system's ability to scale with the number of tenants in extreme load situations, e.g., for the SCALABILITYBENCHMARK, it presents a somewhat pathologic scenario and more importantly does not help to evaluate system characteristics like fairness and performance isolation. A key assumption for multi-tenancy systems is that at no time, all tenants are working simultaneously. Figure 4 shows two tenants' activities, i.e., their workload over time, and it can be seen that their peak loads are at different times. However, the aggregated workload for the entire system, which is less than the sum of both peak workloads, dictates each tenant's performance. A MT-DBMS should take the specific behavior of its tenants into account (as much as possible) and provision for realistic, average load scenarios. In our work, we would like to acknowledge that tenants are different to one another and over time. To relate the concept of activities to our exemplary

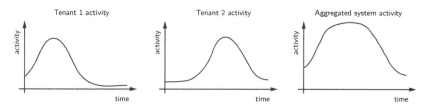

**Fig. 4.** Time Dependent Tenant Workloads—Activities

benchmarks, we briefly discuss their need in context of the benchmark purposes. All three benchmarks will be further discussed in Section 5.

1. SCALABILITYBENCHMARK: A simple constant workload is sufficient to test a system's scalability.
2. FAIRNESSBENCHMARK: To evaluate fairness, tenants can execute constant load over time. However, to evaluate how resources are split among tenants, they must execute possibly different workloads at different stress-levels.
3. ISOLATIONBENCHMARK: To evaluate performance isolation, a tenant's workload must change over time. For example, Tenant 1 can run a constant workload while Tenant 2 executes resource-intensive queries sporadically. The reaction of the first tenant's performance to the second tenant's activity gives an important insight into the MT-DBMS.

To support varying tenant loads, we introduce *time-dependent workloads* or *activities* in our benchmarks. As indicated before, we understand a tenant's *activity* as the combination of the queries that the tenant executes and the timeline that defines, when queries are executed. A design decision in MULTE is that activities are defined per tenant (as opposed to for the whole system) so that tenants can be driven independently and possibly in a distributed fashion.

Given these pre-requisites, the question rises how activities should be defined; an interesting research topic on its own. We shortly introduce how we solve the problem in our implementation of MULTE. However, the framework is flexible enough to support other, more complex approaches in future releases.

*Aggregated or disaggregated workload definition:* The overall goal of the activities is to simulate a system of multiple tenants to get a realistic global view on the system. However, there seem to be two general approaches to achieve this. The *aggregation approach*—which we decided to implement—defines tenants' activities individually such that the resulting aggregated workload fulfills certain requirements or shows certain characteristics. The challenge is to define individual activities that aggregate to the expected global workload. The *disaggregation approach* on the other hand starts with a global load characteristic for the whole multi-tenancy system. Here, the challenge is then to split (or disaggregate) this global workload in a meaningful way to a set of local tenant activities.

*Set of parameters:* A second challenge when defining activities is to find a compromise between the complexity and the expressiveness of the description. To provide a function definition to calculate the activity at any point in time would be one extreme. Although most powerful, this approach seems to be hard to implement. Defining detailed activity functions for tens or possibly hundreds of clients is not a feasible task. The other extreme would be to rigorously simplify a tenant's activity so that it results in a constant or possibly random workload—only one or two parameters are necessary to implement that, but the possibilities for interesting workloads are limited.

We decided to pick the query to execute randomly (with weights). To describe the timeline of an activity, we use four parameters: MEANSLEEPTIME, PARALLELUSERS, ACTIVITY, and ACTIVITYCONSTRAINT—their meanings are shown in Figure 5. This simple set of parameters allows to model tenants with an on/off behavior, i.e., tenants that are active periodically and idle (for a certain amount of time, MEANSLEEPTIME) in between. When tenants are active, multiple parallel users (PARALLELUSERS) run queries against the database, either constraint by a number of transactions or by an amount of time (depending on ACTIVITY and ACTIVITYCONSTRAINT). In our opinion, this approach is a good compromise between complexity and expressiveness but we continuously work on new methods.

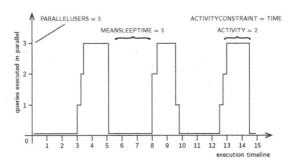

**Fig. 5.** Workload Parameters

*Independent or correlated parameters:* Once the method for describing activities is chosen, the question remains how to determine good values for the parameters. Again, the challenge is to find a compromise between expressiveness and the feasibility of the task to come up with parameters for possibly hundreds of instances. Our approach is to pick parameter values independently from one another. For example, the MEANSLEEPTIME may follow a Gaussian distribution over all tenants while the raw data size is evenly distributed between a minimum and a maximum. However, a tenants's MEANSLEEPTIME is independent from its raw data size and the other parameters. In the future, more complex extensions of MULTE may find it useful to correlate certain parameters, e.g., to simulate that larger tenants access data more often.

## 3.3   A Performance Metric for Multi-Tenant Database Systems

We argue that MT-DBMSs are so diverse and complex that different aspects need to be considered when a benchmark is designed. A single, classic performance metric, like transactions executed per second, is valid for peak performance evaluations and hence can be used for the SCALABILITYBENCHMARK and the FAIRNESSBENCHMARK. However, it is not sufficient to answer the question of how well tenants are isolated from one another, which is the intention of the ISOLATIONBENCHMARK. Hence, with tenants that have activities, a multi-tenancy benchmark needs a new performance metric. Since the tenants' activities are time-dependent, it follows that the new metric should also be time-dependent, i.e., it may differ over the run of the benchmark. Depending on the intention of the executed benchmark, this time-dependent metric may be aggregated to a single value. We propose the *relative execution time over time* as the basic metric for MT-DBMSs.

*Relative execution time:* To learn about a query's execution time under optimal conditions, a *baseline run* is performed in a simulated single-tenant environment. During this baseline run, each tenant is allowed to execute its workload on the otherwise idle system (possibly a couple of times) to collect information about its best-case execution time. During actual *test runs*, each query's execution time is recorded and compared to the baseline execution time. This leads to a *relative execution time* for this query, i.e., a penalty caused by the current overall system load, compared to the best-case scenario. Obviously, this relative execution time can differ significantly for a single query over time depending on the system load and configuration at that time. To reason about a tenant's performance or the overall system performance, individual relative execution times from the queries/transactions can be aggregated.

Having this metric, the question remains how to interpret it to answer different performance questions. We discuss our exemplary benchmarks to illustrate the usage of the new performance metric.

1. SCALABILITYBENCHMARK: To evaluate a system's ability to scale with the number of tenants, different (average) relative execution times measured with different numbers of tenants can be compared.
2. FAIRNESSBENCHMARK: When multiple tenants run their individual workloads, the differences of the relative execution times can be used to reason about the fairness of the system. Similar relative execution times can indicate a fair system. Large differences can indicate the absence (or poor performance) of a load-balancing component. However, large differences may be intentional, e.g., because different tenants have different service levels.
3. ISOLATIONBENCHMARK: To evaluate how well tenants are isolated from one another, all tenants execute a steady, moderate workload. At some point in time, a single tenant starts to execute heavy workload. The changes of other tenants' relative execution times after the workload change indicate how well they are isolated from the respective tenant.

## 4    Benchmark Implementation

In this section, we give an overview of design and implementation decisions that we made for the implementation of MULTE. Detailed information about the implementation can be found in the framework package and a related technical report (to appear with this paper).

### 4.1    Framework Design Principles

Our intention is to provide MULTE as a framework for MT-DBMSs that will be widely used and extended by the community. We committed our work to a number of design principles that shall help to increase the value of the framework.

*Easy-to-use:* We provide an example implementation to create tenants that run the TPC-H benchmark against MySQL or PostgreSQL databases. A user only needs to provide a small number of configuration parameters (e.g., host, port, paths, ...) and a workload definition, e.g., following one of the provided example scripts. The framework then generates and loads tenants. The Java workload driver can be used with a provided sample configuration to run the workload.

*Component Re-use:* We re-use existing components wherever possible to increase a benchmark's acceptance and reliability. From the given database benchmark, we re-use, e.g., data generators and schema definitions. The Java workload driver in MULTE is a modification of the workload driver of the TPoX database benchmark [4]. Hence, the strengths of this well-tested tool as well as the experiences and improvements gathered from using it help to improve MULTE.

*Extensibility:* The framework components to generate and load tenants can be replaced such that both, other benchmarks and other database systems can be supported. Python as the scripting language allows users to easily adopt our example implementations and modify them to fit their needs. The workload driver is designed to be able to run a wide variety of workloads, thus supports different benchmarks. Extending the workload driver to support different database systems is also easily possible as long as they provide a JDBC interface.

### 4.2    Python Scripts—Define, Generate, and Load Tenants

The Python scripts/classes to define, generate, and load tenants follow the structure shown in Figure 6. The full Python functionality can be used to define a tenant's set of activity parameters. We provide two implementations that either specify the parameters' values explicitly or pick them randomly (following a distribution) but independent from one another. Given the tenants' definitions, instances of the respective database benchmarks are generated using both, provided data generators and templates. Other instance generators for other benchmark types can be added by implementing the methods `generateData`, `generateSchema`, and `generateWorkload`. A DBMS-specific database executor

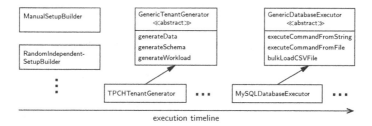

**Fig. 6.** Python Scripts Overview

is used to load all tenants' data into the databases. Our example implementation uses the command line interfaces of MySQL and PostgreSQL to execute SQL statements and to bulk-load data from CSV-files.

### 4.3 Java Workload Driver

As mentioned before, the Java workload driver, which executes all tenants' workloads against a MT-DBMS, is a modification and extension of the workload driver provided with the TPoX database benchmark. A detailed documentation of the original workload driver and its capabilities can be found on the TPoX website. Here, we would like to briefly show some of the modifications that we made (Figure 7). The class structure is closely coupled to the framework conception. The `WorkloadSuite` uses `GlobalSuiteParameters` for the benchmarks, taken from a simple configuration file (here `suite.xml`). The `WorkloadSuite` furthermore drives multiple tenants (`WorkloadInstance`) that in turn use multiple `ConcurrentUsers` to execute statements in the database. All of a tenant's parameters—stored in `WorkloadInstanceParameters`—are taken from an XML configuration file that is automatically generated by MULTE.

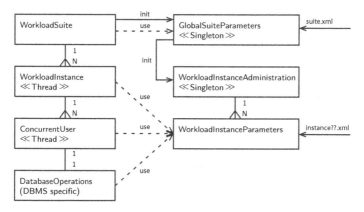

**Fig. 7.** Java Workload Driver Overview

## 5    Exemplary Benchmark Development and Execution

To show the ability of MULTE to help with the development of multi-tenancy benchmarks, we have implemented the three exemplary benchmarks SCALA-BILITYBENCHMARK, FAIRNESSBENCHMARK, and ISOLATIONBENCHMARK on a dual-socket AMD Opteron machine running Ubuntu 11.10 server, Java, Python, R, and MySQL. We used MULTE to generate up to 8 tenants that all run the TPC-H benchmark with 500MB of raw data. All tenants' data is loaded to private databases in a single MySQL server.

In the following, we are only interested in the process of building and executing a benchmark and not the particular results, which is why we do not further detail the system under test and only show relative results without baselines. We do not intent to make any statement about MySQL's multi-tenancy capabilities.

### 5.1    A Multi-Tenancy Scalability Benchmark

Our first benchmark is the SCALABILITYBENCHMARK described earlier. To run the benchmark, we generated and loaded 8 identical tenants that run constant workload with the parameters denoted in Table 1.

**Table 1.** Tenant Parameters for the SCALABILITYBENCHMARK

| Parameter | Value |
| --- | --- |
| TYPE | TPC-H |
| SIZE | 500MB |
| QUERY | TPC-H Query 1 |
| MEANSLEEPTIME | 0 |
| PARALLELUSERS | 5 |
| ACTIVITY | 300 |
| ACTIVITYCONSTRAINT | seconds |

We then collected a baseline for the execution time of TPC-H Query 1 in single-tenant mode. Afterwards, we used the workload driver to run 1, 2, 4, 6, or 8 tenants at the same time and to collect the execution times of all queries. Last, we computed the average relative execution time, an aggregate of our basic metric, the relative execution time over time, as an indicator for the system's ability to scale. The results are shown in Figure 8.

### 5.2    A Multi-Tenancy Fairness Benchmark

The second benchmark that we built is the FAIRNESSBENCHMARK. We generated and executed two different flavors of the benchmark: one with identical tenants, the other one with two different (groups of) tenants that differ in the

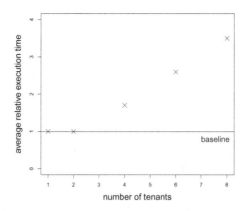

**Fig. 8.** Scalability Benchmark

query they execute. In FAIRNESSBENCHMARK 1, shown in Figure 9a, all tenants execute TPC-H Query 1. In FAIRNESSBENCHMARK 2, shown in Figure 9b, half of the tenants execute TPC-H Query 1 while the other half executes TPC-H Query 8. The metric shown in the bar charts is the average relative execution time per tenant (note the different scales of the y-axes). It can be seen that, on the one hand, with identical queries the relative execution time goes up with the number of tenants, but the available resources are distributed evenly. On the other hand, with tenants running different queries, one group observes a considerably higher relative execution time.

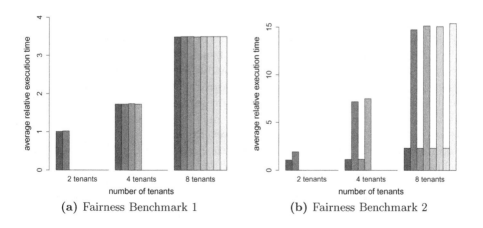

(a) Fairness Benchmark 1          (b) Fairness Benchmark 2

**Fig. 9.** Fairness Benchmarks

## 5.3    A Multi-Tenancy Isolation Benchmark

The last of our exemplary benchmarks is the IsolationBenchmark. To evaluate whether and how much a tenant can influence another tenant's performance we generated two different tenant types using the parameters shown in Table 2.

**Table 2.** Tenants used for the IsolationBenchmark

| Parameter | Tenant 1 | Tenant 2 |
|---|---|---|
| TYPE | TPC-H | TPC-H |
| SIZE | 500MB | 500MB |
| QUERY | TPC-H Query 1 | TPC-H Query 8 |
| MEANSLEEPTIME | 0 | 60 seconds |
| PARALLELUSERS | 5 | 20 |
| ACTIVITY | 50 | 10 |
| ACTIVITYCONSTRAINT | transactions | seconds |

It can be seen that both tenants have different activities. While Tenant 1 is running a constant workload, Tenant 2 is idle for 60 second intervals interrupted by short bursts of heavy query execution. The resulting individual loads imposed on the DBMS as well as the aggregated load are shown in Figures 10a–10c. To learn more about the system's ability to isolate tenants, we collected and charted the relative execution times. The results are shown in Figures 10d and 10e.

## 6    Related Work

There are several standardized benchmarks like TPC-C, TPC-E, TPC-DS, and TPC-H that are provided by the Transaction Processing Performance Council (TPC) [3]. All of these benchmarks aim at benchmarking database servers for different scenarios; TPC-C, for example, provides a database schema, data population, and workload for a typical OLTP scenario. Unfortunately, none of the TPC benchmarks can be used directly to measure the performance of a MT-DBMS. All of them use a fixed schema for only a single tenant. The queries, schema, and data of these benchmarks, however, can be re-used to create load for multiple tenants. Thus, they can form the foundation for any MT-DBMS benchmark that is built and run using MulTe.

Aulbach et al. [9] describe a testbed that is tailor-made for benchmarking MT-DBMSs. The workload relies on a fixed schema (i.e., a customer-relationship schema) and provides OLTP and OLAP queries for multiple tenants that are hosted on a service provider. Curino et al. [10] define multiple fixed workloads to benchmark their MT-DBMS. The workloads are based on TPC-C and have certain time-varying patterns. MulTe allows to use arbitrary and mixed workloads and schemas, hence allows to build more elaborate benchmarks.

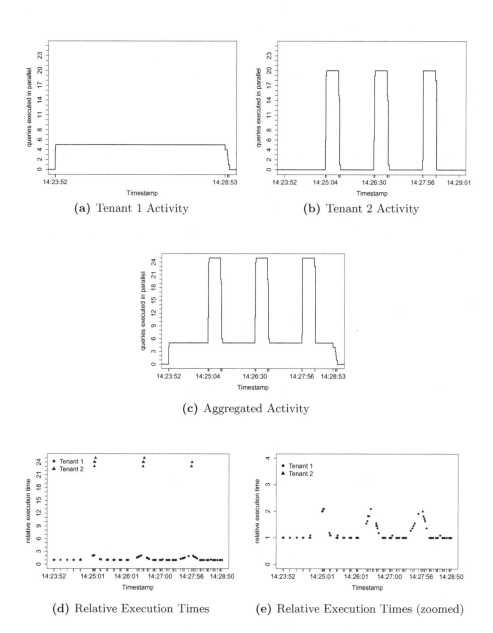

(a) Tenant 1 Activity                    (b) Tenant 2 Activity

(c) Aggregated Activity

(d) Relative Execution Times     (e) Relative Execution Times (zoomed)

**Fig. 10.** Performance Isolation Benchmark—Activities and Relative Execution Times

TPC-V [5] is a benchmark under development of the TPC suite. It is intended to benchmark databases that are hosted in virtual environments. The main focus lies on virtual machines (cf. Figure 2c), but the same concepts are applicable to other multi-tenancy implementations as well. TPC-V uses different database sizes and numbers of queries to emulate tenants with different loads. Furthermore, the load is varied within twelve 10-minute periods to shift the tenants' peak load to different periods as it is usually the case in real-life applications. Although TPC-V aims for the same direction as MULTE does, it has significantly different priorities. Like other TPC benchmarks, it provides strict guidelines to ensure a comparable and long-lasting benchmark. Consequently it is less flexible with respect to the tested scenarios, executed workloads, and other aspects of the benchmark. Moreover, TPC-V rather concentrates on the benchmark specification than the actual implementation which is left to the benchmark sponsor. In contrast, our goal is to support building benchmarks for all classes of MT-DBMSs (cf. Figure 2) and benchmarks that can be adapted to certain scenarios and questions. With the tools provided by MULTE, new benchmarks can be implemented very fast. This flexibility allows users to quickly expose performance, fairness, and other issues in MT-DBMSs.

## 7   Summary

We introduced and provided MULTE, a framework to help with the process of building and running benchmarks for MT-DBMSs. A multi-tenancy benchmark consists of multiple tenants, each running an arbitrary database benchmark. MULTE provides extensible tools to define, generate, and load all tenants as well as drive workloads and analyze results. Our example implementation of the MULTE components supports the TPC-H benchmark on MySQL or PostgreSQL.

In contrast to classic database management systems, multi-tenancy systems have additional requirements for, e.g., fairness and isolation, that need to be addressed in benchmarks. We introduced activities, i.e., time-dependent workloads, and a related performance metric (relative execution time) to account for these new requirements. We showed the necessity for the time-dependent workloads and a new performance metric as well as the capabilities of MULTE with the three exemplary benchmarks SCALABILITYBENCHMARK, FAIRNESSBENCHMARK, and ISOLATIONBENCHMARK.

We would like the community to actively extend MULTE. Additionally, we are also working on extensions for further benchmarks and database systems. To allow all components of the framework to run in a distributed fashion is another planned extension of MULTE that shall ensure its scalability to arbitrarily large MT-DBMSs.

# References

[1] Microsoft: Microsoft Windows Azure (2012),
    http://www.windowsazure.com/en-us/
[2] Amazon: Amazon Relational Database Service (2012),
    http://aws.amazon.com/rds/
[3] TPC: Transaction Processing Performance Council (2012), http://www.tpc.org/
[4] TPoX: Transaction Processing over XML (TPoX) (2012),
    http://tpox.sourceforge.net/
[5] Sethuraman, P., Reza Taheri, H.: TPC-V: A Benchmark for Evaluating the Performance of Database Applications in Virtual Environments. In: Nambiar, R., Poess, M. (eds.) TPCTC 2010. LNCS, vol. 6417, pp. 121–135. Springer, Heidelberg (2011)
[6] Jacobs, D., Aulbach, S.: Ruminations on Multi-Tenant Databases. In: Fachtagung für Datenbanksysteme in Business, Technologie und Web - BTW 2007, Aachen, Germany, pp. 5–9 (2007)
[7] Kiefer, T., Lehner, W.: Private Table Database Virtualization for DBaaS. In: Proceedings of the 4th IEEE International Conference on Utility and Cloud Computing - UCC 2011, vol. 1, pp. 328–329. IEEE, Melbourne (2011)
[8] Soror, A.A., Minhas, U.F., Aboulnaga, A., Salem, K., Kokosielis, P., Kamath, S.: Automatic Virtual Machine Configuration for Database Workloads. ACM Transactions on Database Systems (TODS) 35(1), 1–47 (2010)
[9] Aulbach, S., Grust, T., Jacobs, D., Kemper, A., Rittinger, J.: Multi-Tenant Databases for Software as a Service: Schema-Mapping techniques. In: Proceedings of the 2008 ACM SIGMOD International Conference on Management of Data - SIGMOD 2008, pp. 1195–1206. ACM, Vancouver (2008)
[10] Curino, C., Jones, E.P., Madden, S., Balakrishnan, H.: Workload-Aware Database Monitoring and Consolidation. In: Proceedings of the 2011 ACM SIGMOD International Conference on Management of Data - SIGMOD 2011, pp. 313–324. ACM, Athens (2011)

# BDMS Performance Evaluation: Practices, Pitfalls, and Possibilities

Michael J. Carey

Information Systems Group, Computer Sciences Department,
University of California, Irvine,
Irvine, CA 92697-3435
mjcarey@ics.uci.edu

**Abstract.** Much of the IT world today is buzzing about Big Data, and we are witnessing the emergence of a new generation of data-oriented platforms aimed at storing and processing all of the anticipated Big Data. The current generation of Big Data Management Systems (BDMSs) can largely be divided into two kinds of platforms: systems for Big Data analytics, which today tend to be batch-oriented and based on MapReduce (*e.g.,* Hadoop), and systems for Big Data storage and front-end request-serving, which are usually based on key-value (*a.k.a.* NoSQL) stores. In this paper we ponder the problem of evaluating the performance of such systems. After taking a brief historical look at Big Data management and DBMS benchmarking, we begin our pondering of BDMS performance evaluation by reviewing several key recent efforts to measure and compare the performance of BDMSs. Next we discuss a series of potential pitfalls that such evaluation efforts should watch out for, pitfalls mostly based on the author's own experiences with past benchmarking efforts. Finally, we close by discussing some of the unmet needs and future possibilities with regard to BDMS performance characterization and assessment efforts.

**Keywords:** Data-intensive computing, Big Data, performance, benchmarking, MapReduce, Hadoop, key-value stores, NoSQL systems.

## 1    Introduction (The Plan)

We have entered the "Big Data" era – an era where a wealth of digital information is being generated every day. If this information can be captured, persisted, queried, and aggregated effectively, it holds great potential value for a variety of purposes. Data warehouses were largely an enterprise phenomenon in the past, with large enterprises being unique in recording their day-to-day operations in databases and warehousing and analyzing historical data in order to improve their business operations. Today, organizations and researchers from a wide range of domains recognize that there is tremendous value and insight to be gained by warehousing the emerging wealth of digital information and making it available for querying, analysis, and other purposes. Online businesses of all shapes and sizes track their customers' purchases, product searches, web site interactions, and other information to increase the effectiveness of

R. Nambiar and M. Poess (Eds.): TPCTC 2012, LNCS 7755, pp. 108–123, 2013.

their marketing and customer service efforts; governments and businesses track the content of blogs and tweets to perform sentiment analysis; public health organizations monitor news articles, tweets, and web search trends to track the progress of epidemics; and, social scientists study tweets and social networks to understand how information of various kinds spreads and how it can be effectively utilized for the public good. Technologies for data-intensive computing, search, and scalable information storage – *a.k.a.* Big Data analytics and management – are critical components in today's computing landscape. Evaluating and driving improvements in the performance of these technologies is therefore critical as well.

The goal of this paper is to take an informal look, with a critical eye, at the current state of the art in Big Data platform performance evaluation. The eye in question will be that of the author, who makes no claims about being an actual expert in this area. The author's performance evaluation experience comes mostly from a series of previous forays into benchmarking of other database technologies, and his Big Data experience comes from a current and somewhat counter-cultural project (ASTERIX) that aims to develop a second-generation (meaning post-Hadoop) Big Data Management System (BDMS) at UC Irvine. The paper will start by reviewing some of the history in the previously distinct areas of Big Data technologies and DBMS benchmarking; this part of the paper will end with a summary of where things are today at the intersection of these two areas. The paper will then turn to a series of potential pitfalls – things to be wary of – when attempting to characterize and/or to compare the performance of data management systems; this part of the paper will largely be anecdotal, drawing on lessons that the author has learned either by direct observation or through personal experience. The paper will then turn briefly to the question of future requirements and challenges, presenting one perspective on where future efforts in this area might want to focus; this part of the paper will be based largely on combining inputs that the author has gotten from various industrial colleagues together with some of the lessons covered in the middle part of the paper.

## 2     Background (The Practices)

In this section of the paper we will take quick tours of the history of systems for managing Big Data, of some of the historical efforts to benchmark data management technologies, and of the current state of these two fields (combined).

### 2.1     Big Data Management Systems

The IT world has been facing Big Data challenges for over four decades, though the meaning of "Big" has obviously been evolving. In the 1970's, "Big" meant Megabytes of data; over time, "Big" grew first to Gigabytes and then to Terabytes. Nowadays the meaning of "Big" for data in the enterprise IT world has reached the Petabyte range for high-end data warehouses, and it is very likely that Exabyte-sized warehouses are lurking around the corner.

In the world of relational database systems, the need to scale to data volumes beyond the storage and/or processing capabilities of a single large computer system gave birth to shared-nothing parallel database systems [23]. These systems run on networked clusters of computers, each with their own processors, memories, and disks. Data is spread over the cluster based on a partitioning strategy – usually hash partitioning, but sometimes range partitioning or random partitioning – and queries are processed by employing parallel, hash-based divide-and-conquer techniques. The first generation of systems appeared in the 1980's, with pioneering prototypes from the University of Wisconsin and the University of Tokyo, a first commercial offering from Teradata Corporation, and traditional relational DBMS vendors following suit. The past decade has seen the emergence of a new wave of systems, with a number of startups developing parallel database systems that have been swallowed up through recent acquisitions by IBM, Microsoft, EMC, HP, and even Teradata. Users of parallel database systems have been shielded from the complexities of parallel programming by the provision of SQL as a set-oriented, declarative API. Until quite recently, shared-nothing parallel database systems have been the single most successful utilization of parallel computing, at least in the commercial sector.

In the late 1990's, while the database research community was admiring its "finished" research on parallel databases, and the major database software vendors were commercializing the results, the distributed systems world began facing Big Data challenges of its own. The rapid growth of the World-Wide Web, and the resulting need to index and query its mushrooming content, created Big Data challenges for search companies like Inktomi, Yahoo!, and Google. Their processing needs were quite different, so parallel databases were not the answer, though shared-nothing clusters emerged as the hardware platform of choice in this world as well. Google responded to these new challenges [21] by developing the Google File System (GFS), allowing very large files to be randomly partitioned over hundreds or even thousands of nodes in a cluster, and by coupling GFS with a very simple programming model, MapReduce, that enables programmers to process Big Data files by writing two user-defined functions, map and reduce. The Google MapReduce framework applied these functions in parallel to individual data items in GFS files (map) and then to sorted groups of items that share a common key (reduce) – much like the partitioned parallelism used in shared-nothing parallel database systems. Yahoo! and other big Web companies such as Facebook soon created an open-source version of Google's Big Data stack, yielding the now highly popular Apache Hadoop platform [4] and its associated HDFS storage layer. Microsoft has a different but analogous Big Data stack, the SCOPE stack [19], used in support of its Bing search services.

Similar to the two-worlds history for Big Data back-end warehousing and analysis, the historical record for Big Data also has a dual front-end (*i.e.,* user-facing) story worth noting. As enterprises in the 1980's and 1990's began to automate more and more of their day-to-day operations using databases, the database world had to scale up its online transaction processing (OLTP) systems as well as its data warehouses. Companies like Tandem Computers responded with fault-tolerant, cluster-based SQL systems. Similarly, but again later over in the distributed systems world, the big Web companies found themselves driven by very large user bases (up to 10s or even 100s of millions of Web users) to find solutions to achieve very fast simple lookups and updates to large, keyed data sets such as collections of user profiles. Monolithic SQL databases for OLTP were rejected as too expensive, too complex, and not fast enough, and the scalable key-value stores that are driving today's "NoSQL movement" [18] were born. Again, companies like Google and Amazon each developed their own answers (BigTable and Dynamo, respectively) to meet this set of needs, and the Apache community soon followed suit by creating a set of corresponding open-source clones (*e.g.*, HBase and Cassandra).

So where are things now? Over the past few years, Hadoop and HDFS have grown to become the dominant platform for Big Data analytics at large Web companies as well as within less traditional corners of traditional enterprises (*e.g.*, for click-stream and log analyses). At the same time, data analysts have grown tired of the low-level MapReduce programming model; instead, they are now using a handful of high-level declarative languages and frameworks that allow data analyses to be expressed much more easily and written and debugged much more quickly. The two most popular languages are Hive [5] from Facebook (a variant of SQL) and Pig [6] from Yahoo! (a functional variant of the relational algebra, roughly). Tasks are first expressed in these languages and then compiled into a series of MapReduce jobs for execution on Hadoop clusters. Looking at the workloads on real clusters in the last few years, it has been reported that well over 60% of Yahoo!'s Hadoop jobs and over 90% of Facebook's Hadoop jobs come from these higher-level languages rather than hand-written MapReduce jobs. More and more, MapReduce is being relegated to serving as the Big Data runtime for various higher-level, declarative data languages (which are not so different from SQL) rather than as a solution developers' programming platform. Similarly, and ironically, there are even early efforts looking at providing higher-level, SQL-like query language interfaces to "NoSQL" stores. Figure 1 illustrates the layers in a typical instance of the first-generation, Apache-based Big Data software stack.

The first-generation Hadoop-centric software stack for Big Data dominates today in industry, and batch-oriented data analytics are usually managed separately (both

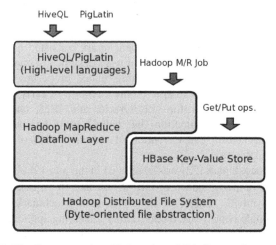

**Fig. 1.** The first-generation, Hadoop-based, Big Data software stack

logically and physically) from the real-time, user-facing, key-value stores in today's overall architectures. ETL-like processes, usually also Hadoop-based, are used to connect the two. In addition to these current architectures, it is important to be aware, when planning Big Data performance studies, that changes are occurring in this space and that performance-related efforts must be ready for the changes. One such trend is towards more specialized systems on the Big Data analytics side. As examples, the increasing availability of very large graph data sets, such as social graphs or derived graphs of user interactions, is leading to the creation of new platforms such as Pregel [27] and GraphLab [26] for graph analytics or programming models; a new platform called SciDB [33] is currently being developed for storing, querying, and analyzing large volumes of array-based science data; and, the development of platforms tailored to large-scale machine learning tasks (*e.g.,* see [12]) is becoming a popular target driven by Big Data analysis requirements. Another potential "trend" is represented by the ASTERIX project at UC Irvine [8], where we are working to deliver a BDMS that is somewhat *less* specialized – one where "one size fits a bunch" – namely, a system that is capable of handling very large quantities of semistructured data and supporting data ingestion, updates, small to medium queries, and large batch analyses over both internally managed as well as externally stored data [9, 11, 1].

### 2.2  Data Management Benchmarks

Benchmarking of database management systems [24] is an activity that has drawn the attention of DBMS practitioners and researchers for over three decades. Two of the most influential early benchmarks were the Wisconsin benchmark and the Debit-Credit benchmark.

The Wisconsin benchmark [22] was developed in the early 1980's and was the first benchmark designed to test and compare the performance of relational database systems. The benchmark was a single-user micro-benchmark consisting of 32 queries chosen to measure the performance of basic relational operations. The benchmark query set included selection queries with different selectivity factors, projections with different degrees of attribute duplication, 2-way and 3-way joins (including select/join queries and full joins), aggregates with and without grouping, and a handful of inserts, deletes, and updates. The database for the benchmark consisted of a set of synthetic relations with attribute value distributions that were designed to enable careful control over the selectivity-related and duplicate-value-related properties of the benchmark queries. The Wisconsin benchmark captured the attention of early relational database vendors, including INGRES, Britton-Lee, Oracle, and IBM, and it served as an important competitive forcing function that helped to drive industry progress in relational query optimization and execution in the early days of relational DBMS technology commercialization.

The Debit-Credit benchmark [32] was developed in the mid 1980's and was designed to test and compare the performance of DBMS transaction processing capabilities. In contrast with the synthetic nature of the Wisconsin benchmark, the Debit-Credit benchmark was a simple benchmark modeled after a banking application. The database for the benchmark consisted of account, teller, branch, and history files whose size ratios and data content were designed to scale in a fairly realistic manner based on the scale of the system being tested. The workload was multi-user, and it consisted of a number of teller terminals generating transactions at a fixed rate; the number of tellers was scaled up until the system being tested became unable to meet a specified goal for the response time distribution. The transaction rate (TPS) for that tipping point was reported as the system's transaction performance, and the cost of the system capable of providing that level of performance was also reported. Much as the Wisconsin benchmark did, the Debit-Credit benchmark captured the attention of the IT industry, and it served to drive significant industrial progress related to transaction processing performance. The Debit-Credit benchmark drew numerous industrial participants, including both software and hardware vendors, and it became so successful that it led to the formation of the Transaction Processing Council (TPC) in order to oversee the first two formal Debit-Credit inspired benchmarks, namely TPC-A and then TPC-B.

As DBMS technology and its functional richness have progressed over the past three decades, together with the performance of the underlying hardware and software platforms that these systems run on, a number of additional benchmarks have been developed with varying degrees of interest and adoption. On the strictly relational front, the TPC has produced a number of widely used benchmarks, including TPC-C, a more complex multi-user transaction processing benchmark based on an inventory management application, and TPC-H (formerly TPC-D), a single-user analysis query benchmark designed to test a system's complex query processing capabilities (somewhat in the spirit of the Wisconsin benchmark, being a series of queries, but with a database schema modeled after an enterprise data warehousing scenario). On the functionality front, a biased sub-sample of interesting benchmarks over the years might include the OO7 benchmark for object-oriented DBMSs [14, 15], the BUCKY benchmark for object-relational DBMSs [16], and the XMark and EXRT benchmarks for XML-related DBMS technologies [31, 17]. Each one of these benchmarks was a micro-benchmark based on an application-oriented database schema: OO7 was based on a computer-aided engineering design data management scenario, while BUCKY was based on a hypothetical university data management scenario; XMark considered an XML-based auction data management scenario, while EXRT based its choice of data on a financial services scenario that it borrowed from TPoX [28].

## 2.3    Existing BDMS Benchmarks

Owing to the importance of and interest in Big Data management solutions, work on benchmarking Big Data Management Systems (BDMSs) has started to appear. To date there have been two major benchmarking exercises that have caught the attention of a significant portion of the Big Data community, one in each of the two major sub-areas of Big Data – namely Big Data analytics and NoSQL data stores.

For Big Data analytics, the most influential study to date has been the work by Pavlo *et al* on "a Comparison of Approaches to Large-scale Data Analysis" [30] (which we will refer to henceforth as the CALDA effort, for brevity). This effort defined a micro-benchmark for Big Data analytics and then used it to compare the performance of Hadoop with that of two shared-nothing parallel DBMS platforms, a traditional parallel relational DBMS (denoted simply as DBMS-X in the study) and a parallel relational DBMS based on column-based data storage and column-oriented query processing techniques (Vertica). The data analysis tasks chosen for use in this benchmark were a *grep*-like selection task (borrowed from the original MapReduce paper), a range-based selection task, a grouped aggregation task, a two-way join task (including subsequent aggregation), and an aggregation task involving a user-defined function. The CALDA benchmark results included reporting of the times required to load and index the datasets for the benchmark, in the case of the two parallel database systems, as well as the execution times for each of the tasks on all three of the alternative Big Data analytics systems. A 100-node cluster was used in producing the reported initial benchmark results.

For NoSQL data stores, the most influential benchmark developed to date has been YCSB, the Yahoo! Cloud Serving Benchmark [20]. The goal of the YCSB effort was to create a standard benchmark to assist evaluators of NoSQL data stores, *i.e.,* of the wide range of new data stores that are targeting "data storage and management 'in the cloud'", based on scenarios of providing online read-write access to large volumes of simple data. YCSB is a multiuser benchmark that has two tiers, a performance tier and a scalability tier. YCSB's performance tier tests the latency of request processing for a loaded NoSQL system under workloads with mixes of reads (single-record gets and range scans) and writes (single-record inserts and updates). The system is tested as an open system; the rate of job arrivals is increased until the system becomes overloaded and response times are averaged per operation type in the workload's mix of operations. Several record popularity distributions are considered as well, including Uniform record access, Zipfian (by key), and Latest (Zipfian by insertion time, with recent records being more popular). The initial YCSB paper's main results came from running three workloads, an update-heavy workload (with 50%-50% reads and updates), a read-heavy workload (with 95% reads and 5% updates), and a short-range workload (with 95% range scans and 5% updates), against four different data stores: Cassandra, HBase, PNUTs, and MySQL. The scalability tier of YCSB examines the static and dynamic scalability of NoSQL systems. The static test is a scaleup test that varies the number of servers (from 1-12 in the initial study) while proportionally adding data as well. The dynamic test fixes the data size and the workload (which is sized to cause a heavy load when the system is small) and then increases the number of servers (from 2-6 in the initial study) over time in order to observe the performance of the system as more servers are added in order to absorb and balance the load on the system. Suggested future YCSB tiers included availability and replication testing.

In addition to these two benchmarks, other existing BDMS benchmarks include GridMix [3], a synthetic multiuser benchmark for Hadoop cluster testing, and PigMix [7], a collection of queries aimed at testing and tracking the performance of the Pig query processor from release to release. Also, the Web site [29] for the recent NSF Workshop on Big Data Benchmarking is a potentially useful resource for seekers of more information about existing Big Data benchmarks and/or about the community's thoughts on future needs and approaches in this area.

# 3    Lessons from Past Benchmarks (The Pitfalls)

The process of benchmarking Big Data systems, more traditional database systems, or most any computer software for that matter, is an interesting and challenging exercise.

Technical challenges often include somehow defining and agreeing upon acceptable domain- and or system-relevant notions of what is "reasonable", "proper", "fair", "normal", "comparable", and/or "steady-state". Challenges also include the level of detail at which a benchmark should be specified, or conversely, how much freedom should be left to eventual implementers of the benchmark. Non-technical challenges usually include dealing with others' reactions to the benchmark, particularly from those individuals or organizations whose systems are being put to the test. This section of the paper discusses a number of potential pitfalls, mostly based on various of the author's first-hand experiences over the years with benchmarking situations, that warrant consideration as this community strives to define useful and influential new Big Data benchmarks.

### 3.1    "Fair" Tuning Is Critical

One of the key challenges in conducting a benchmarking study, particularly one that aims to compare systems, is configuring all of the systems both "properly" and "fairly". When the Wisconsin benchmark [22] was first being developed and run on a collection of early relational database systems, David DeWitt's initial approach to configuring the systems was to run each one with its default configuration settings – *i.e.,* to base the benchmark numbers on each system's "out of box experience". The relational database systems being tested included the INGRES system, developed by Michael Stonebraker and Eugene Wong at UC Berkeley, the Britton-Lee IDM-500 database machine, developed by Bob Epstein and Paula Hawthorn, SQL DS, IBM's commercialization of System-R, and Oracle, based on their own initial clone of the IBM System-R design. I was a graduate student at Berkeley and was in the "INGRES bullpen" on the day that Stonebraker got his first look at the initial DeWitt numbers, which were not very favorable for INGRES, and I seem to remember that it took several of us to pull him down from the ceiling after he'd looked at them. As it turned out, University INGRES was configured to run in a friendly (to other users) way on small Unix systems, so its buffer pool usage was modest and file-system based. In contrast, the IDM-500 was a dedicated box (with special search hardware as well as a very lightweight DB-oriented operating system), so it dedicated most of its vast main memory resources (something along the lines of 2MB ☺) to the buffer pool by default. In addition, the Wisconsin benchmark tables in those initial tests were very small, enough so that the numbers ended up comparing INGRES having to perform I/O against the IDM-500 running as a main-memory database system. I also later remember listening to a very angry Bruce Lindsay, from IBM's System-R team, complaining passionately about how little sense it made to compare systems "out of the box" – as in those days, virtually no system was configured well "out of the box". I didn't hear Oracle's reaction first-hand, but I do know that founder and CEO Larry Ellison apparently attempted to get David DeWitt fired from his faculty position at Wisconsin, so it seems he was not entirely pleased either (☺). The eventual published numbers from the Wisconsin benchmark study were produced using larger tables and only after setting the systems up as comparably as possible. Tuning is important! (It is also far from easy, as very often systems have different knobs, and it can be unclear how in fact to set them all across all systems to be "comparable". We encountered challenges regarding memory settings, roughly thirty years after the initial Wisconsin benchmark, while trying to configure memory settings for several relational and non-relational database systems for the EXRT benchmark [17]).

## 3.2    Expect Unhappy Developers

Another challenge in conducting a benchmarking study is dealing with the human factor – which can easily escalate into the legal factor in some cases. When trying to address the first challenge, *i.e.*, ensuring proper use and tuning of each system, it can be very helpful to interact with experts from the companies or organizations whose software is going to be tested. Such individuals, who are often the lead developers of the products in question, are usually eager to make sure that things are done right, and usually start out being very helpful. Unfortunately, a benchmark is often viewed as a contest of some sort – in effect, it often is – and there must be winners and losers in any contest. Developers often become less enamored with a benchmark when it starts to turn up product "issues" that are going to be hard to address before the end of the study, and/or if their system's showing starts looking for any reason like it's not going to be the winner. This happened to David DeWitt, Jeff Naughton, and I when we worked together on the OO7 benchmark for object-oriented database systems [14, 15]. The systems that we tested included three commercial systems – each of us was actually on the Technical Advisory Board for one of those companies, so we had a "perfect storm" of conflicts of interest that cancelled one another out – so getting initial buy-in and cooperation was easy in each case. However, things got ugly later when the results started to emerge – to the point where Naughton took to shouting "Incoming!" whenever we heard the FAX machine across the hall get a call, as we began receiving threatening "cease and desist" orders from several of the companies' legal representatives. As it turns out, each had a "DeWitt clause" in their system's license agreement – a clause saying that one could not publically report performance results. We had not paid enough attention to this due to the cooperative attitudes of each company initially, but this clause gave the companies the power to order us to not publish results – and in fact, in the end, one of the companies did completely withdraw from the benchmark, and our university lawyers instructed us to not publish their results. Interestingly, the one company that opted out had been doing very well, the best in fact, performance-wise – its system just wasn't winning in absolutely every single test category. Since their product was the OODBMS market leader at the time, their management team decided that no good could come from participating in a contest they couldn't completely sweep – so the OO7 paper ended up having one less participant than it started out with. While this is less likely to happen today, at least for open-source Big Data systems (which don't have software licenses with "DeWitt clauses" in them), it is still almost certain that results from any given benchmarking effort will make the various systems' lead developers unhappy at some point.

## 3.3    Just How Declarative Is a Query?

Yet another challenge in developing a benchmark relates to defining and clearly specifying its operations. For SQL DBMS benchmarks, this is not a huge problem, as one can use SQL to specify the various operations in the benchmark. However, when one ventures into newer territories – like the Big Data territory of interest today – it's a different story. One might, for example, wish to come up with a "Big Data query benchmark" that can be run using "any" Big Data language – such as Pig, Hive, Jaql, or AQL – in which case this problem will arise. When DeWitt and Naughton and I were developing OO7, we faced this issue, as each OODBMS at that time had its own unique API as well as different query languages and capabilities. Some had fairly rich query languages, with expressive power comparable to SQL, while others had persistent, object-oriented programming language APIs with limited filtering options in their looping constructs (meaning that joins had to be hand-coded, among other implications, for the benchmark[1]). As a result, we ended up specifying the benchmark operations and our intentions in English [14, 15], as best we could, but this was not an entirely satisfying manner in which to specify a benchmark. Later, when we set out to benchmark object-relational systems in our Bucky benchmarking effort [16], we faced similar challenges – our work pre-dated the SQL3 standard, so there was no single query language, or even a truly uniform set of O-R extensions, to be used in our specification – so again we faced questions related to how to convey the properties "required" of a "correct" implementation of Bucky. Fast forward to the EXRT relational/XML benchmarking effort [17], of just a few years ago, and *still* this issue arose, albeit in a somewhat narrower form. In EXRT we tested several systems using only two standard XML query languages –SQL/XML and XQuery – so we were able to use those languages to write two specifications for each benchmark operation. However, what we found was that the systems, one of them in particular, were sensitive to the way that the queries were formulated – so we were faced with the question of whether or not it was "fair" to reformulate a query to work around a system's query optimizer blind spots and/or cost model glitches. The bottom line is that it's always something! This is sure to be a big issue for Big Data benchmarks, given the heterogeneity of current systems' languages and user models.

### 3.4    Is This a Reasonable Data Set?

When designing a set of operations for a benchmarking study, one needs data, so the design of a benchmark's database will essentially go hand-in-hand with the design of the benchmark itself. The Wisconsin benchmark used a completely synthetic set of tables (with table names like *1KTUP* and *10KTUP1* and column names like *unique1* and *tenpercent*) whose only purposes were to serve as targets for a series of carefully controlled queries. In contrast, as mentioned in Section 2.2, most of the DBMS benchmarks that followed have taken a more application-inspired approach to their

---

[1] We recently re-encountered this expressive power issue in an internal ASTERIX-related effort to compare our system's performance to that of MongoDB, one of the richest NoSQL stores [18]. The ASTERIX query language supports joins, but in MongoDB, joins have to be coded in client programs. As a result, we had some heated internal arguments about whether or not, and how well if so, to do that (*e.g.,* whether or not a typical client programmer would take the time to program a sort-merge or hash-based join method, and thus what a "fair" and/or "reasonable" implementation of a join would be for a user of MongoDB).

database designs, using a set of tables, a set of object collections, or a collection of documents intended to model something "real" drawn from a likely application area for the set of systems and features being tested. Typically these designs mix the realistic with the synthetic; attribute value distributions are still controlled to aid in the creation of benchmark queries with predictable performance and cardinality characteristics. An example of the latter approach is the XML database design used in the XMark [31] benchmarking effort, which is based on a hypothetical Web-based auction site scenario. As specified, the XMark database is a single and therefore potentially very large XML document containing nested collections of subdocuments about concepts such as people, world regions and items, item categories, and open and closed (finished) auctions. XMark's XML schema and data designs were based on careful consideration of various XML data features that transcend the relationally-representable norm and were therefore deemed to be interesting and important aspects of each system to test. So is this a reasonable design? At the time of its inception, it was felt that the answer was yes, but in retrospect, one could argue that having one humungous XML document containing an entire application database is probably both unrealistic and unwise from an application point of view. Big Data benchmarks will have to face similar choices and come to "reasonable" conclusions. In addition, since scale-up testing is an important aspect of Big Data testing, Big Data benchmarks are faced with the task of designing scale-up strategies for their data values – which is easily done for simple data, but can be quite challenging for data such as social graph data or data where fuzzy-matching properties (*e.g.,* entity-matching data sets) need to be maintained in a "realistic" manner as the data scale grows.

### 3.5    Steady as She Goes!

Well-engineered DBMSs in search of high performance employ techniques such as caching, or deferral and batching of certain operations, in their runtime systems. Database pages containing data are accessed from disk and then cached in memory (buffered) so that temporal locality can be leveraged to avoid subsequent I/Os for re-access; database queries are often compiled the first time they are encountered, and then their query execution plans are cached so that subsequent requests involving the same query, perhaps even with different input parameters, can avoid the cost of query planning by reusing the cached execution plan. For writes, most systems use defer-and-batch approaches at various levels in order to amortize write-related costs over multiple write operations. For example, transaction managers have long used group-commit techniques that delay individual transaction commits so as to commit multiple transactions with a single log write; the Vertica parallel DBMS and many of today's NoSQL data stores utilize LSM-based file structures (LSM = log-structured merge) so that write operations can first be performed on an in-memory tree component and the associated I/O costs occur later, asynchronously, in a batch, when the component is written to disk and/or merged with a disk-resident component of the file. The result of all of these optimizations is that the systems being benchmarked must be run for "long enough", with their initial warm-up period either being excluded or "drowned out", in order for the benchmark results to reflect the systems' steady-state behavior.

An example of how *not* to do this can be found in the last segment of the EXRT benchmark, which tests the performance of systems for a handful of simple update operations [17]. Two of the systems tested were traditional relational DBMSs with XML extensions, and they had traditional DBMS-like storage architectures and buffer managers; the third system was a native XML DBMS that has a different, LSM-like storage and caching architecture. The update-related performance results reported for the native XML system were much faster than for the relational systems due to this architectural difference and the fact that EXRT's update cost measurement approach allowed the update-related I/O's to "escape" beyond the measurement period. Being a micro-benchmark, each operation was run some modest number of times and then the results were averaged, and this simplistic methodology didn't properly capture the update I/O costs for the XML system's deferred-write architecture [17]. As we define new Big Data benchmarks, in a world with very large memory sizes and defer-and-batch mechanisms, benchmark designers need to be cognizant of the these techniques and their implications – and think about how to make benchmarking "fast enough" without losing track of important costs due to steady-state achievement issues.

### 3.6    Single- Versus Multi-user Performance

As we saw in Section 2's tour of prior benchmarks, some of the existing DBMS benchmarks have taken a single-user, query-at-a-time look at DBMS performance, *e.g.,* Wisconsin, OO7, Bucky, EXRT, while others have focused on the performance of DBMS's under multi-user workloads, *e.g.,* the TPC benchmarks A, B, and C. On the Big Data side, the CALDA evaluation of Big Data analytic technologies was a single-user micro-benchmark, while YCSB is a simple multi-user benchmark. When we started our ASTERIX project at UCI, one of our first steps was to make a set of "pilgrimages" with our initial project ideas to visit several major Big Data players – including one provider (Teradata) and several consumers (eBay and Facebook) – to get input on what considerations they viewed as important and what problems they thought we should be sure *not* to ignore in our work. One unanimous message that we received can be paraphrased as: "Real Big Data clusters are never run in single-user mode – they never run just one job at a time. Real clusters are shared and run a concurrent mix of jobs of different sizes with different levels of priority. Doing this sort of scheduling well is important, and nobody is truly there yet." This is important because decisions that one might make to optimize single-user, single-job response time in a Big Data system can be very different than the decisions that one would make once several instances of the job have to share the resources of the cluster, either amongst themselves or with other concurrent jobs. Several clear illustrations of the importance of multi-user thinking can be found in some performance work that we recently did related to a UCI Ph.D. student's summer internship at Facebook [25], where the student's assignment was to tweak Hadoop's runtime mechanisms so that analysts could run large exploratory HiveQL queries with `limit` clauses when investigating new questions and answers over large data sets in their daily work. The student's summer project led to Hadoop changes that enabled jobs to consume their input files in a more incremental fashion, and to cease their execution early when done.

These changes improved single-user Hive query performance on Hadoop only in cases where the job's needs outstripped the parallel resource capacity of the entire cluster (which of course can happen with Big Data's data sizes), but the changes *dramatically* improved Hive's multi-user performance in *all* cases, including multi-user cases with both homogeneous and heterogeneous job mixes sharing a cluster. We also looked briefly at how the default Hadoop scheduler's treatment of job mixes compared to that of one of the popular "fair schedulers" used by some Hadoop installations, and the results were surprising, at least to us – the multi-user performance of the "fair scheduler" was actually worse, at least for the workloads that we considered, due to its overly conservative utilization of the cluster's processing capacity.

### 3.7    Should the World Be Open and/or Classless?

Analytical and simulation-based modelers of the performance of computer systems have long faced questions about how to model a given system under study, and how to model the system's offered workload is an important question. One approach is to use an "open" system model – where jobs arrive and depart independently of how well the system is processing them. This is often an appropriate model when the workload for the system originates from a very large user base with very large per-user inter-request times, *e.g.,* as in a telephone network. Open systems can become overloaded when the load exceeds the system's capacity. Another approach is to use a "closed" system model – where there is a fixed population of users, each submitting one request, waiting for the system's response, thinking about the response, and then submitting their next request. This is often an appropriate model when the system has a more modest number of users, *e.g.,* where the system's user base is a small team of analysts each working interactively with a collection of data. A closed system can never become truly swamped in the fashion of an open system because its finite user population and the serial nature of requests mean that the system just "slows down" – users wait longer as the system's performance degrades, but they ultimately do wait for their answers before asking the next question. Another important workload modeling decision, for closed systems, is how to appropriately associate job classes with users – *i.e.,* whether each user can submit jobs of any class, or whether the system's active user population is better subdivided into different user classes, each with its own finite population, with each class of users submitting jobs with potentially different characteristics. The latter approach is arguably more appropriate for benchmarking DBMS performance under mixes of small and large jobs, *e.g.,* where small update requests or queries are mixed with large read-only requests. Otherwise, a scheduling policy that is somehow biased against one or the other of the workload's job classes may not have the opportunity to properly display its biases [13, 25], in which case the performance study may "miss" an important opportunity to surface a potential performance problem with one or more of the systems under study. This can occur because, without a static division of users into user classes, the system can eventually reach a state where every user is waiting for a response to a job of the class that the system is biased against – *i.e.,* those jobs can pile up, and eventually all users have an outstanding request of that type – and then it can finish at least one of those before it starts getting other kinds of requests again. Unless the actual load of the deployed system can be expected to have this "eventual relief" characteristic in production, it would not be good for a benchmark to give its studied systems such an "out" due to its choice of workload design.

# 4    Towards Future BDMS Benchmarks (The Possibilities)

Given the onslaught of Big Data, and the rapid expansion of Big Data as a platform sector in the IT landscape, opportunities abound for future efforts related to Big Data benchmarking [29]. Given the current status of the work in this area, and in light of the potential pitfalls just discussed, we close this paper by briefly surveying some of the unmet needs and important future possibilities (at least in this author's opinion) regarding BDMS performance characterization and assessment efforts.

*Richer BDMS Micro-Benchmarks:* The CALDA effort on benchmarking Big Data analytics technologies was a good start, clearly, but it really just scratched the surface in this area. There is a clear need for a more comprehensive benchmark, perhaps along the lines of the Wisconsin benchmark or OO7, that could be used in evaluating the emerging generation of BDMS alternatives. Such an effort would consider a much broader range of queries and updates, including small- and medium-sized requests against indexed data in addition to large, MapReduce-influenced jobs.

*Multi-user BDMS Benchmarks:* The YCSB effort on benchmarking Big Data key-value stores was a good start as well, but again it represents a surface scratch relative to the ongoing needs in this area; YCSB studied only a few workload mixes involving very simple operations. Needs here include profiling the workloads of operational clusters in order to identify the kinds of query mixes seen in Big Data analytical settings, in practice, on shared clusters. The results of such profiling could then be used to create synthetic workloads for evaluating the existing Big Data technologies in realistic settings as well to help drive research on cluster resource management. Other needs include the exploration of multi-user workloads involving mixes of both analytical and simple data access requests, *i.e.,* truly heterogeneous workloads.

*Domain-Centric Big Data Benchmarks:* Social graph data, scientific data, spatial data, streaming data (*a.k.a,* "Fast Data" or "high-velocity data") – each of these is the current focus of one or more specialized Big Data platform efforts. To help assess the platform progress in these areas, and to help motivate their engineering efforts, new benchmarks are needed. In each case, the new programming models being proposed, and the associated new data handling mechanisms being developed for them, are sufficiently specialized to justify the development of specialized benchmarks as well. (The "Linear Road" benchmark [2] from the stream data management community is one example of what such a specialized benchmark might look like.)

*Self-Management Benchmarks:* Some of the most attractive features of scalable distributed file systems like HDFS and of key-value stores like HBase and Cassandra are their support for auto-management of storage as new data and/or cluster nodes are added and their support for high availability in the face of data node failures. Good benchmarks that can be used to compare and evaluate these dimensions of Big Data platform functionality are an open problem, and will be important to drive research and development efforts in these areas.

*Challenging Data Benchmarks:* Last but not least, the emerging new generation of BDMS platforms is starting to provide very rich functionality in areas such as flexible schema support, fuzzy searching and matching, and spatial data handling. Again, the result is an opportunity to develop new benchmarks, benchmarks that can proxy for the requirements of emerging Big Data applications, in order to evaluate and drive the work being done in these key new areas of BDMS functionality.

**Acknowledgments.** The work to date on the ASTERIX project at UC Irvine has been supported by NSF IIS awards 0910989 and 0844574, by a grant from the University of California Discovery program with a matching donation from eBay, by a Facebook Fellowship award and several graduate Yahoo! Key Scientific Challenges awards, and through the provision of access by Yahoo! Research to one of their large research computing clusters. The ideas shared here owe much to discussions over the years with the co-developers of prior benchmarks, particularly David DeWitt and Jeffrey Naughton, as well as with the co-leads of the ASTERIX project, particularly Vinayak Borkar and Chen Li at UCI.

# References

1. Alsubaiee, S., Behm, A., Grover, R., Vernica, R., Borkar, V., Carey, M., Li, C.: ASTERIX: Scalable Warehouse-Style Web Data Integration. In: Proc. Int'l. Workshop on Information Integration on the Web (IIWeb), Phoenix, AZ (May 2012)
2. Arasu, A., Cherniack, M., Galvez, E., Maier, D., Maskey, A., Ryvkina, E., Stonebraker, M., Tibbetts, R.: Linear Road: A Stream Data Management Benchmark. In: Proc. VLDB Conf., Toronto, Canada (August 2004)
3. Apache GridMix, http://hadoop.apache.org/mapreduce/docs/current/gridmix.html
4. Apache Hadoop, http://hadoop.apache.org/.
5. Apache Hive, https://cwiki.apache.org/confluence/display/Hive/Home
6. Apache Pig, http://pig.apache.org/.
7. Apache PigMix, https://cwiki.apache.org/confluence/display/PIG/PigMix
8. ASTERIX Project, http://asterix.ics.uci.edu/.
9. Behm, A., Borkar, V., Carey, M., Grover, R., Li, C., Onose, N., Vernica, R., Deutsch, A., Papakonstantinou, Y., Tsotras, V.: ASTERIX: Towards a Scalable, Semistructured Data Platform for Evolving-World Models. Distrib. Parallel Databases 29(3) (June 2011)
10. Borkar, V., Carey, M., Grover, R., Onose, N., Vernica, R.: Hyracks: A Flexible and Extensible Foundation for Data-Intensive Computing. In: Proc. IEEE ICDE Conf., Hanover, Germany (April 2011)
11. Borkar, V., Carey, M., Li, C.: Inside "Big Data Management": Ogres, Onions, or Parfaits? In: Proc. EDBT Conf., Berlin, Germany (March 2012)

12. Bu, Y., Borkar, V., Carey, M., Rosen, J., Polyzotis, N., Condie, T., Weimer, M., Ramakrishnan, R.: Scaling Datalog for Machine Learning on Big Data. arXiv:1203.0160v2 (cs.DB) (March 2012)
13. Carey, M., Muhanna, W.: The Performance of Multiversion Concurrency Control Algorithms. ACM Trans. on Comp. Sys. 4(4) (November 1986)
14. Carey, M., DeWitt, D., Naughton, J.: The OO7 Benchmark. In: Proc. ACM SIGMOD Conf., Washington, DC (May 1993)
15. Carey, M., DeWitt, D., Kant, C., Naughton, J.: A Status Report on the OO7 OODBMS Benchmarking Effort. In: Proc. ACM OOPSLA Conf., Portland, OR (October 1994)
16. Carey, M., DeWitt, D., Naughton, J., Asgarian, M., Brown, P., Gehrke, J., Shah, D.: The BUCKY Object-Relational Benchmark. In: Proc. ACM SIGMOD Conf., Tucson, AZ (May 1997)
17. Carey, M.J., Ling, L., Nicola, M., Shao, L.: EXRT: Towards a Simple Benchmark for XML Readiness Testing. In: Nambiar, R., Poess, M. (eds.) TPCTC 2010. LNCS, vol. 6417, pp. 93–109. Springer, Heidelberg (2011)
18. Cattell, R.: Scalable SQL and NoSQL Data Stores. ACM SIGMOD Rec. 39(4) (December 2010)
19. Chaiken, R., Jenkins, B., Larson, P., Ramsey, B., Shakib, D., Weaver, S., Zhou, J.: SCOPE: Easy and Efficient Parallel Processing of Massive Data Sets. Proc. VLDB Endow. 1(2) (August 2008)
20. Cooper, B., Silberstein, A., Tam, E., Ramakrishnan, R., Sears, R.: Benchmarking Cloud Serving Systems with YCSB. In: Proc. ACM Symp. on Cloud Computing, Indianapolis, IN (May 2010)
21. Dean, J., Ghemawat, S.: MapReduce: Simplified Data Processing on Large Clusters. In: Proc. OSDI Conf. (December 2004)
22. DeWitt, D.: The Wisconsin Benchmark: Past, Present, and Future. In: [24]
23. DeWitt, D., Gray, J.: Parallel Database Systems: The Future of High Performance Database Systems. Comm. ACM 35(6) (June 1992)
24. Gray, J.: Benchmark Handbook for Database and Transaction Systems, 2nd edn. Morgan Kaufmann Publishers, San Francisco (1993)
25. Grover, R., Carey, M.: Extending Map-Reduce for Efficient Predicate-Based Sampling. In: Proc. IEEE ICDE Conf., Washington, D.C (April 2012)
26. Low, Y., Gonzalez, J., Kyrola, A., Bickson, D., Guestrin, C., Hellerstein, J.: GraphLab: A New Parallel Framework for Machine Learning. In: Proc. Conf. on Uncertainty in Artificial Intelligence (UAI), Catalina Island, CA (July 2010)
27. Malewicz, G., Austern, M., Bik, A., Dehnert, J., Horn, I., Leiser, N., Czajkowski, G.: Pregel: A System for Large-Scale Graph Processing. In: Proc. ACM SIGMOD Conf., Indianapolis, IN (May 2010)
28. Nicola, M., Kogan, I., Schiefer, B.: An XML Transaction Processing Benchmark. In: Proc. ACM SIGMOD Conf., Beijing, China (June 2007)
29. NSF Workshop on Big Data Benchmarking, http://clds.ucsd.edu/wbdb2012/
30. Pavlo, A., Paulson, E., Rasin, A., Abadi, D., DeWitt, D., Madden, S., Stonebraker, M.: A Comparison of Approaches to Large-Scale Data Analysis. In: Proc. ACM SIGMOD Conf., Providence, RI (June 2009)
31. Schmidt, A., Waas, F., Kersten, M., Carey, M., Manolescu, I., Busse, R.: XMark: A Benchmark for XML Data Management. In: Proc. VLDB Conf., Hong Kong, China (August 2002)
32. Serlin, O.: The History of DebitCredit and the TPC. In: [24]
33. Stonebraker, M., Brown, P., Poliakov, A., Raman, S.: The Architecture of SciDB. In: Proc. SSDBM Conf., Portland, OR (July 2011)

# Data Historians in the Data Management Landscape

Brice Chardin[1,2], Jean-Marc Lacombe[1], and Jean-Marc Petit[2]

[1] EDF R&D, France
[2] Université de Lyon, CNRS,
INSA-Lyon, LIRIS, UMR5205, F-69621, France

**Abstract.** At EDF, a leading energy company, process data produced in power stations are archived both to comply with legal archiving requirements and to perform various analysis applications. Such data consist of timestamped measurements, retrieved for the most part from process data acquisition systems. After archival, past and current values are used for various applications, including device monitoring, maintenance assistance, decision support, statistics publication, etc.

Large amounts of data are generated in these power stations, and aggregated in soft real-time – without operational deadlines – at the plant level by local servers. For this long-term data archiving, EDF relies on data historians – like InfoPlus.21, PI or Wonderware Historian – for years. This is also true for other energy companies worldwide and, in general, industry based on automated processes.

In this paper, we aim at answering a simple, yet not so easy, question: how can data historians be placed in the data management landscape, from classical RDBMSs to NoSQL systems? To answer this question, we first give an overview of data historians, then discuss benchmarking these particular systems. Although many benchmarks are defined for conventional database management systems, none of them are appropriate for data historians. To establish a first objective basis for comparison, we therefore propose a simple benchmark inspired by EDF use cases, and give experimental results for data historians and DBMSs.

## 1 Introduction

In industrial automation, data generated by automatons – sensors and actuators – are generally used with critical real-time constraints to operate the plant. Beside this operational usage, these data streams – mainly measurements from sensors – may be mined to extract useful information for failures anticipation, plant optimization, etc.

At EDF, a worldwide leading energy company, process data produced in power stations are indeed archived for various analysis applications and to comply with legal archiving requirements. These data consist of timestamped measurements, along with meta-data on data quality, retrieved for the most part from process data acquisition systems.

R. Nambiar and M. Poess (Eds.): TPCTC 2012, LNCS 7755, pp. 124–139, 2013.

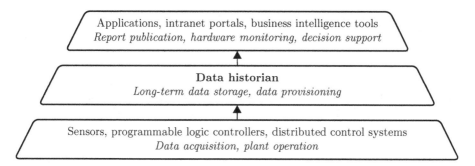

**Fig. 1.** Data historians in the production information system

These archived data – past, but also current values – are used for various applications, including devices monitoring, maintenance assistance, decision support, statistics publication, compliance with environmental regulation, etc. Data mining may also be performed, essentially with signal processing techniques: cross-correlation, filtering, dimension reduction, spectrum analysis, prediction, etc.

Power stations generate large amounts of data for thousands of measurement time series, with sampling intervals ranging from 40ms to a few seconds. This data is aggregated in soft real-time – without operational deadlines – at the plant level by local servers. For this long-term data archiving, EDF relies on data historians for years. Figure 1 gives an overview of power plants information systems at EDF, with data historians as fundamental intermediaries to access production data.

In this paper, we aim at answering a simple, yet not so easy, question: how can data historians be placed in the data management landscape, from classical relational database management systems (RDBMS) to NoSQL systems? From a practical point of view at EDF, answering such a question may have a profound impact on the choice of its data management systems. To answer this question, we first give an overview of data historians and analyze the similarities with three types of systems: RDBMS, data stream management systems (DSMS) and NoSQL systems. We then discuss benchmarking in this context. Although many benchmarks are defined for conventional database management systems, none of them are appropriate for data historians. To establish a first objective basis for comparison, we therefore propose a simple benchmark inspired by EDF use cases, and give experimental results for a data historian (InfoPlus.21), a RDBMS (MySQL) and a NoSQL system (Berkeley DB) – DSMS are not relevant for this benchmark (i.e. no continuous queries).

The purpose of this paper is not to define a new benchmark such as TPC benchmarks, but to introduce a new application lacking adapted comparison tools. All the more so data historians are proprietary systems whose performances are not documented. To the best of our knowledge, we are not aware of similar work.

*Paper organization.* An overview of data historian technologies is given in section 2. In section 3, an analysis of the differences between data historians and other data management systems is proposed. In section 4, we focus on performance comparison and define a benchmark to evaluate differences between these technologies. Results for this benchmark with a data historian, a RDBMS and a NoSQL DBMS are presented in section 5. Section 6 concludes and draws perspectives on this ongoing work.

## 2    Overview of Data Historians

In Supervisory Control And Data Acquisition (SCADA) systems, data acquisition begins with Programmable Logic Controllers (PLC) or Remote Terminal Units (RTU) which retrieve measurements from metering devices and equipment status reports. These data elements – called tags or points – represent a single input or output value monitored or controlled by the system. Tags usually appear as value-timestamp pairs.

After generation, data are eventually sent to other automatons, or monitoring servers to let human operators make supervisory decisions. Coincidentally, data may also be fed to a data historian to allow trending and other analytical auditing.

Data historians – like InfoPlus.21 [3] by AspenTech, PI [8] by OSIsoft or Wonderware Historian [5] by Invensys – are proprietary software designed to archive and query industrial automation time series data. They store time series following a hierarchical data model which reflect the operating environment. This data model should be consistent with the plant organization to ease browsing and group similar time series by subsystem.

Data historians receive data generated, for the most part, by industrial process control – Distributed Control Systems (DCS) or SCADA systems. For these purposes, they provide some business-oriented features which are not typically found within other data management systems: they support industrial communication protocols and interfaces – like OPC [7], Modbus or device manufacturers proprietary protocols – to acquire data and communicate with other DCS or SCADA software. They also receive data from other systems, occasionally provided by external entities, like production requirements or pricing informations from the Transmission System Operator, as well as meteorological forecasts. Additionally, manual insertions may occur to store measurements made by human operators.

Data historians provide fast insertion rates, with capacities reaching tens of thousand of tags processed per second. These performances are allowed by specific buffer designs, which keep recent values in volatile memory, to later write data on disk sorted by increasing timestamps. Acquired data that do not fall in the correct time window are written on reserved areas, with reduced performances, or even discarded.

To store large amounts of data with minimum disk usage and acceptable approximation errors, data historians often rely on efficient data compression engines, lossy or lossless. Each tag is then associated with rules conditioning new values archival – for example: storage at each modification, with a sampling interval, or with constant or linear approximation deviation thresholds.

Regarding information retrieval, data historians are fundamental intermediary in the technical information systems, providing data for plant operating applications – like device monitoring or system maintenance – and business intelligence – like decision support, statistics publication or economic monitoring. These applications might benefit from data historians time series specific features, especially interpolation and re-sampling, or retrieve values pre-computed from raw data. Values not measured directly, auxiliary power consumption or fuel cost for example, key performance indicators, diagnostics or informations on availability may be computed and archived by data historians.

Visualization features are dispensed by standard clients supplied with data historians. They ease exploitation of archived data by displaying plots, tables, statistics or other synoptics. These clients allow efficient time series trending by retrieving only representative inflection points for the considered time range.

Data historians also provide a SQL interface, with proprietary extensions for their specific features, and offer some continuous queries capabilities, to trigger alarms for instance.

Roughly speaking, data historians can be characterized by:

- a simple schema structure, based on tags,
- a SQL interface,
- a NoSQL interface for insertions, but also to retrieve data from time series, eventually with filtering, resampling or aggregate calculations,
- a design for high volume append-only data,
- built-in specialized applications for industrial data,
- no support for transactions,
- a centralized architecture.

# 3   Data Historians and Other Data Management Systems

## 3.1   Data Historians and RDBMS

The hierarchical data model might be convenient to represent data according to the plant organization, but the relational model might be preferred to easily integrate other data. Moreover, data historians mostly acquire time series: other data may not be supported; they can hardly be used for relational databases. Besides, even if data historians support SQL queries, they might have limitations with their query optimizers and their compliance with the entire SQL standard. For these reasons, some data historians can be associated with a RDBMS to store relational data.

Additionally, data historians do not support transactions and might not guarantee data durability for most recent measurements, even if they often provide several levels of buffers across the network to prevent data loss during server or network failures.

## 3.2    Data Historians and NoSQL Systems

Data historians provide a dedicated non-SQL interface for insertion and retrieval. Insertions are functionally comparable to SQL insert statements, with improved performances as these routines avoid parsing and type conversions. The retrieval interface however differ significantly from SQL. Extraction queries can be defined with filtering conditions (typically using value thresholds or status verification), resampling intervals and aggregate calculations over time periods. While filtering conditions are straightforward to translate in SQL, aggregate calculations grouped by time periods (e.g. timestamp÷period) might not be handled efficiently by query optimizers. Interpolated values (with various interpolation algorithms) can be tedious to define, both in SQL and with usual NoSQL interfaces, especially when combining multiple time series with different sampling periods.

Nevertheless, ordered key-value data stores provide closely related NoSQL access methods, like Berkeley DB cursor operations [6]. These cursors can be set to a specified key value, and incremented by key order – to retrieve consecutive values of a time series in this context. However, data historian interface is specialized, and thus combine several usual algorithms and processing techniques besides raw data retrieval.

NoSQL systems can typically be distributed over multiple servers. For data historians, this horizontal scalability is separated between replication and distribution. Load balancing for data retrieval is provided by replication, where multiple servers hold the same data and are individually able to serve extraction queries. However, this architecture does not decrease insertion workloads: data distribution is achieved declaratively, by associating a tag with a specific server – which might then be replicated. Therefore, data historians provide only limited load-balancing and horizontal scalability in comparison with most NoSQL systems. However, data retrieval relies on an efficient NoSQL interface for range queries. Typically, key-value stores using distributed hash tables are not suitable, which makes scalability a complex issue.

## 3.3    Data Historians and DSMS

Data stream management systems provide continuous queries capabilities as an extension of SQL [1] or appear as an extension on top of a classical RDBMS such as Oracle. Such systems typically process data over a relatively short time-window to execute continuous queries.

As far as insertions are concerned, data historians have similar mechanisms as they associate their write buffer with a time window, rejecting or inserting with lower performances data falling out of range. However, in our context, continuous queries are handled by specific monitoring and process control systems, with real-time constraints due to their critical aspect; while long-term data archiving is provided by data historians.

Yet, a new generation of DSMS allows long-term analysis of historical data by warehousing data streams. These stream warehouse systems still focus on continuous queries, which is not the purpose of data historians. As for data transfer and archiving, "a stream warehouse ... receives a wide range of data feeds from disparate, far-flung, and uncontrolled sources" [4], which is not true in the context of industrial automation.

### 3.4   Synthesis

Data historians are products designed and sold for a specific industrial use. Other data management systems might have a wider range of applications, at a possibly lower cost, but do not include most of the business-oriented features included in data historians. These systems typically can neither acquire data from process control systems with industrial communication protocols, nor use lossy compression, interpolation or re-sampling on time series.

To sum up, the match between data historians and other data management systems is clearly imperfect:

− no data distribution,
− no transactions,
− only raw sensor data (no images, no blobs, etc.).

Despite these differences, using a RDBMS or a NoSQL system for industrial data seems feasible with some functional restrictions, even if not yet adopted by the market. As data historian manufacturers advertise high insertion speeds, we ought to investigate the capacity of other data management systems to sustain industrial automation workloads before considering them for production purposes.

Benchmarking these systems would help evaluating performance differences, otherwise unavailable. Still, this comparison turns out to be not so easy, the functionalities, the interfaces, the underlying data model being quite different.

As a matter of fact, we focus on simple data-centric operations (queries) over a generic database schema. To initiate this comparison, we propose a micro-benchmark and run it against a data historian, an ordered key-value store and a RDBMS, which have been optimized for this context.

## 4   Micro-benchmark

Although many benchmarks are defined for relational database management systems, like TPC-C or TPC-H [9,10], to the best of our knowledge, none of them are designed for data historians. The idea of comparing these systems with an existing benchmark − designed for RDBMS − seems natural. However, in the context of industrial data at EDF, it seemed impractical to use one of the Transaction Processing Performance Council benchmarks for the following reasons:

− Data historians are not necessarily ACID-compliant, and generally do not support transactions.

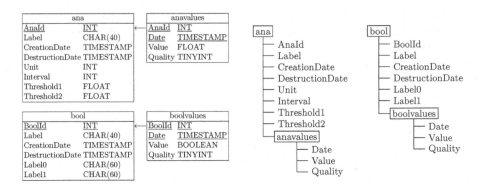

**Fig. 2.** Logical relational schema    **Fig. 3.** Hierarchical schema for data historian

- Insertion is a fundamental operation for data historians. This type of query is executed in real-time, which prevent using benchmarks that batch insertions, like TPC-H.
- Data historians are designed to handle time series data. It is mandatory that the benchmark focuses on this type of data for results to be relevant.

Benchmarks for data stream management systems, like Linear Road [2] can also be considered; but data historians do not comprehensively handle continuous queries. Data historians – and RDBMS for that matter – use a different design by storing every data for future data mining operations. In DSMS benchmarks, even historical queries use a first level of aggregation on raw data, which is not representative of data historian utilizations at EDF.

To compare data historians and RDBMS performances, we defined a benchmark inspired by the scenario of nuclear power plants data historization. In this context, data generated by sensors distributed on the plant site are aggregated by a daemon communicating with the data historian. For insertions, the benchmark simulates this daemon and pseudo-randomly generate data to be inserted.

This data is then accessible for remote users, which can send queries to update, retrieve or analyze this data. After the insertion phase, this benchmark proposes a simple yet representative set of such queries.

### 4.1    Database Schema

This benchmark deals with data according to a minimal database schema, centered upon times series data and simplified from EDF nuclear power plants schema. For each variable type – analog or boolean – a description table is defined (*ana* and *bool*). Measurements are stored in separate tables (*anavalues* and *boolvalues*). Figure 2 shows the logical relational schema for this benchmark.

Each time series is associated with an identifier (AnaId or BoolId), a short textual description – or name – (Label), a creation date (CreationDate) and a destruction date (DestructionDate). For analog values, the description table *ana* also contains the unit of measurement (Unit), which is usually described in a separate table discarded for this benchmark, a theoretical sampling interval (Interval) and two thresholds indicating if the measured value is critically low (Threshold1) or critically high (Threshold2). For boolean values, the description table *bool* contains two short descriptions associated with values 0 (Label0) and 1 (Label1).

Times series are stored in tables *anavalues* and *boolvalues*, which contains the time series identifier (AnaId or BoolId), the timestamp with millisecond precision (Date), the value (Value) and a small array of eight bits for meta-data – data quality – (Quality).

For this benchmark to be compatible with hierarchical data models used by data historians, the relational model defined previously can not be mandatory. In figure 3, we propose an equivalent hierarchical schema, representing the same data and allowing functionally equivalent queries to be executed.

## 4.2 Query Workload

By defining twelve queries, representative of EDF practices, this benchmark aims at giving an overview of data historians or RDBMS prevalence. Parameters generated at run time are in brackets. These parameters are exactly the same between each benchmark execution, to obtain identical data and queries. Queries are executed one by one in a fixed order; interactions are currently not evaluated with this benchmark to keep its definition simple and alleviate performances analysis. As some queries tend to have similar definitions, we do not express every SQL statement in this paper.

**Insertion.** Data insertion is a fundamental operation for data historians. To optimize these queries, the interface and language are not imposed (ie. these queries can be translated from SQL to any language or API call, whichever maximizes performances).

*Q0.1* Analog values insertions

```
INSERT INTO anavalues VALUES
  ([ID],[DATE],[VAL],[QUALITY])
```

*Q0.2* Boolean values insertions

**Updates.** Data updates, retrieval and analysis are usually performed by end-users; performance constraints are more flexible compared with insertions.

*Q1.1* Update an analog value. The Quality attribute is updated to reflect a manual modification of the data.

```
UPDATE anavalues
SET Value = [VAL], Quality = (Quality | 128)
WHERE AnaId = [ID] AND Date = [DATE]
```

*Q1.2* Update a boolean value. The Quality attribute is updated to reflect a manual modification of the data.

**Data Retrieval and Analysis.** This benchmark defines nine such queries to evaluate the performances of each system, and identify specific optimizations for some types of queries. Queries without parameters (Q11.1 and Q11.2) are executed only once to refrain from using query caches – storing results in order not to re-evaluate the query. NoSQL equivalent queries should provide the same results. We provide two exemples, for Q2.1 and Q9, using a cursor-based interface, which can be positioned (`position`) and incremented (`readnext`).

### Raw Data Extraction

*Q2.1* Extract raw data for an analog time series between two Dates, sorted with increasing Date values.

```
SELECT * FROM anavalues
WHERE AnaId = [ID] AND Date BETWEEN [START] AND [END]
ORDER BY Date ASC
```

---
**Algorithm 1:** Q2.1 NoSQL query

---
   **input:** id, start, end

1 `position((`id, start`))`;
2 key, value ← `readnext()`;
3 **while** key < *(*id, end*)* **do**
4    | key, value ← `readnext()`;

---

*Q2.2* Extract raw data for a boolean time series between two Dates, sorted with increasing Date values.

### Aggregate Queries

*Q3.1* Extract data quantity for an analog time series between two Dates.

```
SELECT count(*) FROM anavalues
WHERE AnaId = [ID]
   AND Date BETWEEN [START] AND [END]
```

*Q3.2* Extract data quantity for a boolean time series between two Dates.

*Q4* Extract the sum of an analog time series between two Dates.

*Q5* Extract the average of an analog time series between two Dates.

*Q6* Extract the minimum and maximum values of an analog time series between two Dates.

### Filtering on Value

*Q7* Extract analog values above the threshold indicated in its description (ana.Threshold2).

```
SELECT Date, Value FROM ana, anavalues
WHERE ana.AnaId = anavalues.AnaId
```

```
AND  ana.AnaId = [ID]
AND  Date BETWEEN [START] AND [END]
AND  Value > ana.Threshold2
```

*Q8* Extract analog values above a given threshold.

```
SELECT Date, Value FROM anavalues
WHERE AnaId = [ID]
  AND Date BETWEEN [START] AND [END]
  AND Value > [THRESHOLD]
```

## Aggregate with Value Filtering on Multiple Time Series

*Q9* Identify the time series whose values most often do not fall between its high and low thresholds.

```
SELECT Label, count(*) as count FROM ana, anavalues
WHERE ana.AnaId = anavalues.AnaId
  AND Date BETWEEN [START] AND [END]
  AND (Value > Threshold2 OR Value < Threshold1)
GROUP BY ana.AnaId, Label ORDER BY count DESC LIMIT 1
```

---

**Algorithm 2:** Q9 NoSQL query

---

  **input**: start, end

1 **foreach** id *in* ana.AnaId **do**
2      count[id] ← 0;
3      threshold1 ← ana[id].Threshold1;
4      threshold2 ← ana[id].Threshold2;
5      position((id, start));
6      key, value ← readnext();
7      **while** key < (id, end) **do**
8          **if** value.Value < threshold1 *or* value.Value > threshold2 **then**
9              count[id]++;
10          key, value ← readnext();
11 result_id ← i: ∀ id, count[id] ≤ count[i];
12 return(ana[result_id].Label, count[result_id]);

---

## Sampling Period Verification on Multiple Time Series

*Q10* Identify the time series whose sampling period do not, by the greatest margin, comply with its description

```
SELECT values.AnaId, count(*) as count FROM ana,
(
   SELECT D1.AnaId, D1.Date,
          min(D2.Date-D1.Date) as Interval
```

```
    FROM anavalues D1, anavalues D2
    WHERE D2.Date > D1.Date
      AND D1.AnaId = D2.AnaId
      AND D1.Date BETWEEN [START] AND [END]
    GROUP BY D1.AnaId, D1.Date
) as values
WHERE values.AnaId = ana.AnaId
  AND values.Interval > ana.Interval
GROUP BY values.AnaId ORDER BY count DESC LIMIT 1
```

### Current Values Extraction

*Q11.1* Extract most recent values for each analog time series.

```
SELECT AnaId, Value FROM anavalues
WHERE (AnaId, Date) IN
(
  SELECT AnaId, max(Date) FROM anavalues
  GROUP BY AnaId
)
ORDER BY AnaId
```

*Q11.2* Extract most recent values for each boolean time series.

## 5    Experiments

For the time being, this benchmark has been run against the data historian InfoPlus.21, the RDBMS MySQL, and the NoSQL DBMS Berkeley DB.

Data historians are proprietary softwares with distinctive designs and thus, performances. Given the EDF requirements, we chose InfoPlus.21, one of the most widespread data historians.

We selected the open source RDBMS MySQL due to its ease of use and for being perennial with a large user community, compulsory for industrial use. In our context, tuples are relatively small (e.g. 17 bytes for anavalues), and most columns are typically accessed. Additionally, query selectivity is low – ie. most tuples match the criteria – within the considered key range. These properties narrow down the benefits of using a column-oriented DBMS.

Lastly, we chose the ordered key-value store Berkeley DB, an open source library for embedded databases, for our experiments. This class of NoSQL systems adapts well to our typical usage based on range queries.

*MySQL physical tuning.* The following results have been gathered with the InnoDB storage engine. The MyISAM storage engine has also been tested, but performances did not scale well with the amount of data, except for insertions. Results with MyISAM are not detailed in this paper.

By default, InnoDB uses a clustered index on the primary key – here (AnaId, Date) and (BoolId, Date). Given the queries of this benchmark, and, altogether, typical queries on historical data at EDF, these indexes appear to be efficient for most of these. We did not define any additional index in order not to slow down insertions.

InnoDB is a transactional storage engine, which limits its ability to buffer insertions. As a result, we disabled this functionality by setting the following options:

```
innodb_flush_log_at_trx_commit=0
innodb_support_xa=0
innodb_doublewrite=0
```

To avoid parsing neither queries nor data, the benchmark uses MySQL C API prepared statements for insertions. Additionally, as MySQL allocates only one thread per connection, multi-threading is achieved by opening multiple parallel accesses (4 has been experimentally determined to maximize performances).

With their SQL definitions, queries Q9 and Q10 are not processed efficiently by MySQL – for instance, MySQL does not divide Q9 into multiple smaller range queries (one for each tag). This issue is solved by using stored procedures.

*Berkeley DB physical tuning.* Berkeley DB transactional capabilities are also minimized to improve performances. DB_TXN_NOSYNC is set to disable synchronous log flushing on transaction commit. This means that transactions exhibit the ACI (atomicity, consistency, and isolation) properties, but not D (durability).

Write cursors (one per tag) are configured to optimize for bulk operations: each successive operation attempts to continue on the same database page as the previous operation.

The database is partitioned, with one partition per tag. Without partitions, insertions are about 60% slower.

For all systems, test servers are composed of a Xeon Quad Core E5405 2.0GHz processor, 3GB RAM and three 73GB 10K Hard Disk Drives with a RAID 5 Controller. For our experiments, only one processor core is activated due to a lack of optimization of our data historian for multi-threaded insertions.

Inserted data amounts to 500,000,000 tuples for each data type – analog and boolean – which sums to 11.5 GB without compression (and timestamps stored on 8 bytes). These tuples are divided between 200 time series (100 for each data type), individually designated by their identifier (AnaId or BoolId). 1,000,000 updates for each data type are then queried against the database; followed by up to 1000 SFW queries – 100 for Q9 and Q10, 1 for Q11.1 and Q11.2 – with different parameters. Date parameters for queries Q2 to Q8 are generated to access 100,000 tuples on average. Q9 and Q10 involve all analog time series, therefore each execution access 10,000,000 tuples on average.

Table 1 reports detailed results for each system. For instance, line 1 means thet executing Q0.1 500M times took 8 003.4 seconds for InfoPlus.21, 24 671.7 seconds for MySQL and 2 849.6 seconds for Berkeley DB. Figure 4 gives an overview of performance differences.

**Table 1.** Query execution times

| Query type | | Execution time (in s) | | |
|---|---|---|---|---|
| | (amount) | InfoPlus.21 | MySQL | Berkeley DB |
| Q0.1 | (×500M) | 8 003.4 | 24 671.7 | 2 849.6 |
| Q0.2 | (×500M) | 7 085.8 | 24 086.0 | 3 115.8 |
| Q1.1 | (×1M) | 16 762.8 | 12 239.5 | 9 031.5 |
| Q1.2 | (×1M) | 16 071.3 | 13 088.2 | 9 348.5 |
| Q2.1 | (×1000) | 267.6 | 410.4 | 693.0 |
| Q2.2 | (×1000) | 215.1 | 284.5 | 655.4 |
| Q3.1 | (×1000) | 252.5 | 186.6 | 531.4 |
| Q3.2 | (×1000) | 216.7 | 181.8 | 533.2 |
| Q4 | (×1000) | 263.0 | 192.6 | 536.8 |
| Q5 | (×1000) | 236.7 | 185.7 | 514.0 |
| Q6 | (×1000) | 235.6 | 191.9 | 513.1 |
| Q7 | (×1000) | 234.0 | 234.2 | 507.7 |
| Q8 | (×1000) | 231.2 | 277.7 | 506.5 |
| Q9 | (×100) | 1 640.6 | 1 710.0 | 4 877.7 |
| Q10 | (×100) | 1 688.8 | 7 660.7 | 4 977.5 |
| Q11.1 | (×1) | $9.5 \times 10^{-3}$ | 1.15 | 2.75 |
| Q11.2 | (×1) | $2.8 \times 10^{-4}$ | 1.13 | 4.81 |

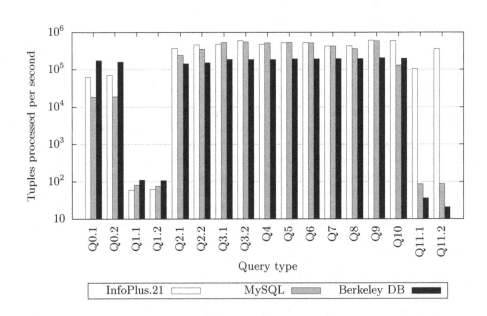

**Fig. 4.** Processing capacity

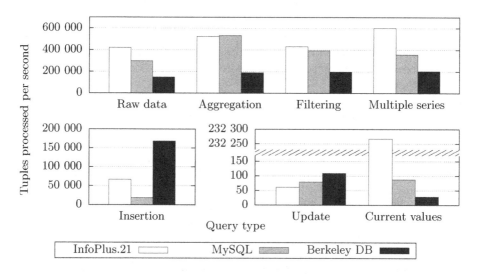

**Fig. 5.** Processing capacity by category

Different queries from the same category reporting similar performances ratios
– ie. Q3, Q4, Q5 and Q6 for aggregate queries, and Q7 and Q8 for value filtering
– are merged in figure 5 to summarize these results.

As advertised, data historians handle insertions efficiently compared to
RDBMS: InfoPlus.21 reaches 66,500 insertions per second (ips), which is about
3.2× faster than InnoDB and its 20,500 ips.

Yet, Berkeley DB reaches 168,000 ips, that is, 2.5× faster that InfoPlus.21.
However, it was used as an embedded library, without inter-process communication, which might significantly improve performances compared with MySQL
or InfoPlus.21.

Current values extractions (Q11.1 and Q11.2) is the second anticipated
strength of data historians, given their particular design with current values
staying in main memory. This operation is performed several orders of magnitude faster than with MySQL (×1 850) or Berkeley DB (×6 140).

Additionally, InfoPlus.21 is faster for queries returning large results (Q2, Q7
and Q8). Since the SQL interface of MySQL involve some parsing overhead due
to type conversions, we believe this overhead is important as we observed the
same behavior with InfoPlus.21 SQL interface.

As for Q9 and Q10, InfoPlus.21 is faster than other systems. Physical data
layouts possibly explain this behavior: InnoDB and Berkeley DB order their data
according to the primary key (AnaId, Date), while data historians sort data by
Date. In contrast with other queries, Q9 and Q10 investigates every time series,
which are gathered in our data historian, but consist in several clusters with
MySQL or Berkeley DB.

Apart from these queries, MySQL is slightly faster than our data historian on
single time series (Q3, Q4, Q5 and Q6).

Overall performances for all systems, although notably different, are of the same order of magnitude, and do not ban RDBMS nor NoSQL systems from archiving industrial process data. Still, before considering any system for production purposes, additional studies with more realistic workloads are mandatory to attest their usability.

## 6   Conclusion

In this paper, we first highlighted data historization as a concurrent market segment with significant industrial needs. We then compared performances between a data historian (InfoPlus.21), a RDBMS (MySQL) and a NoSQL system (Berkeley DB) using a benchmark derived from a significant use case within EDF.

In light of our first experimental results, data historians could still be challenged when abstracting some business-oriented features. Lossy data compression, as well as efficient interpolation and resampling might involve important changes to the core of a DBMS, but industrial communication protocol support and various business-oriented clients supplied with data historians could be provided with independent specific developments. Disregarding business-oriented features, it makes sense to consider conventional DBMS for such industrial applications. Yet, in this context, specific optimizations for time series data insertions would bring value to relational data management systems, as this operation is critical for data historization.

To date, no benchmark is set as a standard to compare data historians together, nor analyze conventional DBMSs performances with regard to industrial automation data management.

## References

1. Arasu, A., Babcock, B., Babu, S., Datar, M., Ito, K., Motwani, R., Nishizawa, I., Srivastava, U., Thomas, D., Varma, R., Widom, J.: STREAM: The Stanford Stream Data Manager. IEEE Data Engineering Bulletin 26(1), 19–26 (2003)
2. Arasu, A., Cherniack, M., Galvez, E., Maier, D., Maskey, A.S., Ryvkina, E., Stonebraker, M., Tibbetts, R.: Linear Road: A Stream Data Management Benchmark. In: VLDB 2004: Proceedings of the Thirtieth International Conference on Very Large Data Bases, pp. 480–491 (2004)
3. Aspen Technology. Database Developer's Manual (2007)
4. Golab, L., Johnson, T.: Consistency in a Stream Warehouse. In: CIDR 2011: Proceedings of the Fifth Biennial Conference on Innovative Data Systems Research, pp. 114–122 (2011)
5. Invensys Systems. Wonderware Historian 9.0 High-Performance Historian Database and Information Server (2007)
6. Olson, M.A., Bostic, K., Seltzer, M.I.: Berkeley DB. In: Proceedings of the FREENIX Track: 1999 USENIX Annual Technical Conference, pp. 183–191 (1999)

7. OPC Foundation. Data Access Custom Interface Standard (2003)
8. OSIsoft. PI Server System Management Guide (2009)
9. Transaction Processing Performance Council. TPC Benchmark C Standard Specification (2007)
10. Transaction Processing Performance Council. TPC Benchmark H Standard Specification (2008)

# Scalable Generation of Synthetic GPS Traces with Real-Life Data Characteristics*

Konrad Bösche[1], Thibault Sellam[2], Holger Pirk[2], René Beier[1], Peter Mieth[1], and Stefan Manegold[2]

[1] TomTom, Berlin, Germany
{first.last}@tomtom.com
[2] Centrum Wiskunde & Informatica (CWI), Amsterdam, The Netherlands
{first.last}@cwi.nl

**Abstract.** Database benchmarking is most valuable if real-life data and workloads are available. However, real-life data (and workloads) are often not publicly available due to IPR constraints or privacy concerns. And even if available, they are often limited regarding scalability and variability of data characteristics. On the other hand, while easily scalable, synthetically generated data often fail to adequately reflect real-life data characteristics. While there are well established synthetic benchmarks and data generators for, e.g., business data (TPC-C, TPC-H), there is no such up-to-date data generator, let alone benchmark, for spatiotemporal and/or moving objects data.

In this work, we present a data generator for spatiotemporal data. More specifically, our data generator produces synthetic GPS traces, mimicking the GPS traces that GPS navigation devices generate. To this end, our generator is fed with real-life statistical profiles derived from the user base and uses real-world road network information. Spatial scalability is achieved by choosing statistics from different regions. The data volume can be scaled by tuning the number and length of the generated trajectories. We compare the generated data to real-life data to demonstrate how well the synthetically generated data reflects real-life data characteristics.

## 1 Introduction

Performance is one of the major selling points of Database Management Systems (DBMSs). However, objectively capturing DBMS performance is hard. The data management community has defined many benchmarks to capture DBMS performance in a single, or at least few, numbers. However, designing a representative benchmark, i.e., one that makes it easy for potential users to extrapolate a DBMS's performance for their application from the benchmark results, is hard. A representative benchmark must contain at least a) a representative query set and b) a representative database that the queries are performed on. A reasonably small, yet representative set of queries is hard to find and beyond the focus of

---

* This publication was supported by the Dutch national program COMMIT.

R. Nambiar and M. Poess (Eds.): TPCTC 2012, LNCS 7755, pp. 140–155, 2013.
© Springer-Verlag Berlin Heidelberg 2013

this paper. A representative dataset for applications of a given domain, however, may be achievable. We focus entirely on the generation of such a representative dataset for the domain of (historical) moving objects data management.

Traditionally, there have been two ways to achieve such a representative dataset. The first is to start with a real-life dataset and stripping it down to the minimal database that is still representative for the application. The second is to synthetically generate a representative dataset from scratch. Both of these approaches have their merits and problems that we discuss in the following.

*Real-Life Data* is a good basis for a representative dataset because it has the desired characteristics. The distribution and correlation of the values, e.g., can have a large impact on the performance of applications on top of the data. These effects will be discovered when evaluating a system using a real-life dataset. However, a real-life dataset lacks the configurability of a synthetic dataset, most importantly, regarding its size. Since a real-life dataset is always a snapshot of the application data at a given time, it can not be used for what-if-analysis. This makes it hard to detect, e.g., future scalability problems. In addition, real-life data is often sensitive with respect to user privacy. Especially when tracking user positions, a dataset could be used to generate presence/absence profiles of people. It could even be matched to an address database to identify individuals. Both of these problems can be addressed by synthetically generating data.

*Synthetic Data* is naturally anonymized since it never contains data about real users. In addition to that, synthetic data can, usually, be generated at any *scale-factor* (i.e., dataset size). However, care must be taken to generate data that resembles the characteristics of real-life data of the targeted applications. This is usually achieved by encoding domain specific rules into the data generator. However, these rules are not only tedious to create. The manual creation of rules is also error prone and might not consider all relevant characteristics of the data.

To resolve the conflict between realistic and scalable representative datasets, we propose to use a hybrid approach that is illustrated in Figure 1. Datasets are based on a "sample" dataset. Statistics are extracted from this sample dataset and combined with a model of the domain to produce a scalable dataset that closely resembles real-life data. In our case we distinguish a user

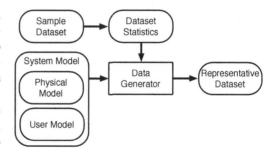

**Fig. 1.** Overview Hybrid Dataset Generation

model and a physical model. The user model represents the intention of a user (e.g., the route a user takes between two points). The physical model captures constraints that are given by the real world (speed limits, traffic lights, ...).

To present our approach, we structured the rest of this paper as follows: In Section 2 we present the requirements for realistic Global Positioning System (GPS) data and other approaches to generate data that fulfills these requirements. In Section 3 we describe our approach to generate GPS data from sample data and a physical model. We evaluate the quality of the generated data as well as the generator performance in Section 4 and conclude in Section 5.

## 2    Background

### 2.1    Use Cases and Requirements

Traffic data is the basis for many applications. To illustrate the benefit of our data generator, we want to briefly discuss the range of applications that can be evaluated using the generated data. We target at least two types of applications that can be classified into the well known domains of Online Transaction Processing (OLTP) and Online Analytical Processing (OLAP): Location Based Services and Traffic Monitoring and Analysis.

Location Based Services aim at providing end-users with answers to geo-spatial queries that involve their current position. Typical queries are: *"What are the three closest restaurants to me?"*, *"What is the best route to avoid this traffic jam?"* or *"Where can I meet up with my husband within half an hour?"*. Low query latency is critical to achieve a good end user experience. However, few queries require historical data which limits the amount of considered data.

Traffic Monitoring and Analysis applications have very different characteristics. The goal is to provide an insight into the traffic at a macro scale, often focusing on trends that develop over time. Queries such as *"Which were the busiest routes in Europe this year?"* or *"What is the impact of a new road on regional traffic?"* naturally involve data acquired over a period of time. On the one hand, the large data volume of traffic monitoring applications poses a challenge. On the other hand, low query latency is less critical.

While targeting all of these cases, we limit our simulation to road-bound vehicles that are tracked using GPS. There are no restrictions on the streets (city or highway), time, or region. However, the generator should produce data that resembles real GPS data, including factors like precision and noise.

In practice, GPS devices produce *fixes* (i.e., samples) that are defined by four attributes: `trace_id`, `longitude`, `latitude` and `time`. The first field is a code that identifies the GPS device for a certain period of time, e.g., one day. The next two fields are the GPS coordinates in degrees at a precision of 5 decimals. The time is the unix timestamp, i.e., time at a resolution of one second.

### 2.2    Spatio-temporal Data Generation

**Moving Objects.** For the last decade, the interest for Moving Objects databases has led to the creation of several dedicated generators.

The *GSTD* algorithm (Generate_Spatio_Temporal_Data) [11] is one of the first contributions. It generates a set of points or rectangular regions according to a predefined distribution (e.g., Gaussian). These objects are then translated and resized by random functions with user-defined parameters. This algorithm is extended in [7] to create more realistic data. New parameters affect the direction shifts, and some objects move in clusters. More importantly, an infrastructure is introduced. The system generates a set of rectangles in which the objects cannot enter. This is the first attempt to impose *constraints* on the movements. The Oporto generator [10] is based on an other approach. It simulates swarms of fish and ships using *attraction* and *repulsion* between the moving objects.

These projects offer different levels of control over the trajectories, and several refinements were introduced to avoid a fully chaotic behavior. Nevertheless, none of them can simulate environment constraints such as road networks.

**Traffic Simulators.** Many traffic simulators have been proposed, with various objectives. The transportation engineering community makes heavy use of micro-scale simulators, that aim at generating short term traffic conditions with physical models. For instance, DRACULA [8] creates urban mobility patterns. The work presented in [9] generates highway traffic with a parallel architecture. Our objective is different. First, we aim at creating large amounts of data in a short time. These micro-simulators target high precision rather than volume. Second, we require realistic data about collective behaviors over large periods of time (e.g., the Netherlands during a month). These solutions target short term vehicle movements at a local scale. The intentions of the travelers (where they come from, where they are going, when the next trip will be) may not be accurate [3].

The data management community proposed several large scale generators. The closest project to ours is presented by Brinkhoff [1]. It is based on network information and routing functions defined by the user. Each edge of the network has a user-specified maximum capacity and speed. Moving objects are created at each timestamp, travel, then "disappear" when they reached their destination. The speed of object creation and their routing is defined by user functions. Our approach differs on two points. First, the data generation does not depend on arbitrary user defined functions or parameters: we use historical data. Second, we maintain consistency between the trips of a same vehicle. The benchmark Berlin-MOD [3] contains a realistic data generation algorithm. Nevertheless, it relies on several rules fine-tuned for the benchmark use-case (the traffic of Berlin).

## 3   Generating Trajectory Data

The simulated GPS data is generated in three steps. First we gather statistics about real world historical GPS data collected from in-car navigation devices and use these to randomly generate Origin-Destination (OD) pairs with similar characteristics. These OD pairs describe the geographical start and end of a sequence of GPS points (i.e., a *trip*). In the next step, we calculate a trajectory between the two points of each OD pair using a route finding algorithm. We use a digital map of the road network in the considered area to compute the fastest route. In the last step, we apply time dependent speed limitations for each edge of the map. In the rest of this section we describe each of these steps in detail.

## 3.1   Generating Origin-Destination Pairs

**Gathering Statistics.** The collection of statistics is the first step of the synthetic trace generation. We used the TomTom GPS archive that contains more than 4 billion hours of GPS data from in-car navigation devices. First, the real-life traces are divided into trips. This is done by simply checking the temporal gaps between each pair of succeeding GPS fixes against a threshold of 15 minutes. If a gap is larger than this threshold the trace is split between the respective fixes. In addition, we use meta-data, namely device events of type "suspend", which are assigned to a certain GPS fix within the belonging trace. Of each trip, we use the first and the last point (origin and destination) for subsequent processing. We build a set of histograms on these points:

- A two dimensional equi-width histogram on the origin coordinates.
- A two dimensional equi-width histogram on the destination coordinates.
  *Note: Naturally, a finer resolution of the histogram yields better results but comes at a performance penalty. During our experiments, we found that a histogram covering the target area at a resolution of 400 by 500 cells (a.k.a. bins or buckets) yields good results at acceptable performance.*
- An equi-width (1 km) histogram on the euclidean distance between origin and destination.
- A set of histograms of the discrete values for the time and date components (year, month, day of week, minute of day) of the origins of the traces.
- A histogram of the discrete values for the GPS sampling rate.
- A histogram of the discrete values for the number of trips per device per day (trips per trace).
- A histogram of the discrete values for the pause between two trips of a device in minutes.

**The Digital Road Network.** In addition to the histograms of the GPS data samples, we use a *Digital Road Network* to simulate vehicles on real roads. In its essence, the network is a directed graph with labels on nodes and edges. Edges represent road segments and are, thus, attributed with labels that describe, e.g., speed limits, road classes or average speeds. Nodes in the digital road network are largely defined by a geographical position. However, the exact definition of a node is hard. Intersections of roads are, naturally, represented as nodes in the digital network. However, a node could also be a change of direction of the road: If two nodes are connected, we assume the connection to represent a straight road. A bent road is, therefore, represented by multiple nodes and edges. Whilst TomTom's digital road network is not disclosed, projects like OpenStreetMap [4] provide publicly available digital road networks that follow the same idea.

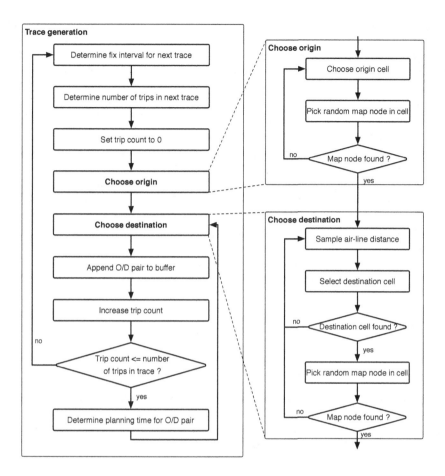

**Fig. 2.** Trace generation algorithm

**Generating OD Pairs.** As basis for the trip generation, we generate OD pairs (see Figure 2 for an overview). We will describe this process in the following.

The first step of the trace generation is setting the trace related parameters[1]. These values are sampled according to the respective histograms and form the basis for the trip simulation. Since, in reality, trips that are acquired using the same GPS device are often correlated, we have to take care to reproduce such correlations in the generated data. To illustrate this, consider the following example: a commuter generates a trip in the morning on the way to work and one trip in the evening on the way home. We call such a set of correlated trips a *trace*. Thus, we generate trips such that all trips of a given device on a given day form a trace[2]. The origin of the first trip of a trace is selected as follows: a

---

[1] GPS sampling interval, number of trips, date and time of first trip.

[2] In practice, our synthetically generated traces can span more than one day, which explains the bias towards an earlier time of day in Figure 5b.

random cell (aka. bucket) is selected according to its relative frequency in the origin histogram. From all the nodes of the digital road network that fall into the selected cell we randomly (uniform) select one to be the start point of the trip. If the cell contains no nodes, we resample a cell. The time of the first (origin) sample of the trip is chosen according to the respective distribution.

The destination of a trip is generated as follows: we randomly select an approximate value for the air-line distance between origin and destination according to the respective distribution. As the origin is already fixed we generate a set of candidate destination cells. This set contains all cells that intersect a circle around the origin with a radius of the set distance. From these, we randomly select one according to the relative frequency in the destination histogram. Within the selected destination cell we randomly (uniform) select one map node as destination. If we fail in one of the described steps, i.e., if there is no map node in the cell selected or the frequencies of the destination cell candidates are all zero, resample a new air-line distance and restart the process.

To determine the starting time of subsequent trips, we add a random idle time to the end time of the previous trip. The idle time is set according to the respective histogram.

## 3.2   Routing

Given the origin and destination of a trip our algorithm will generate GPS points along the fastest path on the digital road network. We utilize TomTom's routing kernel that is also used in their navigation devices. It uses several heuristics for accelerating the search including $A^\star$ [5] and arc-flags [6]. Accelerating shortest path computations in road network has received some attention from the scientific community in recent years [2].

## 3.3   Physical Modeling

**Simulating a Journey.** As the last step we simulate a journey on the calculated route. The idea is to virtually drive along the route and sample the position at uniform time intervals.

To generate GPS data that closely matches the individual speed characteristics of vehicles on each street of the network, we use the speed profiles from the digital road network combined with a physical model based on a set of parameters that we manually selected (see Table 1). As a basis for the speed, we use the average speed on a road segment at the given time of day and day of week. To add a realistic variance to the speed we multiply the traveling speed on each road segment with a stretch factor $ssf$. With a probability $p_{sc}$, $ssf$ is set to a

**Table 1.** Model Parameters

| Symbol | Value |
|---|---|
| $ssf_l$ | .8 |
| $ssf_h$ | 1.2 |
| $p_{sc}$ | .1 |
| $p_{stop}$ | .02 |
| $p_{stop@end}$ | .9 |
| $ts_l$ | 5s |
| $ts_h$ | 40s |
| $\sigma_{shift}$ | 3 meters |
| $p_{shift}$ | .05 |
| $p_{drift}$ | .03 |
| $\sigma_{drift}$ | 10 meters |

random value between $ssf_l$ and $ssf_h$ for a road segment. With probability $1 - p_{sc}$ it is set to the same value as the previous road segment in the trip.

In addition to the variance of the speed, vehicles occasionally have to stop, e.g., for traffic lights. Hence we occasionally stop the virtual journey at likely spots. We simulate a stop on a road segment with a probability $p_s$. The position of the stop on the road segment is determined randomly but biased towards the end of the segment. With a probability $p_{stop@end}$, the stop will occur in the last 20% of the segment (and with $1 - p_{stop@end}$ in the first 80%). The duration of the stop is set randomly between $ts_l$ and $ts_h$ seconds.

**Simulating GPS Noise.** The last step of the simulation covers GPS signal noise. To achieve a realistic noise, a semi-random perturbation is applied to each of the sampled GPS points. Two components make up the simulated noise:

- A random shift for each individual GPS point.
- A random drift over a sub-sequence of GPS points.

The former is simulated by adding a Gaussian noise to each of the two dimensions (longitude and latitude) of each GPS point. We use a distribution with mean value of 0 and with a standard deviation of $\sigma_{shift}$. However, this may lead to successive GPS points having different deviation directions. They would appear to "jump" from one side of a road to the other which is untypical for real GPS samples. To limit this effect we apply such shifts only with a probability of $p_{shift}$ per second[3]. With probability $1 - p_{shift}$ per second[3], we add the deviation of the previous point to the calculated deviation of the current point.

The second noise component, the random drift, is initiated with a probability of $p_{drift}$ per second[3]. "Drift" means a shift along the orthogonal of the current driving direction. More precisely, a shift along the orthogonal of the line defined by the predecessor and the successor of the considered point. Whenever a drift is initiated, a new maximal drift distance is determined according to a Gaussian distribution with mean 0 and standard deviation of $\sigma_{drift}$ meters. The determined maximal drift distance will then be reached from the current drift distance (0 if there is no incomplete preceding drift) within exactly 30 seconds (in case no new drift is initiated along the way). For example, this corresponds to 3 GPS points in case of GPS point interval of 10 seconds. After the maximal drift distance has been reached, the drift distance decreases to zero within 30 seconds again.

## 4    Evaluation

In order to evaluate how well our data generation approach mimics real-life data, we compare the synthetically generated data with real-life data. We do so from two different angles. First, we compare various statistical properties of both synthetically generated and real-life data. This is mainly a sanity check that the

---

[3] The probability is normalized by time between two GPS fixes in order to avoid simulating less/biased noise and drift for traces with a higher GPS sampling rate.

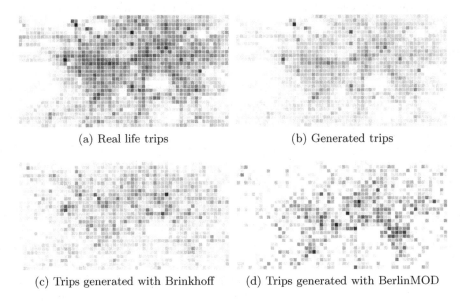

(a) Real life trips          (b) Generated trips

(c) Trips generated with Brinkhoff    (d) Trips generated with BerlinMOD

**Fig. 3.** Spatial distribution of departures

statistics extracted from real-life data are correctly used during the data generation process and thus correctly reflected in the generated data. Second, we compare the spatial distribution of real-life and synthetically generated data. Mostly visual inspection of density plots suggests that our synthetically generated data "looks very similar to" real-life data for various geographical regions at different resolutions. Finally, we assess the performance of our generator to ensure that we can generate large volumes of data in adequate time.

### 4.1 Statistical Properties of the Trips

To assess the quality of the generated data, we compare four sets of trips:

1. An archive of user traces provided by TomTom from February 2011, region of Berlin. There are 217,165 traces. We cropped the dataset to a smaller region to make comparisons possible[4].
2. A set of 135,000 traces containing 289,716 trips generated with our system. The input statistics are extracted from the first set (Berlin area, February 2011) and the generator was setup to cover the baseline region.
3. 28 days of data provided with the BerlinMOD generator. The set is publicly available[5]. We removed all the traces that did not belong to our region. The dataset is made of 111,114 trips, generated by 1589 vehicles.

---

[4] 52.42 °N - 52.56 °N, 13.22 °E - 13.50 °E.

[5] http://dna.fernuni-hagen.de/secondo/BerlinMOD/BerlinMOD.html

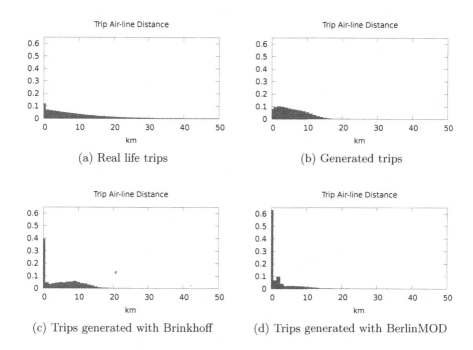

(a) Real life trips

(b) Generated trips

(c) Trips generated with Brinkhoff

(d) Trips generated with BerlinMOD

**Fig. 4.** Distribution of air-line distances

4. A set of 302,400 trips generated by the Brinkhoff generator over the same region. The transportation network was generated from the roads layer of OpenStreetMaps[6]. We used the class DefaultDataGenerator. The parameters were set in a best effort way.

**Geographical Validation.** Figure 3 describes the distributions of departures in the Berlin area for each set of trips. Our data is very close to the TomTom archive. The two other datasets exhibit fairly similar distributions.

We represent the distributions of trip air-line distances in Figure 4. The data created by our generator seems fairly realistic. One major difference is the distribution of very small values (less than 1 km). There is a small but distinct peak in the real data, which is not present in our dataset. This can be explained by the grid that we apply on the network for data generation. A side effect of this method is that very small values are often over-approximated.

The authors of BerlinMOD assume that two kind of trips may be defined. *Work trips* are very short and frequent. They are described by the first peak. Oppositely, *additional trips* are longer, less common and there is more variance in the distribution of their lengths. The same type of behavior appears in the Brinkhoff dataset. This might add realism in more urban regions.

---

[6] http://www.openstreetmap.org/

**Scheduling of the Trips.** An abstract timestamp represents time in the default Brinkhoff generator. There is no notion of hour of the day or calendar, the system has a uniform behavior at each unit of time. Also, it does not group trips in traces. Therefore, we do not consider the Brinkhoff generator in this section.

Figure 5 illustrates the time and day of the trip departures. The shape of the real-life distributions matches an urban traffic scenario: we can identify the early morning rush hours, the weekdays are busier than weekends.

Regarding the distribution of traces among the days of the week, our data is close the the real distribution. Similarly, there are less traces during the weekend in the dataset generated with BerlinMOD. However, the distribution of traces between Saturday and Sunday is different.

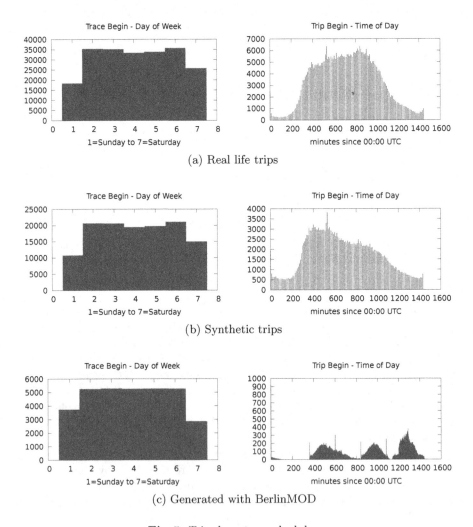

(a) Real life trips

(b) Synthetic trips

(c) Generated with BerlinMOD

**Fig. 5.** Trip departure schedules

The overall shape of the distribution of trips during the day in our dataset is similar to the original. However, it shows a slight bias to the earlier hours as explained in Footnote 2 in Section 3.1. The distributions of the BerlinMOD trips is a direct consequence of how the data is generated. The authors specify several specific times in the day, then distribute departure hours around those with Gaussian distributions. This is represented by the three peaks in the graph.

Figure 6 describes the distribution of trip durations. They are directly related to the distributions of air-line distances (Figure 4). The trips are slightly shorter in our dataset. The fact that simulated vehicles always take the shortest way explains the difference. The BerlinMOD dataset also contains shorter trips. This is a consequence of the shorter air-line distances.

## 4.2   Spatial Comparison

In order to support a spatial comparison of the generated traces with the real world traces we generate density plots at different resolutions. These are pictures where the color of each pixel encodes the number of GPS-points falling into the area represented by the pixel. In case each pixel represents a small area (less than $3 \times 3$ square meters) we give each GPS point a circular shape with radius 3 meter. Remember that the path taken between the origin and the destination of a trip depends exclusively on the digital road map and the weight function of its edges (speeds). Hence, the correctness and precision of the map used has a vital influence on the produced GPS points. As the density of regions differs largely we use a logarithmic scale for the colors. The density plots have been generated on a synthetic trace archive covering whole Europe with 1 million traces.

The first example in Figure 7 shows two pictures with density of GPS points for whole Germany. The left picture is generated from the real world data archive whereas the right picture is made from the synthetic trace archive. The different densities of the real world data are well reflected in the picture of the synthetic traces. In fact, we think it is hard to tell them apart.

The same is true also for the pictures in Figure 8 which show the densities for the region of Amsterdam. In order to use approximately the same number of

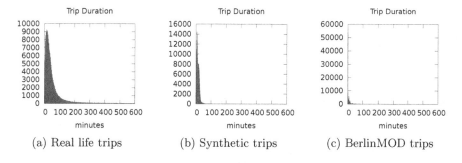

(a) Real life trips          (b) Synthetic trips          (c) BerlinMOD trips

**Fig. 6.** Trip durations

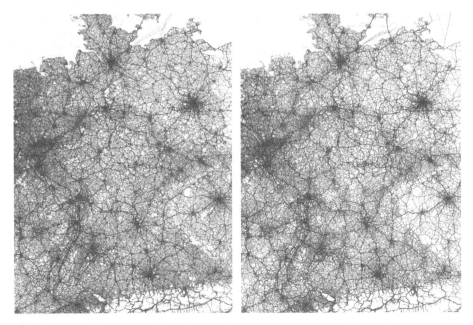

**Fig. 7.** Density of GPS points for Germany. Left: real world data. Right: synthetic data. Color coding with logarithmic scale.

**Fig. 8.** Density of GPS points for Amsterdam. Left: real world data. Right: synthetic data. Color coding with logarithmic scale.

traces we used real world GPS-data for the left picture that has been collected during one day only. The small differences in the pictures mainly come from standing or parking cars that generate a high density as they do not move (uniform sampling in time).

A more detailed view for an urban area in Berlin is shown in the pictures of Figure 9. The high densities on the left picture (real world data) are due to a large percentage of vehicles that have to wait in front of the traffic light.

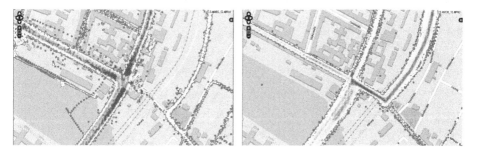

**Fig. 9.** Density of GPS points. Left (real world data): Standing cars in front of traffic lights produce higher density. Right (synthetic data): Many routes use street which is closed in reality.

The street with largest density on the right side (synthetic traces) has no density in the left picture as the road is closed in reality.

Figure 10 shows a big motorway junction south of Berlin. We observe that the real world GPS points exhibit a much smaller deviation from the center of the street compared to the synthetic traces. This is due to the local conditions (no building or trees, wide open sky) that allow much better GPS reception leading to lower noise levels. An opposite situation is shown in Figure 11 covering an urban canyon in Frankfurt/Main with large buildings impairing the GPS quality.

### 4.3   Performance Evaluation

Finally, we measure how much data our generator can generate per time.

**Setup.** The experiments were run on a machine equipped with a 3.4 GHz quad-core Intel(R) Core(TM) i7-2600 CPU (8 hardware threads, 8 MB L3 cache), 8 GB of main memory, and a 7200 RPM 1 TB Seagate Barracuda ES.2 SATA hard disk connected via USB 2.0. To evaluate the performance of our current implementation, we generated 100,000 traces with simulated GPS noise within the bounding box of Germany[7]. For this purpose, we used the following input:

- Trace/trip statistics (O/D grid cell size: 0.02 °x0.02 °) gathered from all traces within the bounding box of Germany contained in TomTom's real-life GPS data archive for 2010.
- A digital map of the entire road network of Europe.

**Results.** The generated data (100,000 traces) consists of 216,875 trips, with 404 GPS fixes per trip on average, i.e., a total of 87.6 million GPS fixes, resulting in a ~4 GB CSV file. With an overall execution time of just under 105 minutes (6279.644 seconds), our generator created on average 15.92 traces per second, respectively 34.54 trips per second (13,954 GPS fixes per second). In other

---

[7] 47.26784 °N - 55.13216 °N, 5.7344 °E - 15.07328 °E.

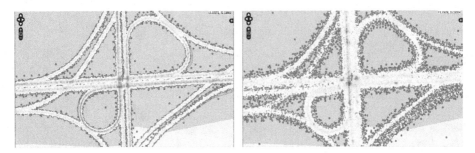

**Fig. 10.** Density of GPS points for motorway junction south of Berlin. Left: real world data, Right: synthetic data. Due to good GPS reception is the noise level of real world data smaller than for the synthetic traces.

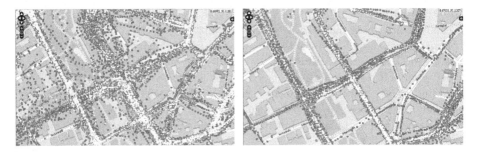

**Fig. 11.** Density of GPS points in urban canyon (Frankfurt/Main). Left: real world data. Right: synthetic data. Due to bad GPS reception, the real world data exhibits more noise than the synthetic traces.

words, it took on average 62.80 ms per trace, respectively 28.96 ms per trip (72 $\mu$s per GPS fix). The total execution time breaks down as follows. Generating the 216,875 OD pairs (one pair per trip) took 6 minutes and 49 seconds (6.5 %). Generating the location queries took 7.5 minutes (7.2 %). Planning the routes between all 216,875 OD pairs took 57.5 minutes, i.e., about 55 % of the total execution time. Generating the 100,000 traces took 6 minutes and 9 seconds (5.8 %). Writing the results to disk took 26.5 minutes (~25 %).

While we believe that these are rather reasonable performance results, we point out that our initial implementation of our generator is purely sequential, i.e., it uses only a single CPU core.

Given that the whole process is for more than 75 % of the time "IO-free" and thus CPU-bound, parallelization is straight-forward, e.g., using spatial partitioning. The given region can be split into sub-regions (e.g., one per available CPU core / hardware thread), and independent generator processes can be run concurrently, one per sub-region.

# 5    Conclusion

We set out to resolve the conflict of real-life and synthetic representative data in the domain of traffic monitoring. To resolve this conflict, we introduced a hybrid data generation technique: Statistics that are gathered from a real-life application set are combined with a system model to generate a scalable dataset that preserves real-life data characteristics. We evaluated the generated dataset against our real life input data using visual inspection as well as statistic analysis. We found that the generated data closely resembles the real-life data and is, thus, a good basis for the evaluation of data management solutions.

# References

1. Brinkhoff, T.: A framework for generating network-based moving objects. GeoInformatica 6(2), 153–180 (2002)
2. Delling, D., Sanders, P., Schultes, D., Wagner, D.: Engineering route planning algorithms. In: Algorithmics of Large and Complex Networks, pp. 117–139 (2009)
3. Düntgen, C., Behr, T., Güting, R.: Berlinmod: a benchmark for moving object databases. The VLDB Journal 18, 1335–1368 (2009),
   doi:10.1007/s00778-009-0142-5
4. Haklay, M., Weber, P.: Openstreetmap: User-generated street maps. IEEE Pervasive Computing 7(4), 12–18 (2008)
5. Hart, P.E., Nilsson, N.J., Raphael, B.: A formal basis for the heuristic determination of minimum cost paths, pp. 100–107 (1968)
6. Hilger, M., Köhler, E., Möhring, R., Schilling, H.: Fast point-to-point shortest path computations with arc-flags. The Shortest Path Problem: Ninth DIMACS Implementation Challenge 74, 41–72 (2009)
7. Pfoser, D., Theodoridis, Y.: Generating semantics-based trajectories of moving objects. Computers, Environment and Urban Systems 27(3), 243–263 (2003)
8. Liu, D.V.V.R., Watling, D.P.: Dracula: Dynamic route assignment combining user learning and microsimulation. In: PTRC, E (1994)
9. Rickert, M., Wagner, P., Gawron, C.: Real-time simulation of the german autobahn network (1997)
10. Saglio, J.-M., Moreira, J.: Oporto: A realistic scenario generator for moving objects. In: DEXA Workshop, pp. 426–432 (1999)
11. Theodoridis, Y., Silva, J.R.O., Nascimento, M.A.: On the Generation of Spatiotemporal Datasets. In: Güting, R.H., Papadias, D., Lochovsky, F.H. (eds.) SSD 1999. LNCS, vol. 1651, pp. 147–164. Springer, Heidelberg (1999)

# S3G2: A Scalable Structure-Correlated Social Graph Generator

Minh-Duc Pham[1], Peter Boncz[1], and Orri Erling[2]

[1] CWI, The Netherlands
{duc,boncz}@cwi.nl
[2] OpenLink Software, U.K.
oerling@openlinksw.com

**Abstract.** Benchmarking graph-oriented database workloads and graph-oriented database systems is increasingly becoming relevant in analytical Big Data tasks, such as social network analysis. In graph data, structure is not mainly found inside the nodes, but especially in the way nodes happen to be connected, i.e. structural correlations. Because such structural correlations determine join fan-outs experienced by graph analysis algorithms and graph query executors, they are an essential, yet typically neglected, ingredient of synthetic graph generators. To address this, we present S3G2: a Scalable Structure-correlated Social Graph Generator. This graph generator creates a synthetic social graph, containing non-uniform value distributions and structural correlations, which is intended as test data for scalable graph analysis algorithms and graph database systems. We generalize the problem by decomposing correlated graph generation in multiple passes that each focus on one so-called *correlation dimension*; each of which can be mapped to a MapReduce task. We show that S3G2 can generate social graphs that (i) share well-known graph connectivity characteristics typically found in real social graphs (ii) contain certain plausible structural correlations that influence the performance of graph analysis algorithms and queries, and (iii) can be quickly generated at huge sizes on common cluster hardware.

## 1 Introduction

Data in real life is correlated; e.g. people living in Germany have a different distribution in names than people in Italy (location), and people who went to the same university in the same period have a much higher probability to be friends in a social network. Such correlations can strongly influence the intermediate result sizes of query plans, the effectiveness of indexing strategies, and cause absence or presence of locality in data access patterns. Regarding intermediate result sizes of selections, consider:

```
SELECT personID FROM person
WHERE firstName = 'Joachim' AND addressCountry = 'Germany'
```

Query optimizers commonly use the *independence assumption* for estimating the result size of conjunctive predicates, by multiplying the estimates for the individual predicates. This would underestimate this result size, since Joachim is more common in

R. Nambiar and M. Poess (Eds.): TPCTC 2012, LNCS 7755, pp. 156–172, 2013.

Germany than in most other countries; similar would happen e.g. when querying for firstName 'Cesare' from 'Italy'. Overestimation can also easily happen, if we would query for 'Cesare' from 'Germany' or 'Joachim' from 'Italy' (i.e. *anti-correlation*).

This correlation problem has been recognized in relational database systems as relevant, and some work exists to detect correlated properties inside the same table (e.g., see [13]). Still, employing techniques for the detection of correlation is hardly mainstream in relational database management, and this is even more so when we start considering correlations between predicates that are separated by joins. Consider for instance the DBLP example of co-authorship of papers that counts the number of authors that have published both in TODS and in the VLDB Journal:

```
SELECT COUNT(*)
FROM paper pa1 JOIN journal jn1 ON pa1.journal = jn1.ID
     paper pa2 JOIN journal jn2 ON pa2.journal = jn2.ID
WHERE pa1.author = pa2.author AND
      jn1.name = 'TODS' AND jn2.name = 'VLDB Journal'
```

The above query is likely to have a larger result size than a query that substitutes 'TODS' for 'Bioinformatics', even though Bioinformatics is a much larger publication than TODS. The underlying observation is that database researchers are likely to co-publish in TODS and The VLDB Journal, but are much less likely to do cross-disciplinary work. For database technology, this example poses (i) a challenge to the optimizer to adjust the estimated join hit ratio of pa1.author = pa2.author downwards or upwards depending on other (selection or join) predicates in the query (ii) provide indexing support that can accelerate this query: the anti-correlated query (Bioinformatics and The VLDB Journal) has a very small result size and thus could theoretically be answered very quickly. However, just employing standard join indices will generate a large intermediate result for the Bioinformatics sub-plan containing all Bioinformatics authors, of which only a minute fraction is actually useful for the final answer.

Summarizing, correlated predicates are still a frontier area in database research, and such queries are generally not well-supported yet in mature relational systems. This holds still more strongly in the emerging class of graph database systems, where we argue the need for correlation-awareness in query processing is even higher.

In the particular case of RDF, its graph data model is expressly chosen to work without need for an explicit schema, such that graph datasets get stored as one big pile of edges (in particular, subject-property-object "triples"). Here we see a dualism between structure and correlation: in the relational model, certain structure is explicit in the schema, whereas in RDF such structure only re-surfaces as structural *correlation*. That is, it will turn out a journal paper (subject) always happens to have one title property, one issue property, one journalName, etc; and that these properties exclusively occur in connection to journal issues. The extreme flexibility of RDF systems in the data they can store, thus poses a significant challenge to SPARQL query optimizers, as they need to understand such correlations to get the planning of even basic queries right. Other graph database systems which use a richer data model, where nodes have a declared structure, suffer less from this problem. Still, when considering that graph analysis queries often involve a combination of (property) value constraints and structural constraints (pattern matching), it is likely that correlations between the structure of the graph and the values in them will strongly affect the performance of systems and algorithms. Yet, systems are not sufficiently aware of this, and existing graph benchmarks do not specifically test for this; and synthetic graphs used for benchmarking do not have such structure correlations. As such, we argue that for *benchmarking* graph data analysis systems and algorithms, it would be very worthwhile if a data generator could generate *synthetic graphs* which such *correlated structure*. To our knowledge, there exists no solution for generating a scalable random graph with value and structure correlations. Existing literature on random graph generation [4,10,6,8] either does not consider node properties at all or ignores correlations between them.

In this paper, we describe the Scalable Structure-correlated Social Graph Generator (S3G2), and its underlying generic conceptual correlated graph generation framework. This framework organizes data generation in multiple phases that each center around a *correlation dimension*. In the case of our social graph use case, these dimensions are (i) education and (ii) personal interests. The data generation workflow is constrained by *correlation dependencies*, where certain already generated data influences the generation of additional data. A graph generator generates new nodes (with property values), and edges between these nodes and existing nodes. The probability to choose a certain value from a dictionary, or the probability to connect two nodes with an edge are thus influenced by existing data values. For instance, the birth location of a person influences probability distribution of the `firstName` and `university` dictionaries. As another example, the probability to create a friendship edge is influenced by (dis)agreement on `gender`, `birthYear` and `university` properties of two person nodes.

A practical challenge in S3G2 is that a naive approach to correlated graph generation would continuously access possibly any node and any edge in order to make decisions regarding the generation of a next node or edge. For generating graphs of a size that exceeds RAM, such a naive algorithm would grind down due to expensive random I/O. To address this challenge, we designed a S3G2 graph generation algorithm following the MapReduce paradigm. Each pass along one correlation dimension is a Map phase in which data is generated, followed by a Reduce phase that sorts the data along the correlation dimension that steers the next pass. We show that this algorithm achieves good parallel scale-out, allowing it e.g. to generate 1.2TB of correlated graph data in half an hour on a Hadoop cluster of 16 machines.

**Contributions** of our work are the following: (1) we propose a novel framework for specifying the generation of correlated graphs, (2) we show the usefulness of this framework in its ability to specify the generation of a social network with certain plausible correlations between values and structure, and (3) we devise a scalable algorithm that implements this generator as a series of MapReduce tasks, and verify both quality of its result as well as its scalability. In our vision, this data generator is a key ingredient for new benchmarks for graph query processing.

**Outline.** In Section 2, we present our framework for the generation of correlated graphs, and describe how such it maps on a MapReduce implementation. In Section 3 we use our framework to generate a synthetic social network graph. In Section 4 we evaluate our approach, confirming that the generated data has typical social network characteristics, and showing the scalability of our generator. Finally, in Section 5, we review related work before concluding in Section 6.

## 2   Scalable Structure-Correlated Social Graph Generator (S3G2)

We first formally define the end product of S3G2 which is essentially a directed graph of objects, and introduce the main ingredients of the S3G2 framework. Then, we describe the MapReduce-based generation algorithm that follows from these ingredients.

S3G2 generates a directed labeled graph, where the nodes are objects with property values, and their structure is determined by the *class* a node belongs to. Such a data model is common in graph database systems, and is more structured than RDF (though it can be represented in RDF, as our S3G2 implementation in fact does).

**Definition 1.** *S3G2 produces a graph $G(V, E, P, C)$ where $V$ is a set of nodes, $E$ is a set of edges, $P$ is a set of properties and $C$ is a set of classes.*

$$V = L \cup \bigcup_{c \in C} O^c$$
$$P = \left\{ P^{L(x)} | x \in C \right\} \cup \left\{ P^{E(x,y)} | x, y \in C \right\}$$
$$E = \left\{ (n_1, n_2, p) | n_1 \in O^x \wedge ((n_2 \in L \wedge p \in P^{L(x)}) \vee (n_2 \in O^y \wedge p \in P^{E(x,y)})) \right\}$$

in which $O^c$ is an object of class $c$ in $C$; $L$ is the set of literals; $P^{L(x)}$ is set of literal properties of class $x$ in $C$; $P^{E(x,y)}$ is the set of properties representing relationship edges that go from instances of class $x$ to class $y$.

We now discuss the main concepts in S3G2, which are (i) property dictionaries, (ii) simple subgraph generation, and (iii) edge generation along correlation dimensions.

**Property Dictionary.** Property values for each literal property $l \in P^{L(x)}$ are generated following a property dictionary specification $PD_l(D, R, F)$, consisting of a dictionary $D$, a ranking function $R$ and a probability function $F$ (if the context is unclear, we can also write $D_l$, $R_l$ and $F_l$).

A dictionary $D$ is simply a fixed set of values: $D = \{v_1, .., v_{|D|}\}$. The ranking function $R$ is a bijection $R : D \rightarrow \{1, .., |D|\}$ which gives each value in a dictionary a unique rank between 1 and $|D|$. The probability density function $F : \{1, .., |D|\} \rightarrow [0, 1]$ steers how the generator chooses values; i.e. by having it draw random numbers $0 \leq p \leq 1$, it chooses the largest rank $r$ such that $F'(r) < p$, where $F'$ is the cumulative version of $F$, that is $F' = \sum_{i=1}^{r} F(i)$. It finally emits the value $v_{pos}$ from dictionary $D$ from position $pos = R(r)$. Thus, our framework can generate data corresponding to any discrete probability distribution.

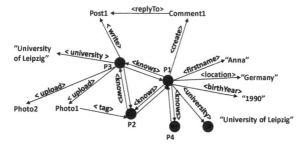

**Fig. 1.** Example S3G2 graph: Social Network with Person Information

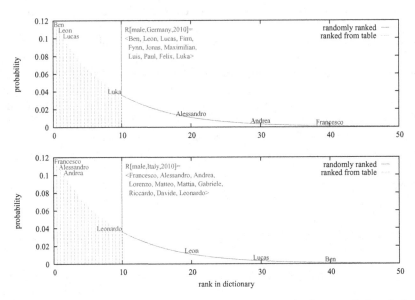

**Fig. 2.** Compact Correlated Dictionary Distributions: boy names in Germany (up) vs. Italy (lo)

The idea to have a separate ranking and probability function comes from generating correlated values. In particular, the ranking function $R[z](c)$ is typically parametrized by some parameters $z$; which means that depending on the parameter $z$, the value ranking is different. For instance, in case of a dictionary of firstName we could have $R[g, c, y]$; e.g. the popularity of first names, depending on gender $g$, country $c$ and the year $y$ from the birthDate property (let's call this birthYear). Thus, the fact that the popularity of first names in different countries and times is different, is reflected by the different ranks produced by function $R()$ over the full dictionary of names. Name frequency distributions do tend to be similar in shape, which is guaranteed by the fact that we use the same probability distribution $F()$ for all data of a property.

Thus, the S3G2 data generator must contain property dictionaries $D_l$ for all literal properties in $l \in P^{L(x)}$, and it also must contain the ranking functions $R_l$, for all literal properties defined in all classes $x \in C$. When designing correlation parameters for a ordering function $R_l$, one should ensure that the amount of parameter combinations such as $(g, c, y)$ stays limited, in order to keep the representation of such functions compact. We want the generator to be a relatively small program and not depend needlessly on huge data files with dictionaries and ranking functions.

Figure 2 shows how S3G2 compactly represents $R[g, c, y]$, by keeping for each combination of $(g, c, y)$ a small table with only the top-$N$ dictionary values (here $N$=10 for presentation purposes, but it is typically larger). Rather than storing an ordering of all values, a table like $R[male, Germany, 2010]$ is just an array of $N$ integers. A value $j$ here simply identifies value $v_j$ in dictionary $D$. The values ranked lower than $N$ get their rank assigned randomly. Given that in a monotonically decreasing probability function like the geometric distribution used here, the probabilities below that rank are very small anyway, this approximation only slightly decreases the plausibility of the generated values. In Figure 2 we see in the top graph that for *(male,Germany,2010)* we keep the 10 most popular boys names, which get mapped on the geometric distribution. All other dictionary values (among which Italian names) get some random rank $> 10$. In the lower graph, we see that for *(male,Italy,2010)* these Italian names are actually the most popular, and the German names get arbitrary (and low) probabilities.

**Simple Graph Generation.** Edges are often generated in one go together with new nodes, essentially starting with an existing node $n$, and creating new nodes to which it gets connected. This process is guided by a degree distribution function $N : h \rightarrow [0,1]$ that first determines how many $h$ such new children (or descendants) to generate. In many social networks, the amount of neighbour edges $h$ is distributed following a *power law* distribution (the probability that a node has degree $h \sim \gamma.h^{-\lambda}$).

In the S3G2 framework, it is possible to have a correlated the degree distribution function $N[n_i](h)$, from which the degree of each nodes $n_i$ is generated, correlated with properties of node $n_i$, e.g. by having these properties influence $\lambda$ or $\gamma$. For instance, people with many friends in a social network will typically post more pictures than people with few friends (hence, the amount of friend nodes in our use case influences the amount of posted comment and picture nodes).

Generating new nodes and connecting them on the fly among mostly themselves and to an existing node $n_i$ leads to isolated subgraphs that are dangling off the main graph connected to it by $n_i$. Typically, such subgraphs are small or have the shape of shallow trees if they are larger.

**Correlation Dimensions.** To generate correlated and highly connected graph data, we need a different approach that generates edges *after* generating many nodes. This is computationally harder than generating edges towards new nodes. The reason is that if node properties influence their connectivity, a naive implementation would have to compare the properties of all existing nodes with all nodes, which could lead to quadratic computational cost and a random access pattern, so the generation algorithm would only be fast as long as the data fits in RAM (to avoid a random I/O access pattern).

Data correlation actually alleviates this problem. We observe that the probability that two nodes are connected is typically skewed with respect to some similarity between the nodes. Given node $n_i$, for a small set of nodes that are somehow similar to it, there is a high connectivity probability, whereas for most other nodes, this probability is quite low. This observation can be exploited by a graph data generator by identifying *correlation dimensions*.

For a certain edge label $e \in P^{E(x,y)}$ between node classes $O^x$ and $O^y$, a correlation dimension $CD_e(M^x, M^y, F)$ consists of two *similarity metric* functions $M^x : n \rightarrow [0,\infty]$, $M^y : n \rightarrow [0,\infty]$, and a probability distribution $F :[1,W.t]\rightarrow[0,1]$. Here the $W.t$ is a window size, of $W$ tiles with each $t$ nodes, as explained later. Note that in case of friends in a social network, both start and end of the edges are of the same class persons ($O^x = O^y$), so a single metric function would typically be used. For simplicity of discussion we will assume $M = M^x = M^y$ in the sequel.

We can compute the similarity metric by invoking $M(n_i)$ on all nodes $n_i$, and sort all nodes on this score. This means that similar nodes are brought near each other, and we observe that the larger the distance between two nodes, their similarity difference monotonically increases. Again, we use a geometric probability distribution for

$F()$ that provides a probability for picking nodes to connect with that are between 1 and $W.t$ positions apart in this similarity ranking. To fully comply with a geometric distribution, we should not cut short at $W.t$ positions apart, but consider even further apart nodes. However, we observe that for a skewed monotonically decreasing distribution like geometric, the probability many positions away will be minute, i.e. $\leq \epsilon$ ($F(W.t) = \epsilon$). The advantage of this window shortcut is that after sorting the data, it allows S3G2 to generate edges using a fully sequential access pattern that needs little RAM resources (it only buffers $W.t$ nodes). An example of a similarity function $M()$ could be `location`. Location, i.e., a place name, can be mapped to (longitude,latitude) coordinates, yet for $M()$ we need a single-dimensional metric that can be sorted on. In this case, one can keep (longitude,latitude) at 16-bits integer resolution and mix these by bit-interleaving into one 32-bits integer. This creates a two-dimensional space filling curve called Z-ordering, also known in geographic query processing as QuadTiles[1]. Such a space filling curve "roughly" provides the property that points which are near each other in the Euclidean space have a small z-order difference.

Note that the use of similarity functions and probability distribution functions over ranked distance drives *what* kind of nodes get connected with an edge, not *how many*. The decision on the degree of a node is made prior to generating the edges, using the previously mentioned degree function $N[n_i](h)$, which in social networks would typically be a power-law function. During data generation, this degree $n_i.h$ of node $n_i$ is determined by randomly picking the required number of edges according to the correlated probability distributions as described before in the example with person who have many friends generating more discussion posts. In case of multiple correlations, we use another probability function to divide the inteded number of edges between the various correlation dimensions. Thus, we have a power-law distributed node degree, and a predictable (but not fixed) average split between the causes for creating edges.

**Random Dimension.** The idea that we only generate edges between the $W.t$ most similar nodes in all correlation dimensions is too restrictive: unlikely connections in a social network that the data model would not explain or make plausible, will occur in practice. Such random noise can be modeled by partly falling back onto uniformly random data generation. In the S3G2 framework this can be modeled as a special case of a correlation dimension, by using a purely random function as similarity metric, and a uniform probability function. Hence, data distributions can be made more noisy by making a pass in random order over the data and generating (a few) additional random edges.

### 2.1 MapReduce S3G2 Algorithm

In the previous discussion we have introduced the main concepts of the S3G2 framework: (i) correlated data dictionaries (ii) simple graph generation (iii) edge generation according to correlation dimensions. We now describe how a MapReduce algorithm is built using these ingredients.

In MapReduce, a Map function is run on different parts of the input data on many cluster machines in parallel. Each Map function processes its input data item and produces for each a result with a key attached. MapReduce sends all produced results to

---

[1] See http://wiki.openstreetmap.org/wiki/QuadTiles

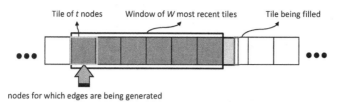

**Fig. 3.** Sliding window of $W$ tiles along the graph

Reduce functions that also run on many cluster machines; the key determines to which Reducer each item is sent. The Reduce function then processes this stream of data.

In the S3G2 algorithm, the key generated between Map and Reduce is used to *sort* the data for which edges need to be generated according to the similarity metric (the $M^x, M^y$ functions) of the next correlation dimension. As mentioned, there may be multiple correlation dimensions, hence multiple successive MapReduce phases. Both the Map and Reduce functions can perform simple graph generation, which includes generation of (correlated) property values using dictionaries, as described before in the example with boys names in Germany vs. Italy. The main task of the Reduce function is sorting on correlation dimension and subsequent edge generation between existing nodes using a sliding window algorithm described in Algorithm 1.

The main idea of the *sliding window* approach to correlated edge generation is that when generating edges, we only need to consider nodes that are sufficiently similar. By ordering the nodes according to this similarity (the metric $M^x, M^y$) we can keep a sliding window of nodes (plus their properties and edges) in RAM, and only consider generating edges between nodes that are cached in this window. If multiple correlations influence the presence of an edge, multiple full data sorts and sequential sliding window passes are needed (i.e. multiple MapReduce jobs). Thus, each correlation dimension adds one MapReduce job to the whole process, that basically re-sorts the data. One may remark that if the simple graph generation activities that kick off graph generation already generate data ordered along the first correlation dimension, we can save one MapReduce job (as data is already sorted).

The sliding window approach is implemented by dividing the sorted nodes conceptually in tiles of $t$ nodes. When the Reduce function accepts a data item, it adds it to the current tile (an in-memory data structure). If this tile is full, and it has $W$ tiles already in memory, the oldest tile is dropped from memory. This is visualized in Figure 3.

The Reduce function generates edges for all nodes in the oldest tile right before it is dropped, using Algorithm 1, implementing the windowing approach and generating edges along a correlation dimension. For each node $u$ in this tile, it sequentially scans nodes in the window, and picks a node to be connected based on a probability function $F()$, until $N(u)$ nodes are connected. Function $F()$ computes the probability of connecting two nodes based on their absolute distance in the window. Using this function nearby nodes are most likely to be picked; since successive nodes do the same, there is a high likelihood that similar (nearby) nodes have some overlapping neighbours (e.g. friends).

In principle, simple graph generation only requires local information (the current node), and can be performed as a Map task, but also as a post-processing job in the

---

**Algorithm 1.** GenerateEdges($t$, $N()$, $F()$)

---

**Input:** $t$: tile of nodes to generate edges for
**Input:** $N$: a function determines the degree of a node
**Input:** $F$: computes probability of connecting two nodes based on their distance
1: **for** each node $u$ in tile $t$ **do**
2:     **for** each node $v$ in window **do**
3:         **if** numOfEdges($v$) = $N(v)$ **then**
4:             continue
5:         **end if**
6:         generate a uniform random number $p$ in [0,1)
7:         $distance$ = position of $v$ - position of $u$;
8:         **if** ($F$(distance) $< p$) & ($u$ not yet connected to $v$) **then**
9:             createEdge($u$,$v$)
10:         **end if**
11:         **if** numOfEdges($u$) = $N(u)$ **then**
12:             break
13:         **end if**
14:     **end for**
15: **end for**
16: flushTile($t$);

---

Reduce function. Note that node generation also includes the generation of the (correlated) properties of the new nodes.

We should mention that data correlations introduce *dependencies*, that impose constraints on the order in which generation tasks have to be performed. For instance, if the firstName property of a person node depends on the birthYear and university properties, then within simple node generation, the latter properties need to be generated first. Also, if the discussion posts forum that a user might have below a posted picture involves the friends of that user, the discussion node generation should follow the generation of all friend edges. Thus, the correlation rules one introduces, naturally determine the amount of MapReduce jobs needed, as well as the order of actions inside the Map and Reduce functions.

## 3 Case Study: Generating Social Network Data

In this section, we show how we applied the S3G2 framework for creating a social network graph generator. The purpose of this generator is to provide a dataset for a new graph benchmark, called the Social Intelligence Benchmark (SIB).[2] As we focus here on correlated graph generation, this benchmark is out of scope for this paper. Let us state clearly that the purpose of this generator is *not* to generate "realistic" social network data. Determining the characteristics of social networks is the topic of a lot of research, and we use some of the current insights as inspiration (only). Our data generator introduces some plausible correlations, but we believe that real life (social network) data is riddled with many more correlations; it is a true data mining task to

---

[2] See: www.w3.org/wiki/Social_Network_Intelligence_Benchmark

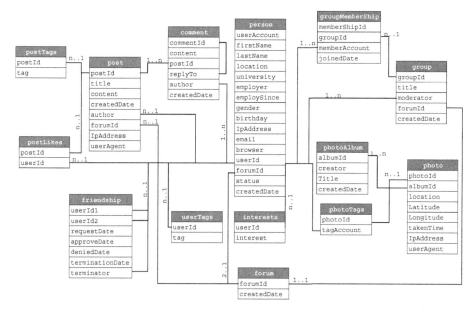

**Fig. 4.** The Generated Social Network Schema (SIB)

extract these. Given that we want to use the generated dataset for a graph database benchmark workload, having only a limited set of correlations is not a problem; as in a benchmark query workload only a limited set of query patterns will be tested.

Figure 4 shows the ER diagram of the social network. It contains persons and entities of social activities (posted pictures, and comments in discussions in the user's forum) as the object classes of $C$. These object classes and their properties (e.g., user name, post creation date, ...) form the set of nodes $V$. $E$ contains all the connection between two persons including their friendship edges and social activity edges between persons and a social activity when they all join a social activity (e.g., persons discussing about a topic). $P$ contains all attributes of a user profile, the properties of user friendships and social activities.

**Correlated Dictionaries.** A basic task is to establish a plausible dictionary ($D$) for every property in our schema. For each dictionary, we subsequently decide on a frequency distribution. As mentioned, in many cases we use a geometric distribution, which is the discrete equivalent of the exponential distribution, known to accurately model many natural phenomena. Finally, we need to determine a ranking of these values in the probability distribution (the $R()$ function). For correlated properties, this function is parameterized ($R[z]()$) and is different for value of $z$. Our compact approximation stores for each $z$ value a top-$N$ (typically $N$=30) of dictionary values.

The following property value correlations are built in ($R_x[z]$ denoted as $z \rightsquigarrow x$):

- (person.location, person.gender, person.birthDay) $\rightsquigarrow$ person.firstName
- person.location $\rightsquigarrow$ person.lastName
- person.location $\rightsquigarrow$ person.university

- `person.location ⤳ person.employer`
- `person.location ⤳ person.employSince`
- `person.location ⤳ person.interests.interest`
- `person.location ⤳ person.photoAlbum.photo.location`
- `person.employer ⤳ person.email`
- `person.birthDate ⤳ person.createdDate`
- `person.createdDate ⤳ person.photoAlbum.createdDate`
- `photoAlbum.createdDate ⤳ photoAlbum.photo.takenTime`
- `photoAlbum.photo.location ⤳ photoAlbum.photo.latitude`
- `photoAlbum.photo.location ⤳ photoAlbum.photo.longitude`
- `friendship.requestDate ⤳ friendship.approveDate`
- `friendship.requestDate ⤳ friendship.deniedDate`
- `(friendship.userId1,friendship.userId2) ⤳ friendship.terminator`
- `person.createdDate ⤳ person.forum.createdDate`
- `forum.createdDate ⤳ forum.groupmembership.joinedDate`
- `forum.createdDate,forum.post.author.createdDate ⤳ forum.post.createdDate`
- `post.createdDate ⤳ post.comment.createdDate`

Our main source of dictionary information is DBpedia [2], an online RDF version of Wikipedia, extended with some ranking information derived with internet search engine scripts. From DBpedia one can obtain a collection of place names with population information, which is used as `person.location`. For the place names, DBpedia also provides population distributions. We use this actual distribution as found in DBpedia to guide the generation of `location`.

The `person.university` property is filled with university names as found in DBpedia. The sorting function $R_{university}[location]$ ranks the universities by distance from the person location, and we keep for each location the top-10 universities. The geometric distribution is used as $F_{university}$ and its parameters are tuned such that over 90% of persons choose one of the top-10. Arguably, it is not plausible that all persons have gone to university, but absolute realism is not the point of our exercise.

From the cities, DBpedia allows to derive country information. DBpedia contains a large collection of person names (first and lastnames) and their country of birth, plus certain explicit information on popularity of first-names per country, which was used as well. Other information was collected manually on the internet, such as a distribution of browser usage, which is not correlated with anything, currently. A special rule for dates is applied that ensures that certain dates (e.g. the date a user joined the network) precede another date (the date that a user became friends with someone). This is simply done by repeating the process of randomly picking a date until it satisfies this constraint.

**Correlation Dimensions.** In our social network graph, the graph with most complex connectivity is the friends graph. The main correlations we have built in are (i) having studied together (ii) having common interests (hobbies). Arguably, the current schema allows more plausible correlations like working in the same company, or living really close, but these can easily be added following our framework. Further, the concept of `interest` is currently highly simplified to favorite musical artists/composers. Consequently, there are three correlation dimensions, where the first is studying together, the second is musical interests and the third is random (this will create random connections). The degree of the persons (function $N[n](h)$) is a power-law distribution that on average produces $h=30$ friends per person node $n$; it is divided over the three correlation dimensions in a 45%, 45%, 10% split: on average we generate 13.5 study friends, 13.5 friends with similar interests and 3 random friends. For having studied together we use the $M_{study}()$ function described before, It depends on gender, university and birthYear, to give highest probability for people of same gender who studied together to be friends. The similarity metric $M_{study}()$ hashes the university to the highest 20 bits of an integer; the following 11 bits are taken by filled with the birthYear and the lowest bit by gender. The musical-interests correlation dimension is also a multi-valued function, because the persons have a list of favorite artists/composers. The similarity metric $M_{interests}$ creates a vector that holds a score for each genre (S3G2 has predetermined genre vectors for all artists, and the result vector contains the maximum value of all favorite artists for each genre). Then, like the previous example with location, z-ordering is used to combine the various genre scores (the genre vector) into a single integer metric.

**Graph Generation.** The generation of the social graph kicks off by generating person nodes; and all its properties. This "simple graph" generation process forms part of the first MapReduce job and is executed in its Map function. The data *is* generated in a specific order: namely location. From location, we generate university in the Map phase and with that (and the uncorrelated gender and birthYear we are able to emit an $M_{study}$ key, that the first Reduce phase sorts on. Because the members of the forum groups of a user (who tag photos and comment on discussions of the user page) and their activity levels are correlated with the user's friends, the objects for these "social activities" cannot be generated before all friends have been generated. Therefore, the algorithm first continues with all correlation dimensions for friendship. The second MapReduce job generates the first 45% percent of friendship edges using the $F_{study}$ probability distribution in its Map function, and emits the $M_{interest}$ keys. Note that we sort person objects that include all their properties and all their generated friendship edges (user IDs); which are stored twice, once with the source node and once at the destination node. The third MapReduce job generates the second 45% percent of friendship edges in its Map function using the $F_{interests}$ probability distribution, and emits the $M_{random}$ keys. The key produced is simply a random number (note that all randomness is deterministic, so the generated dataset is always identical for identical input parameters). The Reduce phase of the third MapReduce job sorts the data on $M_{random}$, but as this is the last sort, it runs the window edge-generation algorithm right inside the Reduce function. This Reduce function further performs *simple graph generation* for the social activities. These social activities are subgraphs with only "local" connections and shallow tree-shape, hence can be generated on-the-fly with low resource consumption. Here, the discussion topics are topics from DBpedia articles, and the comments are successive sentences from the article body (this way the discussions consist of real English text, and is kind-of on-topic). The forum group members are picked using a ranking function that puts the friends of a user first, and adds some persons that are in the window at lower ranks; using a geometric probability distribution.

## 4   Evaluation

We evaluate S3G2 both qualitatively and quantitatively (scalability). Existing literature studying social networks has shown that popular real social networks have the characteristics of a small-world network [12,15,5]. We consider the three most robust measures, i.e. the social degrees, the clustering coefficient, and the average path length of the network topology. We empirically show that S3G2 generates a social graph with such characteristics. In this experiment, we generated small social graphs of 10K, 20K, 40K, 80K, and 160K persons, which on average have 30 friends.

**Table 1.** Graph measurements of the generated social network

| # users | Diameter | Avg. Path Len. | Avg. Clust. Coef. |
|---------|----------|----------------|-------------------|
| 10000   | 5        | 3.13           | 0.224             |
| 20000   | 6        | 3.45           | 0.225             |
| 40000   | 6        | 3.77           | 0.225             |

**Clustering Coefficient.** Table 1 shows the graph measurements of the generated social network while varying the number of users. According to the experimental results, the generated social networks have high clustering coefficients of about 0.22 which adequately follow the analysis on real social networks in [15] where the clustering coefficients range from 0.13 to 0.21 for Facebook, and 0.171 for Orkut. Figure 5(a) shows the typical clustering coefficient distribution according to the social degrees that indicates the small-world characteristic of social networks.

**Average Path Length.** Table 1 shows that the average path lengths of generated social graphs range from 3.13 to 3.77 which are comparable to the average path lengths of real social networks observed in [15]. These experimental results also conform to the aforementioned observations that average path length is logarithmically proportional to the total number of users. Since we used a simple all-pair-shortest-path algorithm which consumes a lot of memory for analyzing large graphs, Table 1 only shows the results of the average path length for a social graph of 40K users.

**Social Degree Distributions.** Figure 5(b) shows the distribution of the social degree with different number of users. All our experimental results show that the social degree follows a power-law distribution with an alpha value of roughly 2.0.

**Scalability.** We conducted scalability experiments generating up to 1.2TB of data on Hadoop a cluster of 16 nodes. Each node is a PC with an Intel i7-2600K, 3.40GHz CPU, 4-core CPU and 16 GB RAM. [3] The intermediate results in the MapReduce program use Java object serialization, and the space occupancy of a person profile+friends is 2KB. The final datasize per person is 1MB: most is in the few hundred comments and picture tags each person has (on average), which contain largish text fields.

In Figure 5(d), for a specific number of nodes, we increase the data size. These results shows that the generation increases linearly with data size. Most of the computational effort is in the first Map function that generates all person nodes and its properties.

---

[3] We used the SciLens cluster at CWI: www.scilens.org

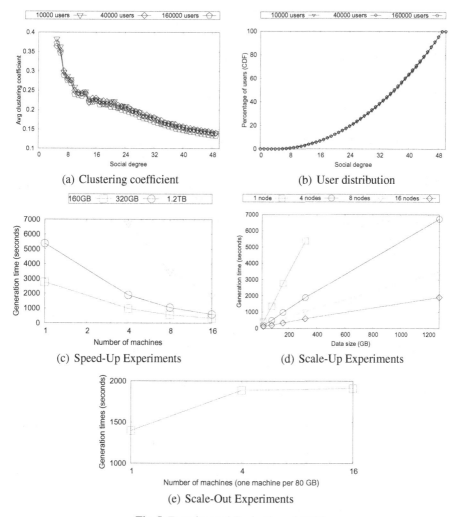

**Fig. 5.** Experimental Evaluation of S3G2

Further, most data volume (and I/O) appears in the last Reduce that generates the social activities (photos, forum posts). Both these first and last steps are time intensive and benefit strongly from parallel execution. Therefore, the cost of data sorting, which is the mainstay of the intermediate steps, and which due to its $N.log(N)$ complexity should causes less than linear scaling, is not visible yet at these data sizes.

Figure 5(c) shows the speed-up of the generator when adding nodes and keeping data size fixed. It shows the MapReduce approach works well, and speed-up is especially good at the larger data sizes.

Figure 5(e) shows the scale-out capability of S3G2 increasing together the dataset size and amount of cluster machines. In these experiments we keep the data generated per machine at 80GB; hence with 4 machines we generate 320GB and with 16 this is 1.2TB. The experimental result shows that performance remains constant at half an hour when scaling out from 4 machines to 16 nodes. This suggests that S3G2 can generate extremely large graphs quickly on a Hadoop cluster with large resources.

## 5   Related Work

There is a lot of work studying the characteristics of social networks [11,7,12,15,5,1,9] and also on the generation of random graphs having global properties similar to a social network [14,3,4,10,6,8]. However, to the best of our knowledge, there is no generator that creates a synthetic social graph with correlations. The existing graph generators mostly consider the topology and the structures of the generated graph, i.e., global properties, not the individual connections of nodes and their correlations.

One of the first studies to generate social-network-like random graph is [14]. This graph generator with small world properties such as a high clustering coefficient and low path lengths, by connecting a node with its k-nearest-neighbors and then rewiring edges. To satisfy the degree distributions [3] introduced the model of preferential attachment which was subsequently improved by [4]. The main idea of this model is that, for a new vertex, the probability that an edge is created between this vertex to an existing vertex depends on the degree of that vertex. Leskovec et al.[10] proposed a tractable graph that matches several properties of a social graph such as small diameter, heavy-tails in/out degree distribution, heavy-tails eigenvalues and eigenvectors by recursively creating a self-similar graph based on Kronecker[4] multiplication. None of these algorithms considers the correlation of a node attributes in the social graph.

Recently, Bonato et al.[6] studied the link structure of a social network and provided a model that can generate a graph satisfying many social graph properties by considering the location of each graph node by ranking each node. In this model, each node is randomly assigned a unique rank value and has a region of influence according to its rank. The probability that an edge is created between a new node and an existing node depends on the ranking of the existing node. Similar to the approach of using influent regions [8] constructed a set of cliques (i.e., groups) over all the users. For each new node (i.e., a new user), an edge to an existing node is created based on the size of cliques they have in common. These models are approaching the realistic observation that users tend to join and connect with people in a group of same properties such as the same location. However, the simulation of realistic data correlations is quite limited and both do not address the correlations between different attributes of the users.

Additionally, all of the existing models need a large amount of memory for storing either the whole social graph or its adjacency matrix. Leskovec et al. [10] may need to store all stages of their recursive graph. Although Batagelj et al. aimed at providing a efficient space-requirement algorithm, the space-requirement is $O(|V| + |E|)$ where $V$ is the set of vertices and $E$ is the set of edges [4].

## 6   Conclusion

In this paper, we have proposed S3G2, a novel framework for scalable graph generator that can generate huge graphs having correlations between the graph structure and

---

[4] http://en.wikipedia.org/wiki/Kronecker_product

graph data such as node properties. While current approaches at generating graphs require holding it in RAM, our graph generator can generate the graph with little memory by using a sliding window algorithm, and exploit parallelism offered by the MapReduce paradigm. It thus was able to generate in half an hour 1.2TB of tightly connected, correlated social graph data, on 16 cluster machines using only limited RAM.

In order to address the problem of generating correlated data and structure together, which has not been handled in existing generators, we propose an approach that separates value generation (data dictionaries) and probability distribution, by putting in between a value ranking function that can be parametrized by correlating factors. We also showed a compact implementation of such correlated ranking functions.

Further, we address correlated structure generation by introducing the concept of correlation dimensions. These correlation dimensions allow to generate edges efficiently by relying on multiple sorting passes; which map naturally on MapReduce jobs.

We demonstrate the utility of the S3G2 framework by applying it to the scenario of modeling a social network graph. The experiments show that our generator can easily generate a graph having important characteristics of a social network and additionally introduce a series of plausible correlations in it.

Future work, is to apply the S3G2 framework to other domains such as telecommunications networks, and a possible direction is to write a compiler that automatically generates a MapReduce implementation from a set of correlation specifications. As we believe that correlations between value and structure are an important missing ingredient in today's graph benchmarks, we intend to introduce the Social Intelligence Benchmark (SIB), that uses S3G2 as data generator, to fill that gap.

# References

1. Ahn, Y., Han, S., Kwak, H., Moon, S., Jeong, H.: Analysis of topological characteristics of huge online social networking services. In: Proc. WWW (2007)
2. Auer, S., Bizer, C., Kobilarov, G., Lehmann, J., Cyganiak, R., Ives, Z.: DBpedia: A nucleus for a web of open data. Semantic Web Journal, 722–735 (2007)
3. Barabási, A., Albert, R., Jeong, H.: Scale-free characteristics of random networks: the topology of the world-wide web. Physica A: Statistical Mechanics and its Applications 281(1-4), 69–77 (2000)
4. Batagelj, V., Brandes, U.: Efficient generation of large random networks. Physical Review E 71(3), 036113 (2005)
5. Benevenuto, F., Rodrigues, T., Cha, M., Almeida, V.: Characterizing user behavior in online social networks. In: Proc. SIGCOMM (2009)
6. Bonato, A., Janssen, J., Prałat, P.: A geometric model for on-line social networks. In: Proc. Conf. on Online Social Networks (2010)
7. de Sola Pool, I., Kochen, M.: Contacts and influence. Elsevier (1978)
8. Foudalis, I., Jain, K., Papadimitriou, C., Sideri, M.: Modeling social networks through user background and behavior. Algorithms and Models for the Web Graph, 85–102 (2011)
9. Kwak, H., Lee, C., Park, H., Moon, S.: What is twitter, a social network or a news media? In: Proc. WWW (2010)
10. Leskovec, J., Chakrabarti, D., Kleinberg, J., Faloutsos, C.: Realistic, Mathematically Tractable Graph Generation and Evolution, Using Kronecker Multiplication. In: Jorge, A.M., Torgo, L., Brazdil, P.B., Camacho, R., Gama, J. (eds.) PKDD 2005. LNCS (LNAI), vol. 3721, pp. 133–145. Springer, Heidelberg (2005)

11. Milgram, S.: The small world problem. Psychology Today 2(1), 60–67 (1967)
12. Mislove, A., Marcon, M., Gummadi, K., Druschel, P., Bhattacharjee, B.: Measurement and analysis of online social networks. In: Proc. SIGCOMM (2007)
13. Stillger, M., Lohman, G., Markl, V., Kandil, M.: Leo-db2's learning optimizer. In: Proc. VLDB (2001)
14. Watts, D., Strogatz, S.: Collective dynamics of "small-world" networks. Nature 393(6684), 440–442 (1998)
15. Wilson, C., Boe, B., Sala, A., Puttaswamy, K., Zhao, B.: User interactions in social networks and their implications. In: Proc. European Conference on Computer Systems (2009)

# Benchmarking in the Cloud: What It Should, Can, and Cannot Be

Enno Folkerts[1], Alexander Alexandrov[2], Kai Sachs[1],
Alexandru Iosup[3], Volker Markl[2], and Cafer Tosun[1]

[1] SAP AG, 69190 Walldorf, Germany
`firstname.lastname@sap.com`
[2] TU Berlin, Germany
`firstname.lastname@tu-berlin.de`
[3] Delft University of Technology, The Netherlands
`A.Iosup@tudelft.nl`

**Abstract.** With the increasing adoption of Cloud Computing, we observe an increasing need for Cloud Benchmarks, in order to assess the performance of Cloud infrastructures and software stacks, to assist with provisioning decisions for Cloud users, and to compare Cloud offerings. We understand our paper as one of the first systematic approaches to the topic of Cloud Benchmarks. Our driving principle is that Cloud Benchmarks must consider end-to-end performance and pricing, taking into account that services are delivered over the Internet. This requirement yields new challenges for benchmarking and requires us to revisit existing benchmarking practices in order to adopt them to the Cloud.

## 1 Introduction

Creating good benchmarks has been considered a "dark art" for a long time because of the many subtleties that ultimately may influence the adoption (and consequently the success) of a benchmark. Nevertheless, the body of related research work suggests a number of widely accepted guidelines and quality criteria which have to be considered in the design and execution of computer system benchmarks.

In this paper, we seek to extent these quality criteria for benchmarking in the Cloud. For the purposes of our discussion, by *benchmarking in the Cloud* we mean the use of Cloud services in the respective (distributed) system under test (SUT). We believe that *building* the benchmark is only half of the story and *execution (operation)* deserves at least as much attention, especially in the discussed complex distributed systems context.

Our work is mainly inspired by *The art of building a good benchmark* [1] by Karl Huppler and *How is the Weather tomorrow? Towards a Benchmark for the Cloud* [2] by Carsten Binnig, Donald Kossmann, Tim Kraska and Simon Loesing. The Dagstuhl Seminar on Information Management in the Cloud held in August 2011 was the starting point for the actual work on the paper. We would like to thank Helmut Krcmar and André Bögelsack who pointed out the business aspect of the topic, as well as Nick Lanham and Dean Jacobs for their suggestions and feedback.

R. Nambiar and M. Poess (Eds.): TPCTC 2012, LNCS 7755, pp. 173–188, 2013.
© Springer-Verlag Berlin Heidelberg 2013

The paper is structured as follows. Section 2 gives an overview of benchmarking in general. Section 3 introduces the topic of benchmarking in the Cloud. In Section 4 and Section 5 we present use cases in the Cloud and go through the necessary steps for building respective benchmarks. Section 6 highlights the challenges for building a good benchmark in the Cloud and proposes first solutions. Finally, Section 7 concludes and presents ideas for future research.

## 2    Benchmarking in a Nutshell

This section gives a brief overview on the topic of benchmarking. We will discuss the objectives of benchmarks, see how benchmarks operate, and then will elaborate how benchmarks try to meet their objectives.

### 2.1    What Is the Task of a Benchmark?

Benchmarks are tools for answering the common question *"Which is the best system in a given domain?"*. For example, the SPECCpu benchmark [3] answers the question *"Which is the best CPU?"*, and the TPC-C benchmark [4] answers the question *"Which is the best database system for OLTP?"*.

The concrete interpretation of *"best"* depends on the benchmarking objective and is the first question that has to be answered when designing a new benchmark. As a systematic approach for answering this question, Florescu and Kossmann suggest to look at the properties and constraints of the systems to be benchmarked [5]. The number one property has to be optimized while lower priority properties give rise to constraints. A benchmark therefore can be seen as a way to specify these priorities and constraints in a well-defined manner. The task of the benchmark then is to report how well different systems perform with respect to the optimized priority under the given constraints.

In practice, benchmarks are used to assist decisions about the most economical provisioning strategy as well as to gain insights about performance bottlenecks.

### 2.2    How Do Benchmarks Do Their Task?

Benchmarks pick a representative scenario for the given domain. They define rules how to setup and run the scenario, and how to obtain measurement results.

Benchmark definitions often refer to the concept of a *System Under Test (SUT)*. The SUT is a collection of components necessary to run the benchmark scenario. The idea of a SUT is to define a complete application architecture containing one or more *components of interest*. In a typical SUT, however, not all components are of principal interest for the benchmark. We refer to the remaining SUT components as *purely functional components*.

Benchmarks measure the the behaviour of a complete SUT. In order to isolate information about the component of interest, complete knowledge about all components involved is essential. That is why all SUT components are subject to strict run and disclosure rules. Benchmark components initiating the workload are called *drivers*, and are not part of the SUT.

## 2.3   Benchmark Requirements

A benchmark is considered to be good if all stakeholders believe that it provides true and meaningful results. There are a number of publications that try to provide guidelines on the subject of benchmark design and implementation. Almost all of them are based on Gray's seminal work [6]. Huppler recently provided a good survey on different benchmarking criteria in [1]. Workload requirements are investigated in [7,8,9,10]. Based on this previous work, we define the following three groups of requirements:

1. *General Requirements* – this group contains generic requirements.
   (a) Strong Target Audience – the target audience must be of considerable size and interested to obtain the information.
   (b) Relevant – the benchmark results have to measure the performance of the typical operation within the problem domain.
   (c) Economical – the cost of running the benchmark should be affordable.
   (d) Simple – understandable benchmarks create trust.
2. *Implementation Requirements* – this group contains requirements regarding implementation and technical challenges.
   (a) Fair and Portable – all compared systems can participate equally.
   (b) Repeatable – the benchmark results can be reproduced by rerunning the benchmark under similar conditions with the same result.
   (c) Realistic and Comprehensive  – the workload exercises all SUT features typically used in the major classes of target applications.
   (d) Configurable – a benchmark should provide a flexible performance analysis framework allowing users to configure and customize the workload.
3. *Workload Requirements* – contains requirements regarding the workload definition and its interactions.
   (a) Representativeness – the benchmark should be based on a workload scenario that contains a representative set of interactions.
   (b) Scalable – Scalability should be supported in a manner that preserves the relation to the real-life business scenario modeled.
   (c) Metric – a meaningful and understandable metric is required to report about the SUT reactions to the load.

In the following sections, we evaluate our results using these requirements and discuss how they can be fulfilled in our scenarios.

## 3   Benchmarking in the Cloud

For a definition of Cloud Computing, we refer to the *NIST Definition of Cloud Computing* [11]. This definition comes with three different service models: *Infrastructure as a Service (IaaS)*, *Platform as a Service (PaaS)*, and *Software as a service (SaaS)*. These service models are commonly referred to as *Service Levels* and can be understood as different levels of software abstraction. These layers do not define a fixed homogeneous set – authors and businesses often introduce new

*Something as a Service (XaaS)* terminologies. Due to space limitations, here we only mention Youseff et al. [12], who extend the three layer model with *Hardware as a Service, Data as a Service*, and *Communication as a Service* concepts.

Under *Benchmarking in the Cloud*, we understand the process of benchmarking services provided by the Cloud. A *Cloud Benchmark* therefore for us is a benchmark in which the SUT contains a Cloud service as component of interest. A good summary of this topic was provided in [13].

### 3.1   Cloud Actors

To introduce the different Cloud actors, we take a business orientated view of Cloud Computing going beyond the simple consumer/provider model. We claim that each service layer brings its own actors who add value to the level below. Different types of actors might have different benchmark requirements for the same SUT. To have a strong target audience, a benchmark has to address the appropriate actors.

Leimeister et al. [14] argue that the actors in the Cloud form a business value network rather than a traditional business value chain. We identify the following actors in a Cloud-centric business value network (Figure 1): *IT Vendors* develop infrastructure software and operate infrastructure services; *Service Providers* develop and operate services; *Service Aggregators* offer new services by combining preexisting services; *Service Platform Providers* offer an environment for developing Cloud applications; *Consulting* supports customers with selecting and implementing Cloud services; *Customers* are the end-users of Cloud services.

Note that [14] uses the term *Infrastructure Provider* for what we call *IT Vendor*. We deviate from [14] to stress the fact that vendors that offer software that enables Cloud services should also be considered part of this actor group. We also use the term *Customer* where others might use the term *Consumer*. We decided to adhere to [14] in this case because service aggregators and service platform providers are consumers just as customers are.

### 3.2   The System under Test

The above definition of a cloud benchmark requires that at least one component of interest within the benchmark SUT is a cloud service. This leads to several implications, which we now briefly discuss.

**SUT Disclosure.** A common benchmark requirement is to lay open all properties of the involved SUT components. This requirement is no longer realistic when the SUT contains public cloud services. We therefore propose to consider the following relaxation: *All properties of SUT components visible to their clients should be laid open.* In terms of white-box vs. black-box benchmarking this leads to nearly white-box IaaS benchmarks, grey-box PaaS benchmarks and black-box SaaS benchmarks. Overcoming the SUT disclosure issue was also recently discussed by the SPEC OSG Cloud Computing Workgroup. Their White Paper [15] provides further information.

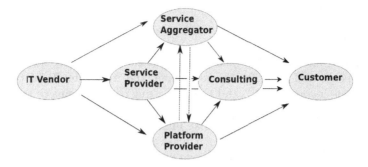

**Fig. 1.** Cloud Actors and their Value Network

**SUT Uniqueness.** Traditional benchmarks run on SUT components copied into an isolated test environment. In a cloud environment, components are modeled as services. These are single instance entities, cannot be copied, and a clear isolation is not possible. During a benchmark run the SUT services most likely will be shared with third party clients, and avoiding external clients is neither possible nor desired.

**Carving Out a SUT.** One possible approach to deal with the disclosure and uniqueness issues discussed above is to carve out a dedicated set of servers within a public cloud and have these deliver the services for the SUT. We believe that this will not lead to relevant results.

## 4 Use Cases

In this section we present a list of sample use cases. The list does not intend to be complete, but rather should help us illustrate the layers and actors defined above and motivate the discussion of different optimization questions. In Section 5 we show how appropriate Cloud benchmarks help answer these questions, and in Section 6 we identify and discuss the most important challenges that these benchmarks should resolve.

### 4.1 Simple IaaS

Businesses use Cloud IaaS for outsourcing of non-critical processes like testing, training and reference landscapes. They buy IaaS resources and install the desired systems, but do not use them all the time. The expected load is moderate to low, being created mainly by non-critical offline processes. Our experience with such scenarios shows systems with 100GB disk space, 32GB memory, and 4 CPU cores. The average load of a running system uses about 10% CPU resources and 25% of memory or disk space.

The IaaS resources are not expected to scale with regard to the load per system. Scalability is expected with regards to the number of systems that can be started and shut down.

## 4.2   Online Gaming Platform

*GameX* is produced by *ACME Games*.

*ACME Games* runs its own server clusters which should host on average hundreds of game and mini-game sessions, each with varying number of users (say between 0 and 5,000 for the core game, and from 5 to 50 for the mini- or smaller game instances [16]), and length ranging of 20-30 mins to several hours.

When players overload the servers, no new player sessions can be established. Waiting to login is one of the worst breaches of the expected Service Level Agreements for *GameX*, so *ACME Games* has to avoid these situations at all cost. Because the resource consumption of interaction operations between players does not always scale linearly with the number of players, and, in fact, in some cases may grow cubically in the number of players, *ACME Games* has to be either overly-conservative in its server capacity estimates or risk severe overloads in some circumstances [17].

Instead of over-provisioning, which as seen is highly undesirable, *ACME Games* can use Cloud technology. They can lease machines on-demand to alleviate sudden surges in their workload. This solution needs to fulfill strict Service Level Agreements in terms of response time, which includes a non-trivial network latency component, and computing workload distribution and interference. For its new games, *ACME Games* may also lease (reserve) instances from a Cloud until the game is properly measured and future workloads can be predicted.

## 4.3   High Workload Analytical Platform

*ACME Analytics* is a start-up that wants to provide Big Data analytics services. Their target customers produce large amounts of data and want to analyze it on a daily or weekly basis. Potential customers may be smart grid or mobile phone providers. The company expects up to 500 TB data per client and as much as 1 PB of data shared among clients. An average task is expected to use 50TB of the private and 1 TB of the shared data. Clearly, using a massively-parallel data processing platform, such as MapReduce, as an off-the-shelf Cloud service is the most lucrative technical solution for *ACME Analytics* because of the low upfront investment and maintenance cost. The first technical decision that *ACME Analytics* has to make therefore is which PaaS to use.

# 5   Building Benchmarks in the Cloud

In this section we go through the previous use cases and try to envision how benchmarks in the respective area could be build.

## 5.1   Simple IaaS

First, we need to refine the optimization question for the use case. The consumer needs many parallel instances of some application for their test or training systems. There is no necessity to scale up a single application instance. It is expected to save cost by shutting down application instances. We can therefore recap the optimization question posed by the use case as follows: *Which IaaS does most effectively host a bunch of parallel mid-size application instances? This includes reducing cost when fewer application instances are active.*

Next, we discuss how the SUT and the workload should look like. We are not interested in a distributed or cluster scenario, so we can adapt a well known workload, say TPC-C, and run it independently on all instances.

To adapt TPC-C, we first pick a `tpmC` value representative for a mid-size load. In addition, we also set the maximum number of independent application instances that will participate for a single benchmark run. Let us put `maxInst=250`.

We will consider two workload variants: (1) running all instances with the same `tpmC`, and (2) running a varying amount of instances over the benchmark runtime. Workload (1) is intended to measure how many IaaS nodes are required to make `maxInst` instances pass the TPC-C SLA requirements. Because different providers are expected to have different nodes, a final comparison of the respective services will only be possible by comparing the price of the services consumed. Workload (2) measures the elasticity of the underlying IaaS by comparing the price of the full workload with the price of the varying workload. For the second workload, we propose a scheduling mechanism with number of active instances defined by the formula:

$$actInstances(\texttt{timeElapsed}) = \left| \frac{\texttt{maxInst}}{2} \times \left( 1 - \cos \left( \frac{3\pi \times \texttt{timeElapsed}}{\texttt{totalRuntime}} \right) \right) \right|$$

These are only a few ideas about a parallel load IaaS benchmark. We list further design questions for such a benchmark.

1. As we are not benchmarking the database we can fix the database system to be used. But this would violate the fairness and portability requirement.
2. Is it allowed to use different schemata of a database instance for different TPC-C instances?
3. Is it allowed to migrate TPC-C instances between server nodes during a benchmark run?
4. Should we rather not design for possible multiple TPC-C per node and scale by increasing the `tpmC` until a node is fully loaded?
5. Where should the Remote Terminal Emulator (the driver) be located?

We discuss these questions in Section 6.

## 5.2   Online Gaming Platform

There currently exists no online gaming benchmark. Relevant prior work on the prerequisites of designing online gaming benchmarks exists, either in the form of game workload characterizations or of benchmarks built for other types of media. The voluminous body of work on game workload characterization has been recently surveyed [18]. For related benchmarks, we refer to ALPBench [19], MediaBench [20], and MiBench [21].

We hold that the Gaming use case rather gives rise to parallel than a distributed scenario. Still, it is much more complex than the Simple IaaS use case. In this case the various types of system operations necessary to fulfill various requests may lead to widely different response times. Another fundamental difference is that requests need to be fulfilled in different amount of times before the users consider their mental Service Level Agreement breached and decide to move to another game. For example, role-playing requests may be fulfilled within 1 second [22,23]. For strategic decisions the response time needs to be around 300 milliseconds [24], and requests for first-person activities need to be fulfilled in under 100 milliseconds [23], [25].

Other important metrics for ACME Games are the 99th percentile of the wait time distribution and the the 99th percentile of the distribution of fraction of dropped requests. These high limits (vs the traditional 95th percentile) stem from the way players join and leave games as the result of positive and negative trends, respectively. Strong community ties between players [26], [27] indicate that a percentage as low as 1% of unhappy players may trigger the departure of 10-20% in a matter of days [17], e.g. via social media rants, in-game negative adverts, and plain group-based discussions.

### 5.3  High Workload Analytical Platform

In this case, *ACME Consulting* acts as service aggregator and has two options. They may either bundle services of an existing analytical platform or deploy their own analytical tools on an existing infrastructure service. To compare the resulting service they need a benchmark build around a set of representative analytical tasks. Most research in the area in done on actual MapReduce benchmarks like MRBench [28] or designing appropriate MapReduce workloads [29]. Pavlo et al. [30] show how to have analytical workload run by both MapReduce and Distributed Databases and compare the results. These approaches make considerable progress defining representative workloads. They do not deal with services and do not intend to define Cloud benchmarks. Here are a few ideas how an analytical Cloud benchmark could look like:

1. Start with a set of analytical tasks from the latest references.
2. For each task find an appropriate runtime SLA defining a 90% percentile.
3. Run the tasks concurrently. Run the whole workload several times.
4. Scale the tasks with the amount of data analyzed. Keep things simple by scaling up all task data sizes with the same linear factor `anScale`.
5. We expect the SUT to acquire more server nodes as the amount of data to be analyzed increases. The primary metric is the maximal `anScale`, that can be reached.
6. Devise a maximal scaling factor `maxAnScaleYYYY`. The benchmark should not scale the load further than `maxAnScaleYYYY`.
7. Also report the price of the services used so that services can be compared if they reach the maximal `anScale`.
8. Periodically (for example once per year) revise and agree on a new (larger) `maxAnScaleYYYY`.

9. Similarly to the Simple IaaS use case report elasticity by running with a varying load.

In the next section we discusses the challenges for the hypothetical benchmarks presented above in more detail.

# 6   The Art of Building and Running a Good Benchmark in the Cloud

We believe, that there are four main steps for building and running a good benchmark in the Cloud. These are *Meaningful Metric, Workload Design, Workload Implementation* and *Creating Trust*. In this section we discuss the inherent challenges in these steps.

## 6.1   Meaningful Metric

A metric is a function that transforms measured results into a form that is easily understood by the system analyst. The most simple metric is the runtime metric, which reports either median, average, maximum or even minimum runtime among transactions run by the SUT. When systems have to deal with concurrent transactions, it makes more sense to consider a throughput metric reporting the maximal number of transactions adhering to some runtime SLA. Some benchmarks (mainly those designed to support business decisions) also report the cost of the underlying system or the cost of running a single transaction at maximal load. There is an ongoing debate if reporting cost makes sense [31]. Kossmann et al. have devoted a sequence of papers to this topic in its Cloud context [5,2,32], arguing that in this case cost should be the primary metric. The argument is motivated by the fact that in theory Cloud technology should provide infinite scalability, which makes the classic throughput metric obsolete. However, in [32] the authors observe that (to no surprise) infinite scalability is an illusion and for most providers breaks down sooner or later due to bottlenecks in the SUT architecture. In that case it makes perfect sense to report how far the load can be scaled up.

**Challenge 1: Price vs. Performance Metric.** For the parallel load of the Simple IaaS use case we had decided to report the number of nodes required to run the 250 TPC-C instances. As nodes of different vendors will most probably have different characteristics, the number of nodes is in fact not a suitable metric. Money is the only possible yardstick and therefore we have to report the price for these nodes. We propose to use the Price Metric as primary metric when dealing with parallel load: *Report the minimal cost to run maxInst of a given application and a given workload on the SUT.*

For a distributed load we propose to use a mixed Price/Performance Metric as suggested by the High Analytical Workload Platform use case: *Scale up the load along a well defined dimension, but do not pass a very ambitious limit of* maxScaleYYYY *which should be reconsidered annually. Also report the price of the SUT. This enables comparison in case systems reach* maxScaleYYYY.

**Challenge 2: Elasticity Metric.** We propose to use a Elasticity Metric as secondary metric. How can elasticity of a service under test be measured? Previous work has introduced for this purpose concepts such as over- and under-provisioning of resources [17,33], or counted the number of SLA breaches [17] during periods of elastic system activity. However, measuring and characterizing elasticity remain activities without theoretical support. Even understanding which periods are elastic, that is, distinguishing between normal fluctuations and significant elastic changes in the system behavior, requires advances in the current body of knowledge. Moreover, the proposal in [17,33] relies on the benchmark being able to collect CPU consumption information of the provider system. In some cases these numbers might not be freely available to the consumer. Consequently a consumer benchmark should not rely on these numbers. Binnig et al. [2] define a Scalability Metric, which does not take into account CPU info and solely relies on the successful interactions under an increasing load. This methodology could be extended to also capture elasticity. Nevertheless, it is of little interest to the consumer if the provider can deal effectively with a varying load. What the consumer needs to know is whether a varied and reduced load leads to a reduced bill. We therefore propose to measure elasticity by running a varying workload and compare the resulting price with the price for the full load. Some details can be found in the discussion of the Simple IaaS benchmark.

**Challenge 3: Percentile.** Which percentiles are appropriate for the response time SLAs of Cloud like interactions? One might argue, that the Cloud calls for higher percentiles. Disappointed users might just move to the next service offered. We hold that percentiles depend on the respective scenario. For the Simple IaaS scenario the 90% percentiles of TPC-C are fine. For the Gaming scenario they are not. We propose not to run the same benchmark (scenario) with different percentiles but to have different benchmarks modeling different scenarios and respective percentiles.

Discussing the metric topic in the Cloud community we were asked to also consider several other metrics like consistency, security, user experience and trust. In our opinion each scenario has its own consistency requirement. The consistency level of a service has to fulfill this consistency requirement. If a service promises a higher degree of consistency than required, this should be stated in the benchmark report. The same more or less holds for security. User experience and trust are hard to capture. We intend to create trust by doing the benchmarking right.

## 6.2   Workload Design

The workload of a benchmark must be designed towards the metric to be used. It has to model real world workloads on a given application scenario. Workload design is a traditional challenge in the design of benchmarks.

**Challenge 4: Limit the Resources Acquired.** Since many Clouds try to provide the illusion of infinite scale, benchmarks cannot merely load the system until it breaks down. This applies in particular for parallel load, where we expect to be able to crash the complete service. This is not realistic and might violate the benchmark requirement to stay within economical boundaries. We have to devise a maximal scaling factor limiting the load. However, having this accepted by the majority of stakeholders poses a serious challenge. We propose to annually renew the maximal scaling factor. We expect a discussion about having a maximal scaling factor or not. Those against could argue, that providers have to take care not to have their services crashed. A benchmark would check implicitly, if this kind of check is in place.

**Challenge 5: Variable Load.** As user-triggered elasticity and automatic adaptivity are expected features of Cloud services, benchmarks can no longer focus solely on steady-state workloads. For the Simple IaaS use case we proposed to use a harmonic variability of the load. In general, capturing and using characteristics of real Cloud workloads might lead to better accepted benchmarks.

**Challenge 6: Scalability.** The benchmark requirements listed in Section 2.3 ask for Scalability. This means that the benchmark has to be enabled to have the load against the SUT increased along a well defined scale. What is the best candidate for a 'well defined scale' for our use case? The answer to this question is not obvious.

Let us return to the Simple IaaS use case and recap the design of its benchmark. The general question is: how well can a service host multiple instances of a given application? To answer this question the benchmark increases the load and reports how far it can get. We have several options to increase the load:

1. Increase the number of users per application instance.
2. Increase the size of the application instance.
3. Increase the number of application instances.
4. Increase the number of application instance per node.

As we do not model for high load per application instance the first two options are not relevant. The third option leaves open the question where to set the limit discussed in the previous challenge. We choose the last option because it addresses resource sharing. Once we deal with distributed load we face different options. In the case of MapReduce scenarios we choose the size of the data to be analysed as 'well defined scale'.

## 6.3  Workload Implementation

**Challenge 7: Workload Generation.** The increased complexity of the workloads also imposes challenges for the implementation of workload generator programs. First, efficient scalability is a hard requirement because of the expected workload sizes. Second, the workload generators should be able to implement all relevant characteristics of the designed application scenario.

As an example, consider the analytical platform use-case from Section 5.3. A relevant benchmark should use test data with similar order of magnitude, so a natural problem that becomes evident here is how to ship benchmark data of that magnitude to the SUT. Clearly, importing data from remote locations or using sequential data generators are not feasible options due to the unrealistic amount of required time (according to our estimates generating 1PB of TPC-H data for instance will take at least a month). The most promising alternative to solve this problem is to utilize the computational resources in the Cloud environment and generate the data and the workloads in a highly parallel manner. Recent work in the area of scalable data generation [34,35] demonstrates how a special class of pseudo-random number generators (PRNGs) can be exploited for efficient generation of complex, update-aware data and workloads in a highly parallel manner. In general, partitionable PRNGs can be used to ensure repeatability and protect against unwanted correlations for all sorts of parallel simulations.

**Challenge 8: Fairness and Portability.** Like Binnig et al. [2] we propose to have Cloud benchmarks model the complete application stack. In case we do not benchmark SaaS services, some party has to provide an implementation of the respective application to be deployed on the service under test. What kind of rules and restrictions should apply for the implementation of this application? We have to take care not to violate the Fairness and Portability requirements. In the Simple IaaS use case we discussed the option to fix a database system for the benchmark. In our opinion, this would violate the Fairness and Portability requirements. Allowing different database systems increases the degrees of freedom. This in turn makes it hard to compare the underlying IaaS SUT. How can this challenge be overcome? Here is our solution:

1. Set application specs without touching implementation details.
2. Service providers are free to provide their own optimal implementation of the respective application.
3. Service providers can require submissions to be based on their own implementation.

With this solution services allowing for good implementations will have an advantage, but this is only fair.

PaaS providers offer a zoo of different languages, data stores and application servers. Some of these follow standards, some do not and others are heading to become the de facto standard. PaaS benchmarks have the choice either to be generic enough to cover all or most of these offers or to restrict themselves to a well defined standard, which is implemented by a considerable group of service providers. We propose to handle the first option like the IaaS case discussed above. This then leads to a single benchmark, which can be used for IaaS and PaaS services. This is the approach of Kossmann et al. [32], who implement the TPC-W benchmark for each of the services under test. The second PaaS option might lead to a reuse of existing benchmarks like SPECjEnterprise in the Cloud.

We conclude the discussion with a short remark about SaaS benchmarks. We cannot expect to have one benchmark for all SaaS offerings. Still, benchmarks for an important application domain like Human Capital Management(HCM) are worth consideration. Their biggest challenge would be to define a set of representative transactions, which most HCM providers offer. The more specialized the services under test are, the more difficult it is to find a common denominator.

## 6.4   Creating Trust

Trust, which is a major concern for any Cloud operation [36], is particularly important for benchmarking Cloud services. Choosing a representative benchmark scenario and properly dealing with above design and implementation challenges supports creating trust. We hold that we must also consider benchmark operations and list three operational challenges.

**Challenge 9: Location.** Benchmarking in the Cloud raises a non-trivial challenge in deciding where each component of the benchmark is located. Should the Cloud provider host the driver? Should the request queues of the user [37] be located close to the Cloud or even in different time zones? Does this decision depend on the workload or not? If yes, is there a general rule of thumb that can help us decide where to place the driver?

**Challenge 10: Ownership.** Which actor, from the group introduced in Section 3.1, should run the benchmark? How to prevent that the Cloud service provider "games" the results, for example by putting more resources into the benchmarked service? Should the Cloud service provider be informed about when the benchmark is being run in their system?

**Challenge 11: Repeatability.** We expect a variability in the results reported by a benchmark and list three possible reasons. a) The performance variability of production IaaS Clouds has been investigated [38] and found to exhibit pronounced time patterns at various time scales. The main reason is that Cloud services time-share and may over-commit their resources. b) Ever-changing customer load may affect the performance of Cloud infrastructures. c) Moreover, providers are liable to change prices, which directly affects the proposed PricePerformance metrics. Thus, benchmarking results may vary significantly over time. In contrast to traditional benchmarking of large-scale computing systems, what is the value of numbers measured at any particular point in time? How to ensure the repeatability of results? Should benchmarks be simply re-run periodically, therefore lowering the economical requirement, or should the repeatability requirement be lowered or even not imposed?

Our first draft of a solution to these operational challenges is to set up an independent consortium. The main tasks of this consortium would be to:

1. Provide a geo-diverse driver Cloud.
2. Run benchmarks without further notice to the provider.
3. Rerun benchmarks periodically.
4. Charge benchmark runs to the provider.
5. Offer different levels of trust by having runs repeated more or less frequently.
6. Store benchmark applications implemented (see Challenge 8) by the provider or third party.

## 7    Conclusion

Benchmarking plays an important role in the wide-spread adoption of cloud computing technologies. General expectations of ubiquitous, uninterrupted, on-demand, and elastic cloud services must be met through innovative yet universally accepted benchmarking practices. In this work we described our understanding what benchmarking should, can, and cannot be. This understanding is governed by general benchmark requirements listed in Section 2.3 . It is also based on a sequence of papers [5], [2], [32] by Kossmann et al. and the respective experiments performed.

We first defined the actors involved in cloud benchmarking, including their value network, and the system under test (SUT). Unlike traditional benchmarking, the SUT includes numerous components that are either black boxes or inherently unstable. Next, we analyzed several use cases where benchmarking can play a significant role, and discussed the main challenges in building scenario-specific benchmarks. Last, we collected the challenges of scenario-specific benchmarks and proposed initial steps towards their solution. Besides proposing solutions for technical challenges we propose founding a consortium, which is able to tackle the operational challenges. We hope to be able to discuss our solutions with the TPC audience and are strongly committed to use our current presence in the related SPEC working groups to foster the adoption of these benchmarking technologies.

## References

1. Huppler, K.: The Art of Building a Good Benchmark. In: Nambiar, R., Poess, M. (eds.) TPCTC 2009. LNCS, vol. 5895, pp. 18–30. Springer, Heidelberg (2009)
2. Binnig, C., Kossmann, D., Kraska, T., Loesing, S.: How is the weather tomorrow?: towards a benchmark for the cloud. In: DB Test. ACM (2009)
3. SPEC: The SPEC CPU2006 Benchmark, http://www.spec.org/cpu2006/
4. TPC: The TPC-C Benchmark, http://www.tpc.org/tpcc/
5. Florescu, D., Kossmann, D.: Rethinking cost and performance of database systems. SIGMOD Record 38(1), 43–48 (2009)
6. Gray, J. (ed.): The Benchmark Handbook for Database and Transaction Systems, 2nd edn. Morgan Kaufmann (1993)
7. Kounev, S.: Performance Engineering of Distributed Component-Based Systems - Benchmarking, Modeling and Performance Prediction. PhD thesis, Technische Universität Darmstadt (2005)

8. Sachs, K., Kounev, S., Bacon, J., Buchmann, A.: Performance evaluation of message-oriented middleware using the SPECjms 2007 benchmark. Performance Evaluation 66(8), 410–434 (2009)
9. Sachs, K.: Performance Modeling and Benchmarking of Event-Based Systems. PhD thesis, TU Darmstadt (2011)
10. Madeira, H., Vieira, M., Sachs, K., Kounev, S.: Dagstuhl Seminar 10292. In: Resilience Benchmarking, Springer (2011)
11. NIST: The NIST Definition of Cloud Computing (2011), http://csrc.nist.gov/publications/nistpubs/800-145/SP800-145.pdf
12. Youseff, L., Butrico, M., Silva, D.D.: Towards a unified ontology of cloud computing. In: Proc. of the Grid Computing Environments Workshop (GCE 2008) (2008)
13. Huppler, K.: Benchmarking with Your Head in the Cloud. In: Nambiar, R., Poess, M. (eds.) TPCTC 2011. LNCS, vol. 7144, pp. 97–110. Springer, Heidelberg (2012)
14. Leimeister, S., Böhm, M., Riedl, C., Krcmar, H.: The business perspective of cloud computing: Actors, roles and value networks. In: Alexander, P.M., Turpin, M., van Deventer, J.P. (eds.) ECIS (2010)
15. SPEC Open Systems Group: Report on cloud computing to the OSG Steering Committee. Technical Report OSG-wg-final-20120214 (February 2012)
16. Shen, S., Visser, O., Iosup, A.: Rtsenv: An experimental environment for real-time strategy games. In: Shirmohammadi, S., Griwodz, C. (eds.) NETGAMES, pp. 1–6. IEEE (2011)
17. Nae, V., Iosup, A., Prodan, R.: Dynamic resource provisioning in massively multi-player online games. IEEE Trans. Parallel Distrib. Syst. 22(3), 380–395 (2011)
18. Ratti, S., Hariri, B., Shirmohammadi, S.: A survey of first-person shooter gaming traffic on the internet. IEEE Internet Computing 14(5), 60–69 (2010)
19. Li, M., Sasanka, R., Adve, S., Chen, Y., Debes, E.: The ALPBench benchmark suite for complex multimedia applications. In: Proceedings of the IEEE International Workload Characterization Symposium, pp. 34–45 (2005)
20. Lee, C., Potkonjak, M., Mangione-Smith, W.H.: Mediabench: A tool for evaluating and synthesizing multimedia and communicatons systems. In: MICRO, pp. 330–335 (1997)
21. Guthaus, M.R., Ringenberg, J.S., Ernst, D., Austin, T.M., Mudge, T., Brown, R.B.: MiBench: A free, commercially representative embedded benchmark suite. In: Proceedings of the Fourth Annual IEEE International Workshop on Workload Characterization, WWC-4 (Cat. No. 01EX538), pp. 3–14. IEEE (2001)
22. Fritsch, T., Ritter, H., Schiller, J.H.: The effect of latency and network limitations on mmorpgs: a field study of everquest2. In: NETGAMES, pp. 1–9. ACM (2005)
23. Chen, K.T., Huang, P., Lei, C.L.: How sensitive are online gamers to network quality? Commun. ACM 49(11), 34–38 (2006)
24. Claypool, M.: The effect of latency on user performance in real-time strategy games. Computer Networks 49(1), 52–70 (2005)
25. Beigbeder, T., Coughlan, R., Lusher, C., Plunkett, J., Agu, E., Claypool, M.: The effects of loss and latency on user performance in unreal tournament 2003. In: Chang Feng, W. (ed.) NETGAMES, pp. 144–151. ACM (2004)
26. Balint, M., Posea, V., Dimitriu, A., Iosup, A.: User behavior, social networking, and playing style in online and face to face bridge communities. In: NETGAMES, pp. 1–2. IEEE (2010)

27. Iosup, A., Lăscăteu, A.: Clouds and Continuous Analytics Enabling Social Networks for Massively Multiplayer Online Games. In: Bessis, N., Xhafa, F. (eds.) Next Generation Data Technologies for Collective Computational Intelligence. SCI, vol. 352, pp. 303–328. Springer, Heidelberg (2011)

28. Kim, K., Jeon, K., Han, H., Kim, S.G., Jung, H., Yeom, H.Y.: Mrbench: A benchmark for mapreduce framework. In: Proceedings of the 2008 14th IEEE International Conference on Parallel and Distributed Systems, ICPADS 2008, pp. 11–18. IEEE Computer Society, Washington, DC (2008)

29. Chen, Y., Ganapathi, A., Griffith, R., Katz, R.H.: The case for evaluating mapreduce performance using workload suites. In: MASCOTS, pp. 390–399. IEEE (2011)

30. Pavlo, A., Paulson, E., Rasin, A., Abadi, D.J., DeWitt, D.J., Madden, S., Stonebraker, M.: A comparison of approaches to large-scale data analysis. In: Çetintemel, U., Zdonik, S.B., Kossmann, D., Tatbul, N. (eds.) SIGMOD Conference, pp. 165–178. ACM (2009)

31. Huppler, K.: Price and the TPC. In: Nambiar, R., Poess, M. (eds.) TPCTC 2010. LNCS, vol. 6417, pp. 73–84. Springer, Heidelberg (2011)

32. Kossmann, D., Kraska, T., Loesing, S.: An evaluation of alternative architectures for transaction processing in the cloud. In: Proceedings of the 2010 ACM SIGMOD International Conference on Management of Data, SIGMOD 2010, pp. 579–590. ACM, New York (2010)

33. Islam, S., Lee, K., Fekete, A., Liu, A.: How a consumer can measure elasticity for cloud platforms. In: [38], pp. 85-96

34. Rabl, T., Poess, M.: Parallel data generation for performance analysis of large, complex rdbms. In: Graefe, G., Salem, K. (eds.) DBTest, p. 5. ACM (2011)

35. Frank, M., Poess, M., Rabl, T.: Efficient update data generation for dbms benchmarks. In: [38], pp. 169–180

36. Armbrust, M., Fox, A., Griffith, R., Joseph, A.D., Katz, R.H., Konwinski, A., Lee, G., Patterson, D.A., Rabkin, A., Stoica, I., Zaharia, M.: A view of cloud computing. Commun. ACM 53(4), 50–58 (2010)

37. Villegas, D., Antoniou, A., Sadjadi, S.M., Iosup, A.: An analysis of provisioning and allocation policies for infrastructure-as-a-service clouds. In: CCGRID (2012)

38. Iosup, A., Yigitbasi, N., Epema, D.H.J.: On the performance variability of production cloud services. In: CCGRID, pp. 104–113. IEEE (2011)

39. Kaeli, D.R., Rolia, J., John, L.K., Krishnamurthy, D. (eds.): Third Joint WOSP/SIPEW International Conference on Performance Engineering, ICPE 2012, Boston, MA, USA, April 22-25. ACM (2012)

# Characterizing Cloud Performance with TPC Benchmarks

Wayne D. Smith

Intel Corporation, JF1-239, 2111 N.E. 25$^{th}$ Avenue, Hillsboro, OR 97124
`Wayne.Smith@intel.com`

**Abstract.** TPC Benchmarks have become the gold standard in database benchmarks. The Companies who publish TPC Benchmarks have a significant investment in the workload, benchmark implementation and publication requirements. We will explore ideas on how TPC Benchmarks with limited modification can be used to characterize database performance in a cloud environment. This is a natural progression beyond the current TPC-VMS Specification that leverages existing TPC Benchmarks to measure database performance in a virtualized environment. The TPC-VMS Specification only addresses the consolidation of multiple databases in a virtualized or cloud environment. In addition to consolidation, we will address the cloud characteristics of load balancing, migration, resource elasticity and deployment.

## 1   Introduction

Cloud computing delivers virtual processors, memory and storage to a community of end-users. The end-users no longer need worry about buying, installing, backing up or maintaining their own hardware servers. In 2011, cloud providers were in the early stages of bringing the technology to market and in 2012 we should see a full range of services for hosting enterprise applications in the cloud [1]. Key to the cloud is virtualization technology that provides a separate virtual machine environment for multiple users. A number of benchmarks currently exist to test virtualization. However there is a lack of a workload that characterizes large database performance in a cloud environment. TPC Benchmarks are the gold standard for large database performance. This paper explores the idea of how TPC Benchmarks with limited modification can be used to characterize database performance in a cloud environment.

## 2   Cloud

A cloud may contain a number of servers distributed geographically over large distances. Each of the servers typically contains a virtualization environment. Cloud management software provides the glue that allows the user to view all of the servers as one large system. Providing a virtualization environment on each of the individual servers is a key technical foundation for the cloud.

R. Nambiar and M. Poess (Eds.): TPCTC 2012, LNCS 7755, pp. 189–196, 2013.
© Springer-Verlag Berlin Heidelberg 2013

## 2.1    Virtualization

Virtualization provides a separate virtual machine (VM) environment for multiple users. Typically each VM includes an operating system and application code. The VM provides security and isolation from other operating systems and application code running in their own virtual machines. A hypervisor provides the virtualization of the underlying hardware by managing the virtual machines.

## 2.2    Cloud Management Software

The Cloud Management Software provides the glue that presents to the user the individual virtualized server environments as one large system or cloud. The Cloud Management software provides the load balancing between servers by deciding where applications or VMs are deployed and provides a centralized management point for server error reporting and backup. Examples of Cloud Management Software are Microsoft's System Center Virtual Machine Manager [5] or VMware's Virtual Center Operations Management Suite [6].

## 2.3    Cloud Characteristics

There are a number of characteristics that can be identified which describe the various functions of a cloud environment.

**Consolidation:** Consolidation is the characteristic of moving multiple applications from their single server system to virtual machines on one server. Consolidation is a characteristic of both a virtualization environment and a cloud environment.

**Migration:** Migration is the characteristic of the cloud where a virtual machine is moved (migrated) from one server in the cloud to another server in the cloud. The operating system and application running in the virtual machine do not have any knowledge of the migration.

**Load Balancing:** Load balancing is the characteristic of moving a VM within a server or between servers for better overall performance. If within a server, the VM virtual processors are moved from busy processors to idle processors which provide better performance for all VMs running on the server. If between servers, a virtual machine is migrated from a busy server to an idle server for overall cloud efficiency and performance.

**Resource Elasticity:** Resource Elasticity is the characteristic of adding or subtracting virtual machine resources (virtual processors or memory) due to performance demands of the application running in the virtual machine. For example if a virtual machine is allocated four virtual processors, additional virtual processors could be added whenever the virtual machine reaches 100% utilization of the four virtual processors. Conversely if the virtual machine is only running 10% utilization for the four virtual processors, some of the virtual processors could be reallocated to another virtual machine.

**Deployment:** Deployment has two definitions or uses. The first definition is the deployment of a new server from installation to activation into the cloud. The second use is the deployment of additional virtual machines to meet a customer's quality of service requirements. Here a cloud customer may have replicated an application into multiple virtual machines. The idea is that additional virtual machines are deployed into the cloud when there is a high demand for the application. For the remainder of this article the second definition will be used.

## 3      Cloud Benchmarks

There are existing virtualization benchmarks such as SPECvirt_sc2010 [2], VMmark[3] and TPC-VMS [4]. However there has yet to emerge an industry standard cloud benchmark. A major problem facing a cloud benchmark is that a cloud by its very nature is designed to scale by the support for easy additional of servers. Thus a new benchmark publication can easily surpass a previous benchmark publication by just adding more servers. For example a test sponsor may publish a top result using 8 servers. The competition need only publish a result with 16 servers. The additional servers could actually hide poor hardware or software performance. The next publication may use 20 servers, the next 40 servers, etc. Thus in order to publish the top result, one need only reach deep into their pockets to configure more servers than the last top publication. The colloquial term for such a benchmark is that it is a "deep pocket benchmark". Such benchmarks only reward the companies with the deepest pockets, not the companies that have the superior products.

   To prevent deep pocket benchmarks, rules will have to be defined that limit the cloud environment such as max number of servers, a max system cost or a max hardware foot print (everything must fit in a 19" rack). Another option is to construct a benchmark with a small number of servers that will characterize a products performance running in a cloud environment. Specifically the benchmark implementation proposed is a method to characterize database performance in a cloud environment.

## 4      TPC-VMS

The TPC Virtual Measurement Single System Specification, TPC-VMS, contains the rules and methodology for measuring and reporting TPC Benchmark metrics running in a virtualized environment. TPC-VMS leverages the TPC-C, TPC-E, TPC-H and TPC-DS Benchmarks by adding the methodology and requirements for running and reporting virtualization metrics. It is simplistic in that it only addresses the characteristic of consolidation as 3 identical VMs are run in a virtualized environment, i.e. 3 TPC-C VMs, 3 TPC-E VMs, 3 TPC-H VMs or 3 TPC-DS VMs. The overriding criterion for TPC-VMS was "time to benchmark" as the need for a TPC virtualized database benchmark was critical. TPC-VMS is the first step for leveraging existing TPC Benchmarks in a virtualization environment. This paper outlines TPC-VMC which is the next step to leverage TPC Benchmarks to characterize database performance in a cloud environment.

# 5    TPC-VMC

The TPC-VMC benchmark is currently under development by the TPC. Various proposals have been discussed. This paper outlines one possible proposal for the TPC-VMC benchmark.

# 6    The TPC-VMC Servers

As TPC-VMC is targeted to characterize database performance in a cloud environment, at least two servers will be required. To limit the cost of the benchmark and for the sake of simplicity, two servers will be used that are identical in hardware and software configuration. The servers are connected to a shared storage subsystem. The option of using a shared storage subsystem is more a choice of simplifying the migration requirements. Another more complex option would be to require separate storage subsystems. As TPC databases typically are several terabytes in size, the simpler shared storage configuration is described in this paper.

# 7    The Measurement Interval

Both TPC-C and TPC-E have a measurement interval where throughput is measured by the number of transactions completed divided by the measurement interval time producing a transactions per time metric. The TPC-H and TPC-DS benchmarks measure the time taken to perform a known quantity of work to produce a work per time metric. The proposed TPC-VMC benchmark will not work for the TPC-H or TPC-DS benchmarks as these benchmarks measure the time for a specific quantity of work to be performed. The proposed TPC-VMC methodology is targeted for TPC-C and TPC-E as both benchmarks define two hour measurement intervals. TPC-VMC splits the two hours into two one hour phases. The first phase is used to characterize load balancing, migration and resource elasticity while the second phase is designed to characterize deployment.

## 7.1    Phase 1 of Measurement Interval

Figure 1 describes the first phase or first 60 minutes of a TPC-C or TPC-E measurement interval. The two servers are configured with 1 active and 1 inactive server, i.e. VMs may only run on one of the servers. Four VMs are deployed on the active server. The bottom dotted line in Figure 1 denotes a transaction rate of zero and indicates the progression of time through the first 60 minutes of the measurement interval. The solid line represents the average TPC-C or TPC-E throughput of the four VMs. As shown the average transaction rate increases from zero to a point where the four VMs are utilizing as much of the active server resources as possible. Typically in a TPC benchmark the test sponsor will run for some amount time to ensure the system is running in a steady state condition. Whenever the test sponsor desires, the cloud management software is informed that the second server is ready to be activated. The activation of the second server denotes the start of the TPC-VMC measurement interval.

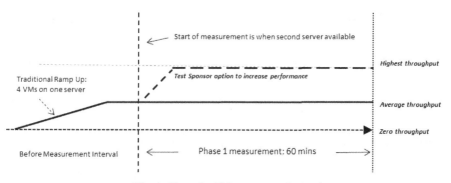

**Fig. 1.** Phase 1 of Measurement Interval

Once the second system is active, the cloud management software may decide to migrate one or more of the VMs to the newly activated server. Migration is not a requirement of the benchmark. It is a requirement that the migration cannot be initiated by user intervention. Here the benchmark is characterizing the load balancing and migration functions of the cloud environment.

At this point the test sponsor has the option to increase the transaction input rate of the four VMs. This is denoted in Figure 1 by the dashed line that increases to the highest average throughput level signified by the horizontal dashed lines at the top of the Figure 1. Thus the benchmark is characterizing resource elasticity as additional resources must be given to the VMs in order to satisfy the additional transaction input. This increase in transaction rate is not required by the benchmark but is highly desirable as the increased performance will significantly impact the published throughput rate. The reason that the load balancing and increased throughput are not required by the benchmark specification is that if they were required it would necessitate a specific kit implementation. The goal of the TPC-VMC is to use the existing TPC benchmark kits.

Phase 1 of the Measurement Interval characterizes load balancing, migration and resource elasticity. The benchmark does not require the test sponsor to demonstrate these characteristics, but the resulting performance throughput is a significant inducement to load balance, migrate and respond to VM resource requests as fast and efficiently as possible.

## 7.2    Phase 2

The second 60 minute phase of the measurement interval is depicted in Figure 2. Starting at plus 60 minutes from the start of the Measurement Interval the test sponsor must deploy 4 additional VMs depicted by a long dash and two short dashes in Figure 2. The VMs are deployed from a VM image that contains an Operating System, Database software and the TPC application software. The 4 TPC databases should have already been created and populated per the TPC-C or TPC-E rules. The VMs are deployed, the databases are started and at this point the test sponsor starts issuing transaction requests to the databases. The 4 VMs are ramped such that all 8 VMs are using all of the resources of the 2 servers, i.e. each server is at or near 100% utilization. This is depicted in the Figure 2 by the lines with a long dash and two short dashes.

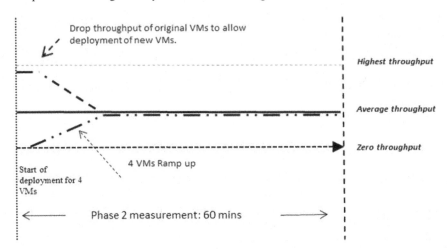

**Fig. 2.** Phase 2 of Measurement Interval

If the test sponsor increased performance of the original 4 VMs as described in Phase 1, the transaction input must be decreased in order accommodate the deployment of the 4 new VMs. If the test sponsor did not choose to increase performance in Phase 1 and no migration took place, then in Phase 2 the 4 new VMs would be deployed onto the idle server. In Phase 2 of the measurement interval the characteristics of resource elasticity and deployment are benchmarked.

# 8     Metric

The complete measurement interval is depicted in Figure 3.

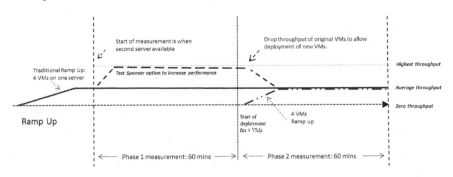

**Fig. 3.** TPC-VMC Measurement Interval

The obvious question is how can one ensure that the test sponsor will follow the rules that each VM is supposed to consume 1/(number of VMs) the resources of the two servers? For example, with 8 VMs and two servers, each VM should consume 25% of a server. The TPC-VMC Specification cannot require that each of the VMs run exactly the same rate as no hardware or software will produce the exact same performance result. So what about roughly equal to 1/VM of the resources? The problem here is what is the definition of roughly? Is there a guard band where the transaction rate from any of the VMs is within 5%, 10% or 15% of any other VM transaction rate? The wording is difficult and prone to disagreement in interpretation. The easy solution is to just require that the lowest transaction rate of the VMs is the reported result. This pushes the issue to the test sponsor who must maximize the lowest VM performance by making sure each VM is using equal amounts of the server resources. Thus the metric is the lowest throughput of the 4 VMs in Phase 1 plus the lowest throughput of the 8 VMs in Phase 2.

VMC Metric = Lowest throughput in Phase 1 + Lowest throughput in Phase 2

The resulting metric provides one number that characterizes the efficiency of the cloud characteristics of consolidation, load balancing, migration, resource elasticity and deployment.

## 9    Issues

A number of issues are still to be resolved.

**Database Ramp Up:** The Phase 2 deployment includes the database ramp up of the TPC transactions. Historically, this process has not been optimized or addressed by the TPC benchmarks but is now part of the metric.

**TPC-C Checkpoints:** The TPC-C benchmark specifies in great detail the checkpoint process that must happen every half hour.   The TPC-VMC migration and deployment requirements may cause the VM TPC-C benchmarks to fail their TPC-C checkpoint requirements.

**Phase 2 Resource Elasticity:** If the Test Sponsor has increased the transaction rate of the first 4 VMs in phase 1, the transaction rate needs to be decreased in Phase 2 to allow the deployment of the second set of 4 VMs.   If the metric is the lowest result of the 8 VMs, then this behooves the Test Sponsor to not gradually decrease throughput but to abruptly decrease performance.   So why have two phases back to back? Another option would be to split the measurement interval with two phases into two separate measurement intervals?

## 10    Summary

As shown it is possible to create a benchmark that characterizes the database performance in a cloud environment without having to create a large cloud environment. The TPC-VMC benchmark uses the existing TPC-C and TPC-E workloads which removes the complex and arduous task of creating a new workload. The TPC-VMC work is still in its infancy as the workload is still being discussed within the TPC. This paper describes one possible solution to the TPC-VMC benchmark.

**Acknowledgements.** The TPC-VMC benchmark is a collaborative of many individuals from several leading companies in the computer industry. The material presented here is the result of the work of the committee members as a whole rather than one author. We would like to acknowledge the contributions of Dave Raddatz, John Fowler, Karl Huppler, Jamie Reding, Rick Freeman, Andy Bond, Shiny Sebastian and Reza Taheri.

# References

1. Gartner Identifies the Top 10 Strategic Technologies for (2012),
   http://www.gartner.com/it/page.jsp?id=1826214
2. SPEC: SPEC Virtualization Committee, http://www.spec.org/virt_sc2010
3. VMware Inc., VMmark: A Scalable Benchmark for Virtualized Systems,
   http://www.vmware.com/pdf/vmmark_intro.pdf
4. TPC: TPC-VMS Specification, http://www.tpc.org
5. Microsoft System Center Virtual Machine Manager,
   http://technet.microsoft.com/en-us/systemcenter/bb545923.aspx
6. VMware Inc., Virtual Center Operations Management Suite, http://www.vmware.com/
   products/datacenter-virtualization/vcenter-operations-
   management/overview.html

# Setting the Direction for Big Data Benchmark Standards

Chaitanya Baru[1], Milind Bhandarkar[2], Raghunath Nambiar[3],
Meikel Poess[4], and Tilmann Rabl[5]

[1] San Diego Supercomputer Center, UC San Diego, USA
`baru@sdsc.edu`
[2] Greenplum/EMC, USA
`Milind.Bhandarkar@emc.com`
[3] Cisco Systems, Inc, USA
`rnambiar@cisco.com`
[4] Oracle Corporation, USA
`meikel.poess@oracle.com`
[5] University of Toronto
`tilmann.rabl@utoronto.ca`

**Abstract.** The *Workshop on Big Data Benchmarking (WBDB2012),* held on
May 8-9, 2012 in San Jose, CA, served as an incubator for several promising
approaches to define a big data benchmark standard for industry. Through an
open forum for discussions on a number of issues related to big data benchmarking—including definitions of big data terms, benchmark processes and
auditing — the attendees were able to extend their own view of big data benchmarking as well as communicate their own ideas, which ultimately led to the
formation of small working groups to continue collaborative work in this area.
In this paper, we summarize the discussions and outcomes from this first workshop, which was attended by about 60 invitees representing 45 different organizations, including industry and academia. Workshop attendees were selected
based on their experience and expertise in the areas of management of big data,
database systems, performance benchmarking, and big data applications. There
was consensus among participants about both the need and the opportunity for
defining benchmarks to capture the end-to-end aspects of big data applications.
Following the model of TPC benchmarks, it was felt that big data benchmarks
should not only include metrics for performance, but also price/performance,
along with a sound foundation for fair comparison through audit mechanisms.
Additionally, the benchmarks should consider several costs relevant to big data
systems including total cost of acquisition, setup cost, and the total cost of ownership, including energy cost. The second Workshop on Big Data Benchmarking will be held in December 2012 in Pune, India, and the third meeting is being
planned for July 2013 in Xi'an, China.

**Keywords:** Big Data, Benchmarking, Industry Standards.

## 1 Introduction

The world has been in the midst of an extraordinary information explosion over
the past decade, punctuated by the rapid growth in the use of the Internet and in the

R. Nambiar and M. Poess (Eds.): TPCTC 2012, LNCS 7755, pp. 197–208, 2013.

number of connected devices worldwide. The data growth phenomenon is global in nature, with Asia rapidly emerging as a major user base contributing to both consumption as well as generation of data, as indicated in Figure 1. A 2010 IDC study [9] estimates the total amount of enterprise data to grow from about 0.5 zettabyte in 2008 to 35 zettabytes in 2020. Indeed, the rate at which data and information are being generated is faster than at any point throughout history. With the penetration of data-driven computing, web and mobile technologies, and enterprise computing, the emerging markets have the potential for further adding to this already rapid growth in data. Data from all sources—from enterprise applications to machine-generated data—continue to grow exponentially, requiring the development of innovative techniques for data management, data processing, and analytics. This motivates the development of evaluation schemes and benchmark standards encompassing hardware and software technologies and products.

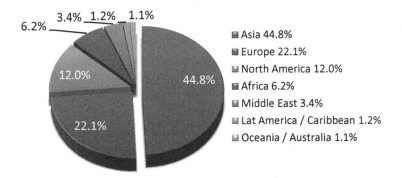

**Fig. 1.** Internet users in the world distributed by regions 2011 [2]

Evaluating alternative technological approaches and assessing the effectiveness of applications and analytic pipelines designed to tackle the challenges of big data require new approaches to benchmarking, especially since current industry standard benchmarks are not designed to cover the most important aspects of big data. Big data is often distinguished from traditional large databases using the three Vs: *volume*, *variety* and *velocity*. In addition, a big data benchmark may also include a fourth V, namely value.

Big data systems deal with large volumes of data, which are sometimes in the multiple petabyte range. Traditional large-scale industry standard benchmarks, such as TPC-H and TPC-DS, only test systems up to 100 Terabyte. Variety in the context of big data systems refers to the ability to deal with differently organized data, such as unstructured, semi-structured and structured data. Current industry standard benchmarks focus on structured data, mostly relational data. Velocity refers to the ability of a big data system to stay in synchronization with operational systems through periodic refreshes, commonly referred to as extraction, transformation and load (ETL) or data integration (DI). While some of the newer industry standard benchmarks, e.g. TPC-DS, include a periodic refresh process and while their refresh methodology, i.e. concurrent updates, is realistic, they do not implement the same scale and frequency at which data is refreshed in big data applications. Finally, "value" refers to big data processing that creates business value to the customer. The benchmarks should be modeled after real-world processing pipelines that create value to the end user.

A big data benchmark must provide objective measures quantifying performance, scalability, elasticity, and price/performance of any system designed to support big data applications. Such a benchmark would facilitate evaluation of alternative solutions and provide for comparisons among different solution approaches. It would also characterize the new feature sets, enormous data sizes, and shifting loads of big data applications, and the large-scale and evolving system configurations and heterogeneous technologies of big data platforms.

The first *Workshop on Big Data Benchmarking (WBDB2012)* held on May 8-9, 2012 in San Jose, CA [7] served as an important incubator towards the development of an industry standard for big data benchmarking. The objective of *WBDB2012* was to identify key issues and launch an activity around the definition of reference benchmarks to capture the essence of big data application scenarios.

Workshop invitees were drawn from academia and industry, and included practitioners as well as researchers with backgrounds in big data, database systems, benchmarking and system performance, cloud storage and computing, and related areas. Each attendee was required to submit a two-page abstract and provide a five minutes "lightning talk". The workshop website (http://clds.sdsc.edu/wbdb2012) provides copies of papers and presentations. The presentations were classified into four categories: *benchmark properties, benchmark process, hardware and software aspects,* and *data generation* for big data workloads.

## 1.1    Workshop Description

A total of about 60 invited attendees represented about 45 different organizations at the workshop[1]. Each day began with three 15-minute introductory talks, followed by presentations in the morning and discussions in the afternoon. The introductory talks on the first day provided an overview of industry benchmarking efforts and standards and discussed desirable attributes and properties of competitive industry benchmarks. On the second day, the talks focused on big data applications and the different genres of big data, such as genomic and geospatial data, and big data generation. The opening presentations were followed by about twenty "lightning talks" of 5-minutes each by the invited attendees. For the afternoon sessions, the attendees were divided into two equal groups, both groups were asked to discuss the same set of topics and report results at a plenary session at the end of the day.

---

[1] See http://clds.sdsc.edu/wbdb2012/participants for a list of participants.
  See http://clds.sdsc.edu/wbdb2012/organizers for a list of organizers.

The rest of this paper summarizes the discussions and findings from the workshop. Section 2 covers the benchmarking context and topics related to the nature of big data and big data applications, and existing big data benchmark efforts; Section 3 discusses guiding principles for the design of big data benchmarks; Section 4 discusses objectives of big data benchmarking, specifically whether such benchmarks should be targeted to encourage technological innovation or primarily for vendor competition; Section 5 probes some of the details related to big data benchmarks; and Section 6 provides conclusions from the workshop discussions and points to next steps in the process.

## 2     Benchmark Context

### 2.1     Application-Level Benchmarking

Workshop attendees were in general agreement that a big data benchmarking activity should begin at the end application level, by attempting to characterize the end-to-end needs and requirements of big data analytic pipelines. While isolating individual steps in such pipelines, e.g. sorting, is indeed of interest, it should be done in the context of the broader application scenario.

### 2.2     Data Genres and Application Scenarios

A range of data genres should be considered for big data benchmarks including, for example, structured, semi-structured, and unstructured data; graphs (including different types of graphs that might occur in different types of application domains, e.g. social networking versus biological networks); streams; geospatial data; array-based data; and special data types such as genomic data. The core set of operations need to be identified, modeled, and benchmarked for each genre, while also seeking similarities across genres.

It may be feasible to identify relevant application scenarios involving a variety of data genres that require a range of big data processing capabilities. An example discussed at the workshop was data management for an Internet-scale business, for example, an enterprise similar to, say, Facebook or Netflix. A plausible use case for such an application can be constructed requiring big data capabilities for managing data streams (click streams), weblogs, text sorting and indexing, graph construction and traversals, as well as geospatial data processing and structured data processing.

At the same time, the workshop attendees agreed that a single application scenario may not realistically capture the full range of data genres and operations that are broadly relevant across a wide range of big data applications. This may necessitate the development of multiple benchmark definitions based on differing scenarios. These benchmarks together would then capture a comprehensive range of variations.

## 2.3    Learning from Successful Benchmarks

Fortunately, there are a number of examples of successful benchmarking efforts that we can learn from and leverage. These include benchmarks developed by industry consortia such as the Transaction Processing Council (TPC) and Standard Performance Evaluation Corporation (SPEC); benchmarks from industry-driven efforts such as VMMark (VMWare) and Top500; and, benchmarks like Terasort [10] and Graph500 [13] designed for specific operations and/or data genres. Can a new big data benchmark be defined by simply building upon and extending current benchmark definitions? While this may be possible, a number of issues need to be considered such as whether:

- The existing benchmarks model application scenarios relevant to big data;
- The existing benchmarks can be naturally and easily scaled to the large data volumes necessary for big data benchmarking;
- Such benchmarks can be used more or less "as is", without requiring significant re-engineering to produce data and queries (operations) with the right set of characteristics for big data applications; and
- The benchmarks have no inherent restrictions or limitations such as, say, requiring all queries to be executed in SQL.

Several existing benchmarking efforts were presented and discussed at the meeting such as the Statistical Workload Injector for MapReduce (SWIM) developed at the University of California, Berkeley [4], GridMix3, developed at Yahoo! [1], YCSB++, developed at the Carnegie Mellon University based on YCSB of Yahoo! [15], and TPC-DS, the latest addition to TPC's suite of decision support benchmarks [4,16,17].

# 3    Design Principles for Big Data Benchmarks

As mentioned, several benchmarks have gained acceptance and are commonly used, including the ones from TPC (e.g., TPC-C, TPC-H [16]), SPEC, and Top500. Some of these benchmarks are impressive in their longevity – TPC-C is almost 25 years old and the Top500 list is just celebrating 20 years – and continue to be used. The workshop discussions focused on features that may have contributed to the longevity of the popular benchmarks. For example, in the case of the Top500, the metric is simple to understand: the result is a simple rank ordering according to a single performance number (FLOPS).

TPC-C, which models an on-line transaction processing (OLTP) workload, possesses the characteristics of all TPC benchmarks, (i) it models an application domain; (ii) employs strict rules for disclosure and publication of results; (iii) uses third-party auditing of results; and (iv) publishes performance as well as price/performance metrics. TPC-C requires that as the performance number increases (i.e. the transactions/minute) the size of the database (i.e. the number of warehouses in the reference database) must also increase. TPC-C requires a new warehouse to be introduced for every 12.5 tpmC. Thus, one cannot produce extremely high transactions/minute numbers while keeping the database fixed at some arbitrarily small database size. This "self-scaling" nature of the benchmark, which may well have contributed to the longevity of TPC-C itself, was recognized as a strength and a key desirable feature of any big data benchmark as well.

Other benchmarks, such as TPC-H, specify fixed, discrete "scale factors" at which the benchmark runs are measured. The advantage of that approach is that there are multiple, directly comparable results at a given scale factor. Arguably, one of the characteristics of the *systems under test (SUT)* in TPC benchmarking is that they tend to be "over-specified" in terms of their hardware configuration. Vendors (*aka* benchmark sponsors) are willing to incur a higher total system cost in order to obtain better performance numbers without much of a negative impact on the price/performance numbers. For example, the SUT can employ 10x the amount of disk for a given benchmark database size, whereas real customer installations will only employ 3-4x the amount of disk. In the case of big data benchmarking, there is the distinct possibility that the SUT is actually *smaller* in overall size and configuration than the actual customer installation, given the expense of assembling a big data system for benchmarking and the rate at which enterprise systems are growing. It may, therefore, become necessary to extrapolate (scale up) system performance based on measured results at a smaller scale. There was discussion on whether, and how well, results at one scale factor could be extrapolated to obtain/infer performance at a different scale factor. A concern was that it is typically not possible to extrapolate performance numbers obtained on small systems running small data sets to performance of large systems running large data sets. However, while such extrapolation may be difficult to achieve across a broad range of scale factors, could it be achieved among neighboring scale factor values? Could a result published at a given scale factor be accompanied by information on the "scalability" of the result for data sizes in the neighborhood of that scale factor, specifying the range of data sizes around that scale factor for which this result can be extrapolated? Facilitating such extrapolation of results may require a more extensive set of system performance and system configuration information to be recorded. Thus, while there are arguments for simplicity of the benchmark metrics, e.g. publishing only one or very few numbers as the overall result of the benchmark, more detailed information may indeed be needed to facilitate extrapolation of performance numbers across a range of data sizes.

A strong motivation for extrapolation is the significant costs involved in running big data benchmarks. The very size and nature of the problem requires large installations and significant amounts of preparation and effort. As a pragmatic matter, the benchmark should not be expensive to run, implying that the end-to-end process should be relatively easy and simple. This can be facilitated by the existence of robust, well-tested programs for data generation; robust scripts for running the tests; perhaps, available implementations of the benchmark in alternative technologies, e.g. RDBMS and Hadoop; and an easy method by which to verify the correctness of benchmarks results.

Other key aspects to consider in the benchmarking exercise are *elasticity* and *durability*, viz., the ability to gracefully handle failures. How well does the system perform under dynamic conditions, for example, when the amount of data is increased; when more resources (e.g. nodes) are added to the system; and when some resource are removed from the system as a consequence of a failure, e.g. node or disk failure? While TPC benchmarks require atomicity, consistency, isolation, and durability (ACID) tests to be performed with the SUT, these are performed as standalone tests, outside the window during which performance measurements are made. For big data systems, elasticity and durability need to be intrinsic to the system and, thus, they need to be part of the overall performance test. Elasticity requires that a system be able to utilize and exploit more resources as they become available. Durability ensures that a big data system can continue to function even in the presence of certain types of system failures.

Finally, the benchmark specification should be technology agnostic as much as possible. The applications, reference data, and workload should be specified at a level of abstraction that does not pre-suppose a particular technological approach. There was discussion on the language to be used for specifying the benchmark workload. At one end is an English-based workload specification; while at the other is a specification that is completely encoded by a computer program (e.g. written in Java or C++). If the primary audience of the benchmark were end customers, then the former is preferable: the benchmark should be specified in "lay" terms, in a manner that allows non-technical audiences to grasp the essence of the benchmark and to relate it to their real-world application scenarios. Using English provides the most flexibility and broadest audience, though some parts of the specification could still employ a declarative language like SQL. However, specification in SQL should not imply that the underlying data system is required to "natively" support SQL.

## 4    Benchmarking for Innovation versus Competition

There was significant discussion at the workshop on the ultimate objective of the benchmarking exercise: whether it served a technical and engineering purpose or a marketing purpose. This choice will obviously influence the nature of the overall exercise. The goals of a technical benchmarking activity are primarily to test alternative technological solutions to a given problem. Such benchmarks focus more on collecting detailed technical information for use in system optimization, re-engineering, and re-design. A competitive benchmark focuses on comparing performance and price/performance (and, perhaps, other costs, such as startup costs and total cost of ownership) among competing products, and may require an audit as part of the benchmark process in order to ensure a fair competition. Furthermore, given that benchmarking can be an expensive activity, it is also important to identify the sponsor of such an activity. The consensus was that this is typically the marketing division, not the engineering division. The workshop discussion made clear that the engineering versus marketing objectives for a benchmark were, indeed, not mutually exclusive. Benchmarks need to be designed initially for competitive purposes—to compare among alternative products/solutions. However, once such benchmarks become successful (such as the TPC benchmarks), there will be an impetus within organizations to use the same benchmarks for innovation as well. Vendors will be interested in developing features that enable their products to perform well on such competitive benchmarks. There are numerous examples in the area of database software where product features and improvement have been motivated, at least in some part, by the desire to perform well in a given benchmark competition. Since a well-designed benchmark suite reflects real-world needs, this means that these product improvements really end up serving the needs of real applications.

In sum, a big data benchmark is useful for both purposes: competition as well as innovation, though the benchmark should establish itself initially as being relevant as a competitive benchmark. The primary audience for the benchmarks are the end customers who need guidance in their decisions on what types of systems to acquire to serve their big data needs. Acceptance of a big data benchmark for that purpose then leads to the use of the same benchmark by vendors for innovation as well. Finally, while competitive benchmarks are useful for marketing purposes, participants from academia are more interested in benchmarking for technical innovation.

# 5     Benchmark Design

In this section, we summarize the outcome of the discussion sessions on the benchmark design; whether the benchmark should be a component or an End-to-End benchmark; whether the benchmark should be modeled after a specific application; where the benchmark should get its data from, i.e. synthetic vs. real-world data and what metric the benchmark should employ.

## 5.1     Component vs. End-to-End Benchmark

A key design question is whether the benchmark specification should focus on modeling and benchmarking one or more "end-to-end" big data application scenarios, or on modeling individual steps of an end-to-end application scenario and measuring the performance of those individual components. We refer to the first type as end-to-end benchmarks and the latter as component benchmarks. The system that is being benchmarked may be the software itself, e.g. different software systems running on a given hardware platform, or may include the software and hardware together.

Component benchmarks measure the performance of one (or a few) components of an entire system with respect to a certain workload. They tend to be relatively easier to specify and run, given their focused and limited scope. For components that expose standardized interfaces (APIs), the benchmarks can be specified in a standardized way and run as-is, for example, using a *benchmark kit*. An example of a component benchmark is SPEC's CPU benchmark (latest version is CPU2006 [3]), which is a CPU-intensive benchmark suite that exercises a system's processor, memory subsystem and compiler. Another example of a component benchmark is TeraSort, which has proved to be a very useful benchmark because, (i) sorting is a common component operation in many end-to-end application scenarios, (ii) it is relatively easy to setup and run, and (iii) it has been shown to serve a useful purpose exercising and tuning large-scale systems.

While end-to-end benchmarks can serve to measure the performance of entire systems, they can also be more difficult to specify. Developing a benchmark kit that can be run *as-is* can be difficult due to various system dependencies that may exist and the intrinsic complexity of the benchmark itself. The TPC benchmarks in general are good examples of such end-to-end benchmarks including for OLTP (TPC-C and TPC-E) and decision support (TPC-H and TPC-DS). TPC-DS for instance, measures a system's ability to load a database and serve a variety of requests including *ad hoc* queries, report generation, OLAP and data mining queries, in the presence of continuous data integration activity on a system that includes servers, IO-subsystems and staging areas for data integration.

## 5.2    Big Data Applications

Big data issues impinge upon a wide range of application domains, covering the range from scientific to commercial applications. Thus, it may be difficult to find a single application that covers all extant flavors of big data processing. Examples of applications that generate very large amounts of data include scientific applications such as in high energy physics (e.g. the Large Hadron Collider, LHC) and astronomy (e.g. the digital sky surveys), and social websites such as Facebook, Twitter, and Linked-in, which are the often-quoted examples of big data. However, the more "traditional" areas such as retail business, e.g. Amazon, Ebay, Walmart, have also reached a situation where they need to deal with big data.

There is also the issue of whether a big data benchmark should attempt to model a concrete application or whether a generic benchmark—using an abstract model based on real applications—would be more desirable. The benefit of a concrete application is that real world examples can be used as a blueprint for modeling the benchmark data and workload. This makes a detailed specification possible, which helps the reader of the specification understand the benchmark and its result. It also helps in relating real world business and their workloads to the benchmark. One approach is to develop a benchmark specification based on retailer model, such as the one used in TPC-DS. This approach has the advantage that it is well understood in the TPC benchmarking community, is well-researched, and accommodates many real world applications scenarios, for example in the area of semantic web data analysis. Another approach is to model the application based on a social website. Large social websites and related services such as Facebook, Twitter, Netflix and others deal with a range of big data genres and a variety of associated processing. In either case, the data will be operated on in several stages, using a data processing pipeline, reflecting the real-world model for such applications. An abstract example of such a pipeline is shown in Figure 2.

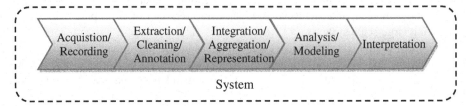

**Fig. 2.** Example for a big data pipeline [8]

### 5.3    Data Sources

A key issue is the source of data for the benchmark. Should the benchmark be based on "real" data taken from an actual, real-world application, or use synthetic data? The use of reference datasets is not practical, since that requires downloading and storing extremely large reference datasets from some remote location. Furthermore, real datasets may reflect only certain properties in the data and not others. And, most important, it would be extremely difficult to scale reference data sets to generate data at different scale factors. Thus, the conclusion was to rely on synthetic data designed to capture some of the key real-world characteristics of data. To efficiently generate very large datasets will require the use of parallel data generators [18]. Different genres of big data will require corresponding data generators.

### 5.4    Metrics

Big data benchmark metrics should include performance metrics as well as cost-based metrics (price/performance). The TPC is the forerunner for setting the rules to specify prices of benchmark configuration. Over the years the TPC has learned "the hard way" how difficult it is to specify rules that govern the way by which hardware and software is priced for benchmark configurations (see [5] for a detailed discussion on this topic). The TPC finalized on a canonical way to measure price of benchmark configurations and defined a pricing specification that all TPC benchmark are required to adhere. While the TPC model can be adopted for pricing, there are also other costs of interest for big data benchmarking. These include *systems setup, or startup cost*, since big data configurations may be very large in scale and setup may be a significant factor in the overall cost, plus some systems may be easier to set up than others; energy cost; and total system cost.

## 6    Conclusions and Next Steps

The first Workshop on Big Data Benchmarking held on May 8-9, 2012 in San Jose, CA took the first step in identifying and discussing a number of issues related to big data benchmarking, including definitional and process-based issues. The workshop concluded that there was both a need as well as an opportunity for defining benchmarks for big data applications to model end-to-end application scenarios while considering a variety of costs, including setup cost, energy cost, and total system cost. Several next steps are underway.

The workshop served as an incubator for several activities that will bring us closer to an industry standard big data benchmark. The "Big Data Benchmarking Community" has been formed (http://clds.ucsd.edu/bdbc/). It is hosted by the Center for Large-scale Data Systems research (CLDS) at the San Diego Supercomputer Center, UC San Diego. Biweekly phone conferences are being held to keep this group engaged and to share information among members. We are excited to hear that members of this community have started to work on prototypes of end-to-end big data benchmarks.

The second Workshop on Big Data Benchmarking will be held on December 17-18, 2012 in Pune, India, hosted by Persistent Systems. A third workshop is being planned for July 2013 in Xi'an, China, to be hosted by the Shanxi Supercomputing Center.

**Acknowledgements.** The WBDB2012 workshop was funded by a grant from the National Science Foundation (Grant# IIS-1241838) and sponsorship from Brocade, Greenplum, Mellanox, and Seagate.

# References

1. Gridmix3,  `git://git.apache.org/hadoop-mapreduce.git/src/contrib/gridmix/`
2. Internet World Stats – Miniwatts Marketing Group (December 2011),
   `http://www.internetworldstats.com/stats.html`
3. SPEC CPU2006: `http://www.spec.org/cpu2006/`
4. Statistical Workload Injector for MapReduce (SWIM), `https://github.com/SWIMProjectUCB/SWIM/wiki`
5. TPC: TPC Benchmark DS Specification, `http://www.tpc.org/tpcds/spec/tpcds_1.1.0.pdf`
6. TPC: TPC-Pricing Specification,
   `http://www.tpc.org/pricing/spec/Price_V1.7.0.pdf`
7. Workshop On Big Data Benchmarking (2012), `http://clds.ucsd.edu/wbdb2012`
8. Agrawal, D., Bernstein, P., Bertino, E., Davidson, S., Dayal, U., Franklin, M., Gehrke, J., Haas, L., Halevy, A., Han, J., Jagadish, H.V., Labrinidis, A., Madden, S., Papakonstantinou, Y., Patel, J., Ramakrishnan, R., Ross, K., Shahabi, C., Suciu, D., Vaithyanathan, S., Widom, J.: Challenges and Opportunities with Big Data. Community white paper (2011)
9. Gantz, J., Reinsel, D.: The Digital Universe Decade – Are You Ready? IDC report (2010),
   `http://www.emc.com/collateral/analyst-reports/idc-digital-universe-are-you-ready.pdf`
10. Gray, J.: Sort Benchmark Home Page, `http://sortbenchmark.org/`
11. Hogan, T.: Overview of TPC Benchmark E: The Next Generation of OLTP Benchmarks. In: Nambiar, R., Poess, M. (eds.) TPCTC 2009. LNCS, vol. 5895, pp. 84–98. Springer, Heidelberg (2009)
12. Huppler, K.: Price and the TPC. In: Nambiar, R., Poess, M. (eds.) TPCTC 2010. LNCS, vol. 6417, pp. 73–84. Springer, Heidelberg (2011)

13. Murphy, R.C., Wheeler, K.B., Barrett, B.W., Ang, J.A.: Introducing the Graph 500. Sandia National Laboratories (2010)
14. Nambiar, R., Poess, M.: The Making of TPC-DS. In: VLDB 2006, pp. 1049-1058, (2006)
15. Patil, S., Polte, M., Ren, K., Tantisiriroj, W., Xiao, L., López, J., Gibson, G., Fuchs, A., Rinaldi, B.: YCSB++: Benchmarking and Performance Debugging Advanced Features in Scalable Table Stores. In: SOCC 2011, pp. 9:1-9:14 (2011)
16. Poess, M., Floyd, C.: New TPC Benchmarks for Decision Support and Web Commerce. SIGMOD Record 29(4), 64–71 (2000)
17. Poess, M., Nambiar, R., Walrath, D.: Why You Should Run TPC-DS: A Workload Analysis. In: VLDB 2007, pp. 1138–1149 (2007)
18. Poess, M., Smith, B., Kollár, L., Larson, P.: TPC-DS, Taking Decision Support Benchmarking to the Next Level. In: SIGMOD 2002, pp. 582–587 (2002)
19. Rabl, T., Frank, M., Sergieh, H.M., Kosch, H.: A Data Generator for Cloud-Scale Benchmarking. In: Nambiar, R., Poess, M. (eds.) TPCTC 2010. LNCS, vol. 6417, pp. 41–56. Springer, Heidelberg (2011)

# Author Index